STREET FRENCH

How to Speak and Understand French Slang

STREET FRENCH

*How to Speak and Understand
French Slang*

David Burke

A Self-Teaching Guide

John Wiley & Sons, Inc.
New York • Chichester • Brisbane • Toronto • Singapore

Publisher: Stephen Kippur
Editor: Katherine Schowalter
Managing Editor: Ruth Greif
Editing, Design, and Production: Publication Services
Illustrator: Brian Pendley

This publication is designed to provide accurate and authoritative information in regard to the subject matter covered. It is sold with the understanding that the publisher is not engaged in rendering legal, accounting, or other professional service. If legal advice or other expert assistance is required, the services of a competent professional person should be sought. FROM A DECLARATION OF PRINCIPLES JOINTLY ADOPTED BY A COMMITTEE OF THE AMERICAN BAR ASSOCIATION AND A COMMITTEE OF PUBLISHERS.

Library of Congress Cataloging-in-Publication Data
Burke, David, 1956-
    Street French.

      1. French language—Slang. 2. French language—
Text-books for foreign speakers—English.
I. Title.
PC3739.B87   1987   447'.09   87-3011
ISBN 0-471-62876-X
Printed in the United States of America
    10 9 8 7

THIS BOOK IS DEDICATED TO MY FATHER. . .

A WORD ABOUT
STREET FRENCH

Speak standard, "correct," grammatical French, and you will no doubt be understood by French natives. You will make yourself acceptable in all social situations. When you write, you should of course use the same standard language, except for very informal correspondence.

But is standard French always enough? Will you be able to understand the natives who address you in their unselfconscious, everyday, familiar language? Will you miss much of a movie dialogue heavily laced with slang? Fail to grasp the idiomatic imagery of a popular song? And wouldn't you love to have right there, at the tip of your tongue, that single, well-chosen phrase—absent *hélas,* from the textbooks—that will give true meaning to the expression "Excuse my French?" If the answer to these questions is yes, this is the book for you.

I have written textbooks for the teaching and learning of French for many years, often wishing that, beyond the classic language one must necessarily learn first, some attention could be given to that "other" French. So, when David Burke showed me the manuscript of his lively, witty *Street French,* I was glad to see that at last, everyday language and yes, even slang, have finally been recognized and treated with the humor and lightness of touch they deserve.

Read this thoroughly enjoyable book, study it, share the author's delight in those picturesque terms of today's French, and enjoy the knowledge that you too can be called *branché.**

Yvone Lenard
Author of
Parole et Pensée, 5th edition
Fenêtres sur la France

* branché: with it, tuned in

PREFACE

STREET FRENCH, geared for the student who has had three or more years of French study, is a step-by-step approach to teaching the actual spoken language of France that is constantly used in movies, books, and day-to-day business, as well as among family and friends. The book is destined to open new doors quickly as you enter the "secret" world of slang and learn the "inside" language that even a ten-year veteran of formalized French would not understand!

STREET FRENCH is designed to teach the essentials of colloquial French and slang in fifteen lessons. The material is organized to teach the reader first *how* to speak—i.e., how to use colloquial language, including the structure of a sentence, contractions, and shortcuts—then *what* to speak—i.e., slang.

The book is divided into five parts:

1. **DIALOGUE:** Here you will encounter about thirty new French slang words in context to demonstrate how to use slang in a given situation. An English translation immediately follows the French dialogue.
2. **VOCABULARY:** This section gives a detailed explanation of each term so that you can rest assured that you will not be led into an embarrassing situation by having just insulted a host, shopkeeper, or policeman! *Note:* A literal translation will always be given when possible.
3. **VOCABULARY PRACTICE:** These drills will allow you to test yourself along the way on the slang from the prior dialogue. Feel free to write directly on the page since this is your workbook. (The pages providing the answers are indicated in the beginning of this section).
4. **GRAMMAR:** This section introduces unconventional "rules" regarding the usage of slang and colloquialisms in a clear, concise, and easy-to-understand style.
5. **EXERCISES:** This section presents a new set of drills to help test you on the previous **GRAMMAR** section. The *last* **GRAMMAR** exercise of each chapter will include slang words from the preceding dialogue as a final review before continuing to the next chapter. (The pages providing the answers are indicated in the beginning of this section).

a. Following each sequence of five chapters is a summary review encompassing all the words and expressions learned up to that point.
b. Also, unique to this book is a thesaurus that offers you easy reference to a list of slang synonyms for a given term.

The secret to learning **STREET FRENCH** is by following this simple checklist:

- Make sure that you have a good grasp on each section before proceeding to the drills. If you've made more than two errors in a particular drill, simply go back and review...then try again! *Remember:* This is a self-paced book, so take your time. You're not fighting the clock!
- It's very important that you feel comfortable with each chapter before proceeding to the next. Words learned along the way *will* crop up in the following dialogues. *So feel comfortable before moving on!*
- Make sure that you read the dialogues and drills aloud. This is an excellent way to get comfortable speaking colloquially and thinking like a native!

Important

Slang must be used with discretion because it is a casual "language" that certainly should not be practiced with formal dignitaries or employers that you are trying to impress! This is why you need to pay close attention to the English equivalents and literal translations given in the **VOCABULARY** section. Their connotations are the same in the English definitions as in French. Therefore, a general rule: *Use your own judgment.*

Just as a student of formalized English would be rather shocked to run into words like *pooped, zonked,* and *wiped out* and discover that they all go under the heading of *tired,* you too will be surprised and amused to encounter a whole new array of terms and phrases usually hidden away in the French language and reserved only for the native speaker.

Welcome to the expressive and "colorful" world of slang!

LEGEND

adj.	adjective	**onom.**	onomatopoeia
adv.	adverb	**pers. pron.**	personal pronoun
exclam.	exclamation	**prep.**	preposition
exp.	expression	**q.**	quelqu'un (someone)
f.	feminine	**qch.**	quelque chose (something)
interj.	interjection	**s.t.**	something
(lit);	literal meaning	**pl.**	plural
m.	masculine	**v.**	verb
n.	noun		

ACKNOWLEDGMENTS

Needless to say, after fifteen years of preparing this book, I have several people I would like to thank: Jerri Simon Borack whose inspiration was the catalyst for my interest in pursuing the French language; My family and friends in France for their unyielding help and patience in spending hours at a time going over the latest slang words and expressions with me: Mimi, Patrice, Carole, Christophe, Régis, Nélie, Essie, Deborah, and Serge; Pascale Ledeur and Mark Maisonneuve for all their help, support, and counsel; Yvone Lenard, whose encouragement came at the perfect time. Her belief in the book was the single most important factor in my pursuit of its publication.

I am especially grateful to Susan Pearlman who had the greatest influence on me and the conception of this book. Her unflagging enthusiasm for the French culture was overwhelmingly contagious and she remains responsible for instilling in me a love and fascination for the French language and traditions. Special thanks go to my agents Michael Larsen and Elizabeth Pomada as well as my editor Katherine Schowalter of John Wiley & Sons. Their encouragement, enthusiasm, and efforts will never be forgotten. Most of all, I want to thank my family. The patience, love, and unrelenting support from my mother, Nancy, and Tom was the driving force behind the book.

CONTENTS

UNIT ONE

LEARNING
FRENCH SLANG
AND COLLOQUIALISMS

UN PIQUE-NIQUE TYPIQUE...

DIALOGUE

En sortant de la pâtisserie...

David: Tu sais, je viens de **fusiller** tout mon **fric** sur la **bouffe**. Je dois être **carrément dingue**.

Carole: Quel **gueuleton**! On **se tire** pour trouver un **bled peinard** pour **se taper la cloche**.

David: Tiens! C'est **génial**, ici! Regarde tous les **piafs**!

Carole: Ah, non! Il commence à **lancequiner** et j'ai pas de **pébroc**.

David: **J'en reviens pas,** moi! Mais, quelle **poisse**!

Carole: Quel **temps de chien**. Il **tombe des cordes**!

David: Oh, mais j'**en ai marre**! En été on **crame** et en hiver on **caille**. La **lancequine journaille** et **neuille**. Que ça **dégringole**!

Carole: Oh, ça passera. Demain, il y aura du **bourguignon** et on pourra **se lézarder**.

David: **Saucée de malheur**! Encore un pique-nique qui **s'en est allé en eau de boudin**. (soupir)

A TYPICAL PICNIC. . .

DIALOGUE

While leaving the pastry shop. . .

David: Ya know, I just blew all my money on food. I've gotta be totally crazy!

Carole: What a feast! Let's go find a quiet place to go scarf out.

David: Hey! This place is great! Just look at all the birds!

Carole: Oh no! It's starting to rain and I don't have an umbrella.

David: I can't get over it! What lousy luck!

Carole: What rotten weather. It's raining cats and dogs!

David: I've really had it! In the summer we fry and in the winter we freeze! Rain day and night! Look at it come down!

Carole: Oh, it'll pass. Tomorrow, the sun will be out and we can lie there and bake.

David: Darn storm! Another picnic down the tubes. (sigh)

VOCABULARY

aller en eau de boudin (s'en) exp. said of something that does not turn out / *Note:* **boudin** m. blood sausage.

bled m. place in general (*from Arabic*).

bouffe f. food, "grub" / *Note:* **bouffer** v. (*extremely popular*) to eat, "to chow down."

bourguignon m. sun / **Il fait du bourguignon aujourd'hui**; It's sunny today.

cailler v. to be extremely cold / (lit); to curdle, clot, congeal / *Also:* **se les cailler** = (lit); to freeze them off / Here, "les" refers to "les miches" meaning "the loaves." / **Je me les caille**; I'm freezing them (my "buns") off.

carrément adv. completely / (lit); squarely.

cramer v. to burn / **Je crame**; I'm burning up. / **J'ai cramé le dîner**; I burned the dinner.

dégringoler v. to tumble down / **Il a dégringolé l'escalier**; He tumbled down the stairs.

de malheur adj. darned; that which causes unhappiness / (lit); of unhappiness.

dingue adj. crazy.

fric m. money (*extremely popular*).

fusiller v. to spend; to blow one's money / (lit); to shoot.

génial(e) adj. terrific, wonderful (*extremely popular*).

gueuleton m. a huge blow-out of a meal / *Note:* **gueule** f. mouth or (lit); the mouth of an animal. When used in reference to a person, it becomes very derogatory and should be used with discretion. **Gueule** is usually used only when talking with friends and parents. / *Also:* **Ta gueule!**; Shut up!

journaille f. day.

lancequine f. (1) rain; (2) urine

lancequiner v. (1) to rain; (2) to urinate / *Note:* **lance** f. (1) water; (2) urine

lézarder (se) v. to bake in the sun / (lit); to act like the lizard / *Also:* **faire le lézard.**

marre (en avoir) exp. to be fed up / **J'en ai marre de ce cours!**; I'm fed up with this class!

neuille f. night.

pébroc m. umbrella.

peinard(e) adj. quiet, calm, "mellow(ed out)" / **Je suis peinard aujourd'hui**; I'm mellow(ed out) today.

piaf m. bird.

poisse f. bad luck / *Note:* **avoir la poisse**; to have bad luck / *Note:* **poissard(e)**; unlucky individual.

revenir (ne pas en) v. to disbelieve / **J'en reviens pas!**; I can't get over it!

saucée f. downpour / *Also:* scolding; thrashing / **Elle lui a donné une vraie saucée**; She gave him a real thrashing.

taper la cloche (se) v. to eat well.

temps de chien m. bad weather / (lit); a dog's weather.

tirer (se) v. to leave, "split" / (lit); to pull oneself.

tomber des cordes exp. to rain heavily, "to rain cats and dogs" / (lit); to fall
    cords (of rain).

PRACTICE THE VOCABULARY

[Answers to Lesson 1, pp. 45–46]

**A. Replace the word(s) in parentheses with the slang synonym from
the right column.**

1. Prends ton (parapluie) —————— . Il com-
    mence à pleuvoir.
2. S'il fait beau demain, on ira à la plage pour
    (se chauffer au soleil) —————— .
3. Qu'il fait chaud! Je (brûle) —————— !
4. J'espère qu'on aura du (soleil) ——————
    en vacances.
5. Quel (temps affreux) —————— !
6. J'ai (dépensé) —————— tout mon argent au
    marché aux puces.
7. Regarde comme ça tombe! Mais, quelle
    (averse) —————— !
8. Il (pleut) —————— des cordes!
9. En hiver, les (oiseaux) —————— volent vers
    le sud.
10. Je suis en retard! Je dois (partir)
    —————— tout de suite!
11. Tu habites dans un bon (endroit) —————— .

A . **tombe**
B . **bourguignon**
C . **crame**
D . **pébroc**
E . **temps de chien**
F . **piafs**
G . **saucée**
H . **se lézarder**
I . **fusillé**
J . **me tirer**
K . **bled**

B. Underline the appropriate word.

1. Regarde ce fou-là! Mais, il est (**doux, dingue, drôle**)!
2. Il fait froid aujourd'hui! Je (**caille, colle, me cache**)!
3. Je ne gagne jamais. J'ai de la (**pomme, poisse, poire**).
4. Quel bon restaurant! C'est sûr qu'on va se taper la (**crabe, clef, cloche**).
5. La (**bouffe, bague, barbe**) est délicieuse!
6. Je n'ai pas assez de (**fleurs, farine, fric**) pour acheter cette voiture.
7. Il est (**carrément, correctement, calmément**) bizarre, lui!
8. Cette pièce de théâtre s'en est allée en eau de (**bourbon, ballon,
    boudin**).

C. Match the French with the English translations.

1. — J'ai trop bouffé ce matin.
2. — J'en reviens pas!
3. — Ces devoirs de malheur!
4. — J'en ai marre d'y aller!
5. — On a mangé un gueuleton ce soir!
6. — Il pleut journaille et neuille ici.
7. — Il commence à lancequiner.
8. — Cette voiture est géniale!
9. — Je suis peinard aujourd'hui.
10. — Il a dégringolé l'escalier.

A. It's starting to rain.
B. I ate too much this morning.
C. This car is fantastic!
D. This darn homework!
E. I can't believe it!
F. I'm so mellowed out today.
G. He fell down the stairs.
H. I'm fed up with going there!
I. It rains day and night here!
J. We scarfed out tonight!

GRAMMAR I: CONTRACTIONS

A. The omission of *e*

As in English, contractions are extremely important in conversational French. This is perhaps one of the most important aspects of understanding the spoken language and conversing like a native! (Make sure to learn this section thoroughly before going on to the following chapters.) Below are some commonly heard contractions:

je = j'
Je veux aller en vacances.
J'veux aller en vacances.

ce = c'
Tu comprends ce qu'il dit?
Tu comprends c'qu'il dit?

me = m'
Il me parle.
Il m'parle.

de = d'
Elle a décidé de partir.
Elle a décidé d'partir.

te = t'
Tu vas te coucher maintenant?
Tu vas t'coucher maintenant?

le = l'
Elles vont le faire plus tard.
Elles vont l'faire plus tard.

se = s'
Il se met en colère facilement.
Il s'met en colère facilement.

que = qu'
Il faut que tu partes.
Il faut qu'tu partes.

Notes

1. When **je** is followed by **me**, the contraction becomes either **j'me** or **je m'**:
J'me lève; Je m'lève

2. When **j'** (**je**) is followed by a word beginning with **c, f, p, q, s,** or **t,** it is pronounced **sh.** In the following examples, **j'** is pronounced **sh:**

   J'compte sur toi.   **J'quitte la maison.**
   J'fais ça facilement.   **J'sais pas.**
   J'peux pas y aller.   **J'te parle.**

3. When **j', c', m', d', t', l'** or **s'** is followed by the same letter, the sound of that letter is simply held a little longer:

   Elle a décidé de danser.   Il va le lire.
   Elle a décidé d'danser.   **Il va l'lire.**

4. In some cases, you may wish *not* to drop the **e** if there are too many consonants surrounding it. In this case, retaining the **e** might actually make the articulation easier:

   Je coupe le fil.   Tu risques de te faire du mal.
   J'coupe le fil.   **Tu risques de t'faire du mal.**

   It would actually be more difficult to articulate the previous sentences if every **e** were contracted:

   J'coupe l'fil.   **Tu risques d't'faire du mal.**

   This is *absolutely* at the speaker's own discretion. The rule in slang is, "Whatever feels easier, do!"

B. The omission of *ne*

In spoken French, **ne** is omitted entirely:

   Il **ne** va pas y aller. = Il va pas y aller.
   Je **n'**aime pas sortir la nuit. = J'aime pas sortir la nuit.
   Je **n'**ai pas d'argent sur moi. = J'ai pas d'argent sur moi.
   Ne bouge pas! = Bouge pas!
   Je **ne** sais pas. = J'sais pas. (pronounced: "shay pa")

C. The omission of *u* in *tu*

The letter **u** in **tu** may frequently be muted when followed by a vowel:

   tu es = t'es ≠ t'es pas
   tu annonces = t'annonces ≠ t'annonces pas
   tu ouvres = t'ouvres ≠ t'ouvres pas
   tu invites = t'invites ≠ t'invites pas

Example:

Tu avoues que tu es toujours devant le réfrigérateur quand tu as faim?
T'avoues que t'es toujours devant le réfrigérateur quand t'as faim?

Note:

It is certainly correct to pronounce the previous sentence entirely with contractions:

   T'avoues qu't'es toujours devant l'frigo quand t'as faim?

D. The omission of *re*

In everyday speech, when something is difficult to pronounce, it may simply be slurred over or even dropped. When the **re** ending is followed by a consonant, it is not easy to articulate quickly even for the native speaker of French. For this reason, the **re** sound is often omitted entirely:

le pauvre chat = le **pauv'**chat
un, deux, trois, quatre, cinq = un, deux, trois, **quat'**, cinq
notre maison = **not'**maison

The same applies to the **re** verbs.

Example:

Il va mettre son cahier sur la table.
Il va mett'son cahier sur la table.
Je vais prendre le train à onze heures pour être chez vous à midi.
J'vais prend'l'train à onze heures pour êt'chez vous à midi.

Notes

1. The **d** in **prend** is silent.
2. The **re** sound can only be dropped when it *ends* a word. Therefore, words like apprendre, comprendre, contrepoint, montrer, etc., must retain the **re** sound.

EXERCISES

A. Rewrite the portion in parentheses using contractions.

Example:

Tu peux (me téléphoner) **m'téléphoner** demain?
(Je ne sais pas) **J'sais pas** si (je peux) **j'peux.**

1. (Tu as) _____ faim?
2. (Je te) _____ présente mon amie, Pascale.
3. (Je comprends) _____ bien (ce que) _____ tu dis.
4. (Je vais) _____ (le voir) _____ plus tard.
5. (Tu n'entends pas) _____ le tonnerre dehors?
6. (Je veux) _____ (prendre) _____ mes vacances demain!
7. (Je dois) _____ finir mes devoirs.
8. (Je peux) _____ (prendre) _____ (le métro) _____ si (je me) _____ dépêche.
9. Qu'est-ce que (je vais) _____ (mettre) _____ ce soir?
10. (Je pars) _____ tout (de suite) _____ pour (être) _____ chez toi à midi.
11. (Je n'ai pas) _____ très faim.
12. (Je ne peux pas) _____ (le faire) _____ .

B. In the following paragraph, draw a slash through the letter(s) where a contraction would be appropriate. (Read the corrected paragraph aloud several times until you feel comfortable pronouncing the contractions.)

Example:

J¢ n¢ vais pas prendr¢ votr¢
voiture parc¢ que les freins n¢ marchent pas bien.

Aujourd'hui, je vais me lever de bonne heure pour passer la journée en ville. Je dois arriver vers midi pour prendre le déjeuner avec mes amis Irène et Jacques à notre café préféré. J'aime bien ce café parce que les prix ne sont pas astronomiques! Après, on va aller au parc pour prendre de la glace comme dessert! Si on a le temps, on se promènera dans le jardin de Versailles.

GRAMMAR II: COMMONLY HEARD CONTRACTIONS

A. The following contractions are commonly used in everyday conversation. However, these contractions are rarely ever seen in written form except in direct quotations.

celui = **c'ui**	Tu connais celui-là? **Tu connais c'ui-là?**	Only used with -ce or -là pronounced **sui-là**.
c'est un(e) = **c't'un**	C'est un(e) bon(ne) ami(e). **C't'un(e) bon(ne) ami(e).**	Also: past tense = c'était un(e) = **c't'ait un(e)**
elle(s) = **è**	Elle m'parle. **E m'parle.** Elles sont belles. **E sont belles.**	Only when followed by a consonant.
il faut = **faut**	Il faut que je parte. **Faut qu'je parte.**	**il** may be dropped in all tenses: **faudrait** (que), **fallait** (que), etc.
il y a = **y a**	Il y a du monde ici! **Y a du monde ici!**	**il** may be dropped in all tenses: **y aurait, y avait, y a eu**, etc. *Note:* When used as an abbreviation of **il y a, y a** is articulated as one syllable: **ya.**

il = **y**	Il a une nouvelle voiture. **Y a une nouvelle voiture.**	When used to mean **he** or **it, y** is articulated as a *separate* syllable even when followed by a vowel: **y a** = **y-a** *not* **ya.**
ils = **y**	Ils vont au magasin. **Y vont au magasin.**	Only when followed by a consonant.
ils = **z**	Ils ont de la chance. **Z'ont de la chance.**	Only when followed by a vowel.
lui = **'ui**	Tu lui parles souvent? **T'ui parles souvent?**	**lui** does *not* take on the form of **'ui** at the end of a sentence: **C'est pour lui**; *not* **pour 'ui**
parce que = **pasque** **(and parc'que)**	Il sourit parce qu'il est content. **Il sourit pasqu'il est content.**	
petit(e) = **p'tit(e)**	Il est petit. **Il est p'tit.**	
peut-être = **p't'êt'**	Peut-être qu'elle est malade. **P't'êt'qu'elle est malade.**	
plus = **pu**	Je n'ai plus faim. **J'ai pu faim.**	
puis = **pis**	Je vais au zoo et puis au cinéma. **J'vais au zoo et pis au cinéma.**	
puisque = **pisque**	Il ne vient pas puisqu'il pleut. **Il vient pas pisqu'il pleut.**	
quelques = **quèques**	Tu peux me donner quelques francs? **Tu peux m'donner quèques francs?**	
s'il te plaît = **s'te plaît**	Passe-moi le sel, s'il te plaît. **Passe-moi l'sel, s'te plaît.**	

EXERCISES

A. Write in the appropriate contraction.

1. _____ c'est un
2. _____ il y a
3. _____ celui-là
4. _____ il faut
5. _____ puis
6. _____ quelques
7. _____ plus
8. _____ c'est une
9. _____ il y avait
10. _____ elle

B. Fill in the blanks with the contraction of the underlined word(s). (There is one slang word in each sentence below from the dialogue. Can you recognize it?)

1. Il faut que _____ je lui _____ donne mon pébroc.
2. Il _____ va très bien parce _____ qu'il _____ va se tirer _____ pour les vacances.
3. C'est un _____ film génial.
4. Il y a _____ beaucoup de _____ piafs dehors.
5. Tu peux me _____ prêter du fric s'il te plaît _____ ?
6. Ils ont _____ mangé un gueuleton ce soir.
7. Je crois _____ qu'elle _____ veut me _____ parler de _____ sa poisse d'hier.
8. Je n'ai _____ plus _____ faim.
9. J'en ai marre! Je ne sais _____ pas ce qu'il _____ me _____ dit!
10. Ils _____ vont à la plage puisqu'il _____ lancequine pas.

Note:

The basic dialogues in the following chapters have been written with contractions as learned in this lesson. Once again, make sure that you feel comfortable with GRAMMARS I and II before continuing.

Leçon Deux

AU RESTAURANT...

DIALOGUE

Régis et Nélie sont assis dans le restaurant...

Régis: J'espère qu'c'est pas un **boui-boui** comme celui d'hier soir. Y était **cradingue** c'ui-là!

Nélie: T'inquiètes pas! C'**resto**, y est **d'première bourre**. Regarde comme c'est **nickel**!

Régis: **Ouais,** c'est vrai. J'commence à avoir les **crocs**, moi. J'vais **m'goinfrer** ce soir. J'ai envie d'**piquer** d'la **bidoche**.

Nélie: Moi aussi! J'm'**en lèche les babines** d'avance!

Régis: T'as vu ces prix-là? Dix milles **balles** pour une **boutanche d'brouille-ménage**? J'suis pas **rupin**, moi!

Nélie: A mon avis, la **boustifaille** ici, è vaut plus qu'ça. J'ai la **pépie**, moi. Tu prends un **apéro** ou d'la **moussante**, toi? **V'là l'barman**!

Régis: C'**guindal** d'**flotte**, ça m'suffit. Quand j'**picole**, j'deviens **bourré** en un rien de temps... un vrai **soûlard**!

Nélie: Mais l'serveur, y pourrait toujours t'**filer** du **caouah**. Qu'est-c'qu'y est devenu au fait!?

Régis: Génial! Pas d'**douloureuse**!

Nélie: Et pas d'**pourliche**! S'y **s'pointe** pas en deux **z'condes**, j'vais **faire figaro**!

Lesson Two

AT THE RESTAURANT...

DIALOGUE

Régis and Nélie are seated in the restaurant...

Régis: I hope this isn't a dive like the one last night. It was trashed!

Nélie: Don't worry! This restaurant's the best. Look how spotless it is!

Régis: Yeah, that's true. I'm getting kind of hungry. I'm gonna pork out tonight. I feel like getting some meat.

Nélie: Me too! My mouth is already watering!

Régis: Did you see these prices? One hundred francs for a bottle of ordinary red wine? C'mon, I'm not loaded with money!

Nélie: In my opinion, the food here is worth even more than that. You want a cocktail or a beer? There's the barman!

Régis: This glass of water is just fine. When I drink, I get bombed in no time flat ... a real drunk!

Nélie: But the waiter could always give you some coffee. What happened to him anyway!?

Régis: Terrific! No check!

Nélie: And no tip! If he doesn't show up fast, he's gonna get stiffed!

VOCABULARY

apéro m. cocktail; apéritif.

balle f. one centime (*extremely popular*) / **Tu peux m'prêter cent balles?**; Can you loan me a franc? / *Note:* 100 balles = 1 franc; 200 balles = 2 francs; etc. Of all the slang synonyms for money, this is one of the most popular!

barman m. barman / (see Unit II, **English Words That Are Used in Spoken French**).

bidoche f. meat (usually of inferior quality) / **sac à bidoche**; sleeping bag.

boui-boui m. bad restaurant; "dive," "greasy spoon."

bourré(e) (être) adj. to be very drunk / (lit); to be stuffed (with alcohol) / *Note:* **bourrer** v. (lit); to stuff, cram, pack tight.

bourre (de première) f. excellent, first-rate / *Note:* **bourre** f. (lit); flock for stuffing or padding.

boustifaille f. food; "grub" / *Note:* **boustifailler** v. to eat, "to chow down."

boutanche f. bottle.

brouille-ménage m. humorous for red wine / *Note:* **brouiller** v. to mix up; stir up / **ménage** m. household / This literally translates as "something that stirs up the household" since husbands and wives would get into fights after having too much to drink.

caouah m. coffee / *Note:* This is derived from Arabic.

cradingue adj. very dirty, filthy / *Also:* **crado**.

crocs (avoir les) m.pl. to be very hungry / *Note:* (1) The "cs" in **crocs** is silent; (2) **crocs** m.pl. teeth.

douloureuse f. bill (in a restaurant) / (lit); that which causes pain / *Note:* Derived from the noun **douleur** f. pain.

figaro (faire) m. to leave no tip; "to stiff a waiter."

filer v. to give; hand over / **File-moi ça tout d'suite!**; Hand it over now!

flotte f. (1) water; (2) rain / *Also:* **flotter** v. to rain / (lit); to float.

goinfrer (se) v. to eat a lot; to "pork out" / *Note:* **goinfre** m. one who makes a pig of himself.

guindal m. glass (of water).

lécher les babines (s'en) exp. To lick one's lips over something / (lit); to lick one's chops over something / *Note:* **babines** f.pl. lips (of an animal); chops.

moussante f. beer / *Note:* This comes from **mousse** f. (lit); foam.

nickel adj. very clean, "spotless."

ouais interj. "yeah" (*extremely popular*).

pépie (avoir la) f. to be very thirsty / *Note:* **la pépie** (lit); a disease of the tongue of fowl.

picoler v. to drink alcohol / *Note:* **pictance** f. alcohol.

piquer v. to get; to take (illegally) / **J'vais piquer un somme**; I'm gonna take a nap. **Y a piqué ma montre**; He stole my watch.

pointer (se) v. to arrive; show up / *Note:* **pointer** v. (lit); to sprout up.

pourliche m. tip / *Note:* This comes from the French word **pourboire** meaning "tip" or literally "for to drink." Here, **boire** has been replaced by its slang synonym **licher**.

resto m. abbreviation of "restaurant."

rupin(e) adj. rich.

soûlard(e) n. drunkard / *Note:* **se soûler** v. to get drunk.

v'là interj. a commonly heard contraction of **voilà**.

z'conde f. pronounced "z'gonde" / a commonly heard contraction of **seconde**.

PRACTICE THE VOCABULARY

[Answers to Lesson 2, pp. 46–47]

A.   Underline the synonym.

1. **boustifaille**	a. boisson	b. nourriture	c. eau
2. **guindal**	a. fille	b. verre	c. restaurant
3. **flotte**	a. ventre	b. vent	c. eau
4. **rupin**	a. artiste	b. fatigué	c. riche
5. **cradingue**	a. sale	b. beau	c. grand
6. **balle**	a. centime	b. voiture	c. maison
7. **filer**	a. montrer	b. donner	c. parler
8. **soûlard**	a. garçon	b. ivrogne	c. lit
9. **picoler**	a. marcher	b. courir	c. boire
10. **se pointer**	a. arriver	b. partir	c. attendre

B.   Complete the phrase by choosing the appropriate word from the list. Give the correct form of the verb.

bidoche	bourré	douloureuse
boutanche	ouais	se goinfrer
moussante	barman	faire figaro
pépie	caouah	lécher les babines

1.   Quel repas fabuleux! J'm'en _____ d'avance!
2.   Je m'sens _____ pasque j'ai trop bu!
3.   Regarde cette _____ ! Y est cher, c'café!
4.   Les végétariens mangent pas la _____ .
5.   Y fait si chaud dehors qu'j'ai toujours la _____ .
6.   Si j'bois du _____ la nuit, j'peux pas dormir.

7. J'veux d'l'alcool, moi. Où est l' _____ ?
8. E m'a donné une _____ d'vin rouge comme cadeau.
9. Y est horrible, c'serveur! J'ai l'intention d' _____ .
10. Y est bon c'restaurant, tu crois? Mais _____ !
11. En Allemagne, la _____ est très populaire.
12. On va _____ au restaurant ce soir.

C. Answer the question by replacing the underlined word with its slang synonym in the right column. Make sure to use contractions where appropriate. (Since *ouais* is as popular in France as *yeah* is in English, practice using it when answering each question.)

Example:

As-tu <u>mangé</u> de la soupe?
Ouais, j'ai bouffé d'la soupe.

1. Tu vas laisser un <u>pourboire</u>?	A.	**nickel**
_____ .	B.	**brouille-ménage**
2. Aimes-tu le <u>vin rouge</u>?	C.	**piquer**
_____ .	D.	**les crocs**
3. Connais-tu ce <u>restaurant</u>?	E.	**pourliche**
_____ .	F.	**de première bourre**
4. Veux-tu de <u>l'eau</u>?	G.	**flotte**
_____ .	H.	**boui-boui**
5. Veux-tu <u>prendre</u> un dessert?	I.	**apéro**
_____ .	J.	**resto**
6. Désires-tu un <u>apéritif</u>?		

7. Trouves-tu le café <u>excellent</u>?

_____ .

8. Est-ce un <u>mauvais restaurant</u>?

_____ .

9. Est-ce une maison <u>très propre</u>?

_____ .

10. Est-ce que tu as <u>faim</u>?

_____ .

GRAMMAR I: THE STRUCTURE OF A QUESTION

A. Inversion and *est-ce que* forms

The structure of a question is extremely important when trying to speak like a native. Even in English, there is a "relaxed" way of speaking. Often, questions are phrased as statements:

Example: "You're going to Europe next week?"

This construction is even more important in slang. If one were to use slang in a sentence that was constructed and articulated perfectly, it would sound unnatural:

Example: "Do you think she is going to be so ticked off at him that she will wig out in front of the whole class?"

More informal pronunciation actually sounds less jarring:

Example: "Ya think she's gonna be so ticked off ad'em she's gonna wig out in fronna the whole class?"

In colloquial French, a question is almost *always* constructed this way: as a statement with a question mark at the end. Traditionally, the inversion and **est-ce que** forms are used in questions:

       Inversion form: Veux-tu déjeuner chez moi?
       est-ce que form: Est-ce que tu veux déjeuner chez moi?

However, in colloquial French, these two forms are rarely used:

Veux-tu déjeuner chez moi?   Est-ce que tu vas mieux?
Tu veux déjeuner chez moi?   **Tu vas mieux?**

Note:

BECAUSE SLANG IS A CASUAL AND INFORMAL "LANGUAGE," THE STRUCTURE OF ANY SENTENCE CONTAINING SLANG SHOULD BE CASUAL AND INFORMAL AS WELL OR IT MAY TEND TO SOUND PHONY!

B. Structure of a question when using interrogative pronouns

The previous rule also applies to interrogative pronouns: **combien (de)**, **comment, où, pourquoi, quand, quel(le), qui** and **quoi**. The interrogative pronoun is placed at the beginning of the statement, transforming it into a question.

combien: Combien pèses-tu?
(how much)   **Combien tu pèses?**

combien de: Combien d'enfants a-t-elle?
(how many,   **Combien elle en a, des enfants?**
how much)   *Note:* This is a strange one! In scholastic French, we are taught that **de** always follows **combien** when meaning "how many." However, in colloquial French the object is placed at the end of the question *as well as* between the subject and verb in the form of the pronoun **en**.

comment:	Comment vas-tu? **Comment tu vas?**
où:	Où vas-tu maintenant? **Où tu vas maintenant?** *Note:* This also applies to **d'où. D'où tu viens?**
pourquoi:	Pourquoi as-tu acheté ça? **Pourquoi t'as acheté ça?**
quand:	Quand est-ce qu'ils veulent venir chez nous? **Quand ils veulent venir chez nous?**
quel(le):	Quelle heure est-il? **Quelle heure il est?**
qui: (as an object)	Qui rencontres-tu à l'aéroport? **Qui tu rencontres à l'aéroport?** *Note:* This also applies to **à qui, avec qui, pour qui,** etc. **A qui tu parles? Avec qui tu danses? Pour qui t'as fait ça?**
quoi:	Qu'est-ce qu'y prend avec lui? **Y prend quoi avec lui?** *Note:* **quoi** is a little different from the other interrogative pronouns because it never begins a statement but rather follows the verb. *Also:* **c'est quoi, ça?** is an extremely common colloquial substitute for "qu'est-ce que c'est?"
à quoi:	A quoi penses-tu? **A quoi tu penses?**
de quoi:	De quoi parles-tu? **De quoi tu parles?**

PRACTICE ASKING A QUESTION

A. Rewrite the question in colloquial French using contractions where appropriate.

Example:

      Pourquoi as-tu fait ça?   Qu'est-ce qu'y veut, lui?
      Pourquoi t'as fait ça?   **Y veut quoi, lui?**

1. Qui vas-tu aider? _____ ?
2. Quand veux-tu partir? _____ ?

3. Quelle heure est-il? _____ ?
4. Pourquoi n'aimes-tu pas ça? _____ ?
5. Comment va-t-il aller au cinéma? _____ ?
6. Qu'est-ce que tu écris? _____ ?
7. D'où vient-il? _____ ?
8. Combien de pantalons as-tu? _____ ?
9. Désires-tu m'accompagner? _____ ?
10. Prends-tu l'autobus? _____ ?
11. Sais-tu conduire? _____ ?
12. Aimes-tu ça? _____ ?

B. Write the question that goes with the answer. (There is one slang word in each sentence below from the dialogue. Can you recognize it?)

Example:

Y va aller au resto avec Nicholas.
(avec qui) **Avec qui y va aller au resto?**

J'vais prend'd'la boustifaille.
(quand) **Quand tu vas prend'd'la boustifaille?**

1. J'vais parler du boui-boui à ma mère.
   (à qui) _____ ?
2. E regarde le soûlard.
   (quoi) _____ ?
3. J'vais acheter d'la moussante.
   (pourquoi) _____ ?
4. J'vais commander cette boutanche d'vin.
   (quelle) _____ ?
5. J'vais inviter l'barman à la soirée.
   (qui) _____ ?
6. J'suis devenu rupin!
   (comment) _____ ?
7. Elle a trois maisons.
   (combien) _____ ?
8. Y va aller s'goinfrer.
   (où) _____ ?
9. E va picoler avec Robert.
   (avec qui) _____ ?
10. Y va laver c'guindal.
    (quel) _____ ?

Leçon Trois

LE CAMBRIOLAGE. . .

DIALOGUE

Jean parle à Léon de son aventure. . .

Léon: **Salut**, Jean. Mais, t'as l'air **lessivé**!

Jean: **Tu parles!** Hier soir, j'étais dans mon **plumard** quand j'ai entendu un **mec** qui **s'baladait** à l'extérieur d'la **baraque** à côté d'chez moi.

Léon: C't'ait un **casseur**?

Jean: Ah, ouais! Au début, y essayait d'y **encarrer** par la **lourde**. Mais comme c'était trop **duraille**, y a **bousillé** la **vanterne**! Quel **charivari**!

Léon: Probablement qu'y voulait **barboter** n'importe quoi . . . la **téloche**, la **flâneuse**, ou même le **bigophone**!

Jean: C'est sûr . . . pour les **mettre au clou**! Alors, j'ai appelé la **flicaille** bien sûr.

Léon: Z'ont **radiné** tout d'suite?

Jean: Ouais, mais l'mec y s'est **carapaté fissa**! J'suppose qu'y s'est **planqué** quèque part.

Léon: Ouais! S'y s'**fait agrafer**, on l'**fourrera** dans l'**placard** pour **écoper** quèques **piges**!

Jean: Alors, après qu'on m'a **cuisiné** pendant une heure, j'pouvais pas m'rendormir.

Léon: Quelle aventure!

Lesson Three

THE ROBBERY...

DIALOGUE

Jean is speaking to Léon about his adventure...

Léon:	Hi Jean! You look wiped out!
Jean:	You said it! Last night, I was in my bed when I heard a guy walking around the house next to mine.
Léon:	Was it a robber?
Jean:	Oh, yeah! At first, he tried to get in through the door. But since that was too hard, he broke the window! What a racket!
Léon:	He probably wanted to grab anything... the television, the armchair, or even the telephone!
Jean:	Sure... to hock them! So, of course I called the cops.
Léon:	Did they show up right away?
Jean:	Yeah, but the guy darted away fast! I suppose he hid somewhere.
Léon:	Yeah! If he got himself caught, they'd stick'm in the slammer and slap'm with a couple of years!
Jean:	So, after getting the third degree for an hour, I couldn't get back to sleep.
Léon:	What an adventure!

VOCABULARY

agrafer (se faire) v. to get arrested / (lit); to fasten by means of a hook, clasp, or clip; to staple / *Note:* **agrafer** v. to arrest.

balader (se) v. to stroll / *Note:* **balade** f. stroll / **faire une balade**; to take a stroll.

barboter v. to steal, "swipe" / *Note:* **barboteur** m. thief.

baraque f. house (*extremely popular*) / (lit); hut.

bigophone m. telephone / *Note:* Derived from **bigorne** f. (lit); a two-headed anvil whose shape looks something like a telephone receiver *Also:* **bigophoner** v. to telephone someone.

bousiller v. to break, damage / *Also:* "to botch up" / **J'ai bousillé mon examen**; I botched up my test.

carapater (se) v. to leave quickly; "to scram."

casseur m. robber / *Note:* **casser** v. to rob; break in / (lit); to break.

charivari m. loud noise, racket.

cuisiner v. to interrogate; to pump, to grill someone for information / (lit); to cook.

duraille adj. hard / *Note:* Derived from **dur** adj. hard.

écoper v. to receive something that is unwanted / **C'est toujours moi qui écope!**; It's always me who gets it (the blame)!

encarrer v. to enter / *Note:* **encarrade** f. entrance / **décarrade** f. exit.

fissa adv. quickly / *Note:* **fissa** is derived from Arabic.

flicaille f. the police (in general) / *Note:* **flic** m. policeman; "cop."

flâneuse f. chair / (lit); loafer / *Note:* **flâner** v. to loaf around.

fourrer v. to cram; to stick / **Où t'as fourré tes clés?**; Where did you stick your keys?

lessivé(e) (être) adj. to be exhausted / (lit); to be washed out.

lourde f. door / (lit); the heavy thing.

mec m. guy; "dude."

mettre au clou exp. to hock / (lit); to put on the nail.

pige f. year / **Elle a deux piges**; She's two years old.

placard m. jail / (lit); closet.

planquer v. to hide / *Note:* **planque** f. hiding place.

plumard m. bed / *Note:* **se plumarder** v. to go to bed.

radiner v. to show up, arrive / *Note:* Although the verb **arriver** is conjugated with **être**, its slang synonym **radiner** is conjugated with **avoir**: **J'suis arrivé = J'ai radiné.**

salut interj. "hi" / *Note:* **salut** is also used to mean "good-bye" depending on the context.

téloche f. television.

tu parles! exp. you said it! / *Also:* **Tu parles, Charles!**

vanterne f. window.

PRACTICE THE VOCABULARY

[Answers to Lesson 3, pp. 47–48]

A. Complete the phrase by choosing the appropriate word from the list. Make all necessary changes to the verbs.

agrafer	balader	écoper
fourrer	plumard	baraque
salut	planquer	flicaille
bousiller	placard	lourde

1. Le voleur, y s'est fait _____ par la police.
2. En entrant, y a fermé la _____ .
3. Elle a _____ un mois d'prison.
4. J'ai habité dans cette _____ toute ma vie.
5. On m'a _____ en prison.
6. J'te verrai plus tard. _____ !
7. On a volé mon portefeuille! Appelle la _____ !
8. J'suis vraiment fatigué. J'vais aller au _____ .
9. Quelle journée splendide. J'ai envie d'me _____ .
10. Si tu voles ça, tu risques de t'faire mett'dans l' _____ !
11. Qui a _____ mon rasoir électrique? Y marche plus!
12. La police! On doit s' _____ !

B. Replace the word(s) in parentheses with the slang synonym from the right column. Make all necessary changes to the verbs.

1. J'suis (très fatigué) _____ c'matin.	A. fissa
2. Y m'a (interrogé) _____ pendant une heure!	B. cuisiner
	C. charivari
3. Elle est entrée par la (fenêtre) _____ .	D. bigophone
4. Quel (bruit) _____ dehors!	E. piges
5. Quand è va (arriver) _____ ?	F. vanterne
6. J'ai 18 (ans) _____ aujourd'hui.	G. se carapater
7. Y l'a mangé (vite) _____ !	H. radiner
8. Le voleur, y (est parti vite) _____ !	I. lessivé
9. Y adore parler au (téléphone) _____ .	J. duraille
10. C'est pas (dur) _____ d'apprend'l'argot!	

C. Translate each sentence into French by replacing the underlined word(s) with its slang synonym in parentheses. Make all necessary

changes to the verbs. (Always make sure to use contractions where appropriate.)

Example:

This is a beautiful <u>house</u>!
(baraque) **C't'une belle baraque!**

1. He <u>stole</u> the bike.
    (**piquer**) _____ .
2. I want to watch <u>T.V.</u>
    (**téloche**) _____ .
3. I <u>blew</u> my test.
    (**bousiller**) _____ .
4. There's the <u>robber</u>!
    (**casseur**) _____ .
5. Do you want <u>to go in</u>?
    (**encarrer**) _____ .
6. You know that <u>guy</u>?
    (**mec**) _____ .
7. We could always <u>hock it</u>!
    (**mettre au clou**) _____ !
8. What time did she <u>show up</u>?
    (**radiner**) _____ ?
9. Do you want to <u>stroll</u> after diner?
    (**se balader**) _____ ?
10. I'm <u>pooped</u>!
    (**lessivé**) _____ !

GRAMMAR I: THE STRUCTURE OF A SENTENCE

A. Subject followed by a personal pronoun

In the previous lesson, we learned how to construct a question in spoken French. The structure of a statement is equally important. In colloquial French, the subject is always followed by a personal pronoun such as: **il (y)**, **elle(s) (è)**, and **ils (y or z)**. The verb then follows:

Cécile m'fait toujours rire.   Ce pantalon m'va bien.
Cécile, è m'fait toujours rire.   **Ce pantalon, y m'va bien.**

B. Subject/object at the end of a sentence

Another *very* popular construction is one in which the subject or object appears at the end of the sentence:

SUBJECT	OBJECT
Cécile m'fait toujours rire.	J'vois ma mère souvent.
E m'fait toujours rire, Cécile.	**J'la vois souvent, ma mère.**
Ce pantalon m'va bien.	T'as parlé à ta sœur hier?
Y m'va bien, c'pantalon.	**T'ui as parlé hier, à ta sœur?**

C. Interrogative pronouns at the end of a phrase

The structure illustrated above, in which a complete sentence is formed first then the subject thrown in at the end, also applies to questions with interrogative pronouns:

combien, comment, où, pourquoi, quand, quel(le), qui and **quoi**

As learned in Lesson 2, these interrogative pronouns (with the exception of **quoi**) can be placed at the beginning of a statement to transform it into a question:

Quand tu dois partir?
Comment tu vas faire ça?
Combien elle en a, des enfants?

It is equally common to form a question by placing the interrogative pronoun at the *end* of a statement:

Tu dois partir **quand**?
Tu vas faire ça **comment**?
Elle en a **combien**, des enfants?

Note:

In the previous example, **combien** ends the phrase with the subject thrown in at the end for more emphasis:

"She has how many of them ... children (that is)?"

EXERCISES

A. Rewrite each sentence with (a) the appropriate personal pronoun after the subject and (b) the subject at the end.

Example:

Jean, va bientôt arriver.
a. **Jean, y va bientôt arriver.**
b. **Y va bientôt arriver Jean.**

1. Ce gâteau est délicieux.
   a. _____ .
   b. _____ .

2. Suzanne est très jolie.
    a. _____ .
    b. _____ .
3. Le dîner est ruiné.
    a. _____ .
    b. _____ .
4. Cette robe me va comme un gant.
    a. _____ .
    b. _____ .
5. Le film était fantastique.
    a. _____ .
    b. _____ .
6. Ma mère m'appelle.
    a. _____ .
    b. _____ .
7. Les jours passent vite.
    a. _____ .
    b. _____ .
8. Cette voiture est toute neuve.
    a. _____ .
    b. _____ .
9. Mon petit frère est très grand.
    a. _____ .
    b. _____ .
10. Serge te demande au téléphone.
    a. _____ .
    b. _____ .

B.   Rewrite the question in French by: (1) replacing the underlined word(s) with its appropriate synonym from this list and (2) placing the interrogative pronoun at the end of the phrase (with the exception of *quoi*). Give the correct form of the verb.

Example:

> What did he <u>throw</u> on the table?
> (quoi) **Y a jeté quoi sur la table?**

lessivé	charivari	piquer
planquer	fourrer	téloche
baraque	bousiller	radiner
flic	se balader	fissa

1. Why are you making this <u>noise</u>?
    (pourquoi) _____ ?
2. What did you <u>break</u>?
    (quoi) _____ ?

3. Which <u>house</u> are you going to buy?
   (quelle) _____ ?

4. When did he <u>steal</u> it?
   (quand) _____ ?

5. Whom are you trying to <u>hide</u>?
   (qui) _____ ?

6. Why are you eating <u>quickly</u>?
   (pourquoi) _____ ?

7. When is he going to talk to the <u>cop</u>?
   (quand) _____ ?

8. How many <u>televisions</u> do you have?
   (combien) _____ ?

9. Whom did she <u>show up</u> with?
   (qui) _____ ?

10. Where are you going to go <u>stroll</u>?
    (où) _____ ?

11. Why are you <u>pooped</u>?
    (pourquoi) _____ ?

LA FAMILLE...

DIALOGUE

Richard parle de sa réunion familiale...

Daniel: Alors, elle était comment la grande réunion?

Richard   Au début, j'm'**en suis payé une tranche** mais pas vers la fin! Z'ont eu une vraie **bagarre** ma **vieille** et mon **vieux!**

Daniel: Y **s'bouffaient l'nez** tes **vieux**, hein?

Richard: Tu parles! Pour commencer, ma **frangine** è **s'engueulait** avec mon **beauffe** sans arrêt.

Daniel: Mais pourquoi?

Richard: Dès l'commencement, z'avaient déjà la **tête près du bonnet** pasqu'leurs p'tits **fiston** et **fistonne**, y faisaient qu'**chialer!**

Daniel: Mon **frangin**, y veut pas d'**moutards** à cause d'ça.

Richard: Alors, ma **frangine-dabuche**, elle voulait faire quèque chose mais mon **frangin-dab**, y 'ui a dit qu'**c'était pas ses oignons.**

Daniel: Et les **beaux-vieux**...y s'amusaient?

Richard: **Tu rigoles!** Ma **belle-doche**, elle était **d'mauvais poil** pasqu'mon **beau-dab**, y **faisait la gueule** toute la soirée!

Daniel: Z'ont l'air vraiment charmants!

Richard: Donc...j'ai passé la soirée comme arbitre! Ah, la joie d'êt'**bouchon!**

Daniel: Si jamais j'décide d'**signer un bail**, j'espère qu'ma **régulière s'entendra** bien avec ma **smala**.

Lesson Four

THE FAMILY...

DIALOGUE

Richard is talking about his family reunion...

Daniel: So, how was the big reunion?

Richard: In the beginning, I had a great time but not toward the end! My mom and dad had a real blow-up!

Daniel: Your parents really got into it, huh?

Richard: You're not kidding! To start off with, my sister kept chewing out my brother-in-law non-stop.

Daniel: Why was that?

Richard: Right from the start, they were already ticked off because their little son and daughter didn't do anything but cry!

Daniel: My brother doesn't want any kids because of that.

Richard: So, my aunt wanted to do something but my uncle told her it was none of her business.

Daniel: What about the parents-in-law ... did they have fun?

Richard: You gotta be kidding! My sister's mother-in-law was in a lousy mood because the father-in-law just frowned the whole evening!

Daniel: They sound truly charming!

Richard: So, I got to spend my evening as referee! Ah, the joy of being the youngest!

Daniel: If ever I decide to get hitched, I hope my wife gets along with my family.

VOCABULARY

bagarre f. a fight; scuffle (of crowd and police) / *Note:* **se bagarrer** v. to have a fight or quarrel / *Also:* **chercher la bagarre;** to look for a fight.

beauffe m. brother-in-law; "beau-frère."

beau-dab m. father-in-law; "beau-père."

beaux-vieux m.pl. parents-in-law, "beaux-parents."

belle-doche f. mother-in-law; "belle-mère."

bouchon m. youngest member of the family / (lit); stopper, plug, cork (of a bottle).

bouffer l'nez (se) exp. to fight / (lit); to eat each other's nose / *Note:* This humorous expression describes two people yelling extremely close to each other's face.

c'est pas tes oignons exp. "It's none of your business" / (lit); it's none of your onions.

chialer v. to cry.

de mauvais poil (être) exp. to be in a bad mood / (lit); to be of bad hair / *Note:* être de bon poil; to be in a good mood.

engueuler v. to yell (at someone) / *Note:* This comes from the slang word **gueule** f. derogatory for "mouth" / (lit); this might be literally translated as "to mouth off at (someone)." / *Also:* **s'engueuler avec quelqu'un;** to yell *at* someone.

entendre (s') v. to get along with someone; to understand each other / (lit); to hear each other. / This could be compared to the American colloquialism "I hear 'ya; where you're coming from."

faire la gueule exp. (1) to pout, frown; (2) to give someone the cold shoulder / *Note:* The difference between these two definitions depends on the context.

fiston m. son; "fils."

fistonne f. daughter.

frangin m. brother.

frangine f. sister.

frangin-dab m. uncle / (lit); brother-father.

frangine-dabuche f. aunt / (lit); sister-mother.

moutards m.pl. children, "kids."

payer une tranche (s'en) exp. to have a great time / *Note:* **se payer** v. to treat oneself / (lit); to treat oneself to a slice (of it).

régulière f. wife / (lit); "regular one."

signer un bail v. to get married / (lit); to sign a lease.

smala f. (large) family or household.

tête près du bonnet (avoir la) exp. to be on the verge of getting angry / (lit); to have the head close to the bonnet.

tu rigoles exp. "you're kidding" / *Note:* **rigoler** v. to laugh / *Also:* **sans rigoler?;** no kidding?

vieille f. mother / (lit); old woman.

vieux m. father / (lit); old man.
vieux m.pl. parents / (lit); old people, "old folks."

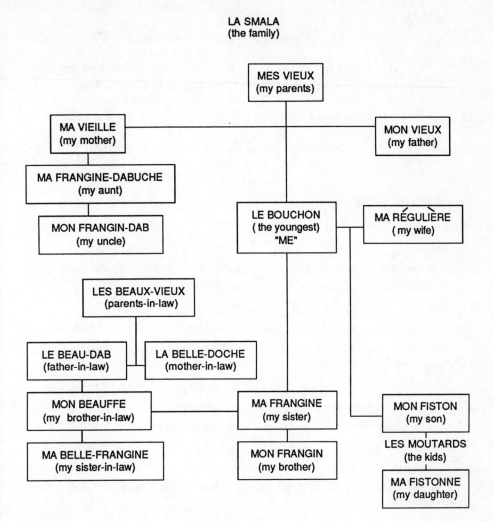

LA SMALA
(the family)

MES VIEUX
(my parents)

MA VIEILLE
(my mother)

MON VIEUX
(my father)

MA FRANGINE-DABUCHE
(my aunt)

MON FRANGIN-DAB
(my uncle)

LE BOUCHON
(the youngest)
"ME"

MA RÉGULIÈRE
(my wife)

LES BEAUX-VIEUX
(parents-in-law)

LE BEAU-DAB
(father-in-law)

LA BELLE-DOCHE
(mother-in-law)

MON BEAUFFE
(my brother-in-law)

MA FRANGINE
(my sister)

MON FISTON
(my son)

LES MOUTARDS
(the kids)

MA BELLE-FRANGINE
(my sister-in-law)

MON FRANGIN
(my brother)

MA FISTONNE
(my daughter)

PRACTICE THE VOCABULARY

[Answers to Lesson 4, pp. 48–49]

A. Match the French with the English translation.

1. __ On s'en paie une tranche ici.   A. It's none of your business.
2. __ Je m'suis engueulé avec mon   B. You're kidding!
    ami.

3. __ C'est pas tes oignons.   C. I'd like you to meet my wife.
4. __ Pourquoi tu fais la gueule?   D. They fight all the time.
5. __ Y va signer un bail   E. He's in a bad mood.
   aujourd'hui.
6. __ J'te présente ma régulière.   F. They get along well together.
7. __ Tu rigoles!   G. What a fight!
8. __ Y font qu'chialer.   H. I had a fight with my friend.
9. __ Elle a la tête près du bonnet. I. They do nothing but cry.
10. __ Y est d'mauvais poil.   J. Why are you frowning?
11. __ Y s'entendent bien ensemble.   K. We're having a great time here.
12. __ Quelle bagarre!   L. She's about to get angry.
13. __ Y s'bouffent l'nez tout   M. He's going to get married today.
   l'temps.

B. Underline the synonym.

1. **bouchon**   a. cadet   b. l'aîné   c. enfant

2. **fistonne**   a. fils   b. frère   c. fille

3. **moutards**   a. mères   b. cadets   c. enfants

4. **frangin**   a. père   b. frère   c. fille

5. **vieux**   a. frère   b. père   c. fils

6. **fiston**   a. fils   b. bébé   c. enfant

7. **frangine**   a. sœur   b. mère   c. tante

8. **smala**   a. sœur   b. tante   c. famille

9. **vieille**   a. mère   b. tante   c. famille

10. **beauffe**   a. frère   b. beau- frère   c. belle-sœur

11. **beaux-vieux** a. beaux-parents   b. beaux-frères   c. famille

12. **beau-dab**   a. beau-père   b. beau- frère   c. cadet

C. Complete the family tree on the next page using the list below as a reference.

frangine-dabuche	frangin-dab	beaux-vieux
vieille	vieux	vieux
frangine	beauffe	fiston
fistonne	frangin	moutards
belle-doche	beau-dab	belle-frangine
bouchon	régulière	smala

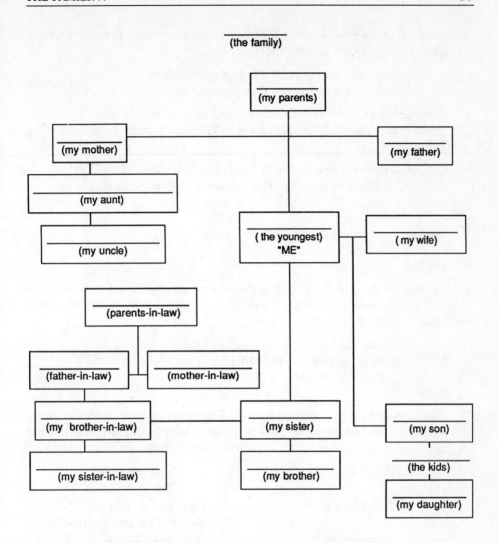

(the family)

(my parents)

(my mother)   (my father)

(my aunt)

(my uncle)   (the youngest)   (my wife)
                                    "ME"

(parents-in-law)

(father-in-law)   (mother-in-law)

(my brother-in-law)   (my sister)   (my son)

(my sister-in-law)   (my brother)   (the kids)

                                                                 (my daughter)

GRAMMAR I: WORDS THAT ADD EMPHASIS

A. *ce, cet,* and *cette* = *c'te*

1. Very often in street conversation, **c'te** replaces the demonstrative adjectives, **ce, cet,** and **cette**. It is commonly used to add emphasis to the noun that it modifies:

Regarde cette maison!
Regarde c'te maison!

Y est délicieux, ce gâteau!
Y est délicieux, c'te gâteau!

2. When **c'te** modifies a noun that begins with a vowel, the **e** is dropped and replaced by an apostrophe:

    > **Y a beaucoup d'énergie, cet enfant.**
    > **Y a beaucoup d'énergie, c't'enfant.**

3. Depending on the context, **c'te** can also be used to add contempt to the noun that it modifies. In this case, **c'te** becomes a package-deal meaning "this darn...."

    > **J'en ai marre d'c'te voiture!**; I'm fed up with this "darn" car!
    > **C'te fille è m'énerve!**; This "darn" girl is bugging me!

Note:

c'te does not replace **ces**.

B. *un peu*

The adverb **un peu** is used *after* the verb to emphasize an imperative or command. It is used in much the same way as "just" is used in English to add emphasis to the verb that it modifies:

> **Ecoute un peu la musique!**; Just listen to the music!
> **Regarde un peu c'te maison!**; Just look at that house!

C. *ben*

1. The adverb **ben**, pronounced like the French word **bain**, is an extremely popular synonym for **bien**. However, **ben** is very frequently used like the emphatic **mais** to emphasize a question, a statement, or an imperative:

QUESTION:	Mais où tu vas?
	Ben où tu vas?
STATEMENT:	Mais elle est très gentille!
	Ben elle est très gentille!
IMPERATIVE:	Mais regarde!
	Ben regarde!

    Unlike **un peu**, **ben** always *preceeds* the verb in the imperative form:

    > Regarde **un peu**!
    > **Ben** regarde!

2. In the imperative form, **ben** may be used with **un peu** to add greater emphasis:

    > **Ben** regarde **un peu**!
    > **Ben** arrête **un peu**!

3. **Ben** is also frequently used to emphasize **oui** and **non**:

> Y t'plaît comme professeur? **Ben oui!**
> C'est ton bébé? **Ben non!**

Note:

> **Ben** is also used to mean "so" / **Eh ben? Ben quoi?**; So? So what?

D. *alors*

1. The adverb **Alors** is often used to emphasize a question, an imperative, or an interjection:

QUESTION:	Pourquoi tu pars **alors?**
	Où tu vas **alors?**
IMPERATIVE:	Viens **alors!**
	Arrête **alors!**
INTERJECTION:	Quelle chance **alors!**
	Fantastique **alors!**

2. **Alors** is also used to emphasize **oui** and **non**. Unlike **ben, alors** follows **oui** and **non**:

> Y t'plaît comme professeur? Oui **alors!**
> C'est ton bébé? Non **alors!**

Note:

> **Alors** is also very often used with **ben** to add even stronger emphasis to **oui** and **non**:

> **Ben oui alors!**; Well yes!
> **Ben non alors!**; Well no!

3. In the imperative form, **alors** may be used together with **ben** to add even greater emphasis:

> **Ben** arrête **alors!**
> **Ben** fais-le **alors!**

Note:

> **Ben alors?**; So?!

Note 1:

> **Ça alors!** is an idiomatic expression meaning "wow!"

Note 2:

> In the imperative form, **alors** usually follows the verb as does **un peu.** Again, **ben** preceeds the verb.

Regarde **alors!**
Regarde **un peu!**
Ben regarde!

Note 3:

It is very possible to use **c'te, un peu, ben,** and **alors** together in the same sentence:

Ben écoute **un peu c'te** musique **alors!**

PRACTICE *C'TE, UN PEU, BEN,* AND *ALORS*

A. Rewrite the following by using the word(s) in parentheses to add emphasis to the phrase.

Example:

Regarde cette robe!
(c'te) **Regarde c'te robe!**

1. Ecoute cette musique!
    (**un peu**) _____ !
2. Ecoute cette musique!
    (**c'te**) _____ !
3. Ecoute cette musique!
    (**un peu/c'te**) _____ !
4. Ecoute!
    (**ben**) _____ !
5. Ecoute!
    (**alors**) _____ !
6. Oui!
    (**ben**) _____ !
7. Oui!
    (**alors**) _____ !
8. Oui!
    (**ben/alors**) _____ !
9. Regarde cette architecture!
    (**c'te**) _____ !
10. Regarde ce livre!
    (**un peu**) _____ !
11. Regarde ce livre!
    (**un peu/c'te**) _____ !
12. Cours!
    (**alors**) _____ !

13. Viens!
    (ben/alors) _____ !
14. Regarde ce bâtiment-là!
    (ben/un peu/c'te) _____ !

B. Fill in the blank using _c'te, un peu, ben,_ or _alors._ (There is one slang word in each sentence below from the dialogue. Can you recognize it?)

1. J'adore _____ smala!
2. C'est ta frangine? Oui _____ !
3. _____ pourquoi tu fais la gueule?
4. Tu crois qu'c'est pas ses oignons? _____ non!
5. Regarde _____ ces moutards!
6. Tu t'es engueulé avec ton beauffe! _____ oui _____ !
7. J'en ai marre de _____ bagarre!
8. _____ ferme _____ la porte!
9. J'déteste _____ cours d'géométrie!
10. _____ viens _____ regarder _____ magicien! Y est super
    _____ !

Leçon Cinq

LA SOIREE. . .

DIALOGUE

Marc a emmené son frère cadet à sa première grande soirée. . .

Marc: C'est **chouette**, c'te **boum**!

Paul: Mais **mate** un peu comme y sont tous si bien **nippés**!

Marc: Ben pourquoi tu **t'fais d'la bile**? T'es pas **mal ficelé**, toi. Tiens! C'te **nana**-là, è t'**bigle**! P't'êt'qu'elle **en pince pour toi**! Va la **brancher**!

Paul: Rien à **chiquer**! J'aurais la **trouille**.

Marc: Tu **déjantes**! T'es pas venu pour **draguer**? Ben écoute! J'crois qu't'as besoin d't'**en jeter un derrière la cravate** comme moi. C'est moi paie la première **tournée**.

Paul: T'as **perdu la boule**, non! T'essaies de m'faire **tomber dans les pommes**? Si j'm'**humectais les amygdales** avec c'te **tord-boyaux** qu't'as dans la **paluche**, j'serais **rond comme une queue d'pelle**.

Marc: Alors, si t'as la pépie plus tard, tu peux toujours **grenouiller**.

Paul: Tu sais? C'est **marrant**. . .tout l'monde ici parade avec une **clope** dans la **gargue**. La fumée, ça **schlingue**!

Marc: J'ai l'impression qu't'es pas fait pour les soirées, **mon vieux**!

38

Lesson Five

THE PARTY...

DIALOGUE

Marc has taken his younger brother to his first big party...

Marc: This party's really great!

Paul: But get a load of how everyone is so decked out!

Marc: What are you getting all worked up for! You're not badly dressed. Hey! That girl over there is giving you the eye. Maybe she's got the hots for you! Go talk to her!

Paul: No way! I'd be scared to death.

Marc: You're crazy! Didn't you come here to cruise? Listen! I think you need to get yourself something to drink like me. I'll pay the first round.

Paul: Have you lost it? You trying to get me to pass out? If I downed that rot-gut that you've got in your hand, I'd get bombed off my rocker.

Marc: So, if you get thirsty later, you can always drink water.

Paul: Ya know? It's funny... everyone here is parading around with a cigarette in his mouth. Smoke stinks!

Marc: I have a feeling that you're just not cut out for parties, pal!

VOCABULARY

bigler v. to look from the corner of one's eye.

boum f. big party; "a bash."

brancher v. to talk to someone / (lit); to plug into.

chiquer v. to chew tobacco / *Note:* This is commonly seen as **rien à chiquer;** nothing doing, no way.

chouette interj. terrific, neat.

clope f. cigarette (*extremely popular*).

déjanter v. to talk nonsense; to go crazy.

draguer v. to cruise (for sexual encounters) / **Y m'drague;** He's cruising me.

faire de la bile (se) exp. to get all worked up; to worry / (lit); to make oneself bilious.

ficelé(e) (être mal) adj. to be poorly dressed / (lit); to be badly strung together.

gargue f. mouth / This comes from the verb **se gargariser** meaning "to gargle."

grenouiller v. to drink water / (lit); to act like a frog / *Note:* This comes from **grenouille** f. frog.

humecter les amygdales (s') exp. to drink; to wet one's whistle / (lit); to moisten one's tonsils.

jeter un derrière la cravate (s'en) exp. to drink / (lit); to throw one behind the tie.

marrant(e) adj. funny; bizarre / *Note:* **marrant** is used in the same way as the French word **drôle** whose meaning is: (1) funny and (2) strange.

mater v. to look.

mon vieux exp. "my pal," "my (old) friend."

nana f. girl, "chick" (*extremely popular*).

nippé(e) (être bien) adj. to be well dressed / *Note:* **se nipper** v. to dress / *Also:* **nippes** f.pl. clothes.

paluche f. hand.

perdre la boule exp. to lose one's mind, to lose "it" / (lit); to lose the ball.

pincer pour quelqu'un (en) exp. to have a mad crush on someone, to have the hots for someone.

rond(e) comme une queue de pelle (être) exp. to be totally bombed / (lit); to be "round" like a handle of a shovel.

schlinguer v. to stink.

tomber dans les pommes exp. to faint, pass out / (lit); to fall in the apples.

tord-boyaux m. very strong alcohol; rot-gut / (lit); gut-twister.

tournée f. round (of drinks) / (lit); a turn.

trouille (avoir la) f. to be scared silly.

PRACTICE THE VOCABULARY

[Answers to Lesson 5, p. 49.]

A. Complete the phrase by filling in the blank with the appropriate word from the list. Give the correct form of the verb.

boum	mater	ficelé
clope	schlinguer	déjanter
nana	brancher	trouille
bigler	marrant	boule

1. J'ai envie d'fumer. Passe-moi une _____ s'te plaît.
2. Ben tu peux pas entrer comme ça! T'es mal _____ !
3. J'veux rencontrer c'te _____ . J'vais la _____ .
4. T'as perdu la _____ , non? Tu peux pas l'faire!
5. Y est _____ c'te mec! Y m'fait toujours rire!
6. C'film de monstres, y m'donne la _____ .
7. J'suis nerveux pasqu'è m' _____ d'l'aut'côté d'la classe.
8. Oh, ça _____ dans c'te poissonerie!
9. Mais quelle histoire! Tu _____ , non?
10. _____ un peu c'te voiture! C'est génial!
11. On s'est bien amusé à la _____ .

B. Choose the appropriate slang synonym of the underlined word(s) by filling in the blank with the corresponding letter.

1. __ C'est fantastique c'film.
2. __ J'vais m'évanouir si j'mange pas fissa!
3. __ Comme j'dois conduire, j'vais boire d'l'eau.
4. __ Y a toujours une cigarette dans la bouche.
5. __ Y a toujours une cigarette dans la bouche.
6. __ Rien à faire!
7. __ Comment ça va mon ami?
8. __ Quand j'l'ai rencontré, y m'a serré la main.
9. __ Y passe son temps à regarder la télévision.
10. __ J'suis amoureux de mon professeur.
11. __ Pourquoi t'es pas encore habillé?
12. __ J'avais très peur, moi!

A. gargue
B. nippé
C. paluche
D. rien à chiquer
E. chouette
F. tomber dans les pommes
G. en pince pour
H. grenouiller
I. vieux
J. téloche
K. clope
L. la trouille

C. Underline the word that goes with the phrase.

1. Ben pourquoi tu t'fais d'la (bile, boum, boule)? Tout va bien!
2. J'ai la pépie. J'vais en (piquer, parler, jeter) un derrière la cravate.

3. C't'alcool, y est trop fort! Quel tord-(**bras, boyaux, bouche**)!
4. Regarde un peu c't'ivrogne. Y est (**riche, carré, rond**) comme une queue d'pelle.
5. Y fait chaud dehors! J'vais m'humecter les (**amygdales, oreilles, pieds**).
6. J'sais pas comment y arrive à fumer c'te (**flâneuse, téloche, clope**) avant l'p'tit déjeuner.
7. Quand j'ai vu l'casseur dans ma baraque, j'suis tombé dans les (**poires, pommes, pêches**).
8. J'aimerais bien la rencontrer. J'vais la (**brûler, brancher, lancequiner**).
9. Mais y est beau c'mec! J'en (**pince, prie, cours**) pour lui.
10. Le chien, y essayait d'm'attaquer! Mais j'avais la (**truite, boue, trouille**)!
11. Elle est belle, c'te fille! J'vais la (**droguer, draguer, tirer**).
12. Quel costume (**moussant, pébroc, marrant**)!
13. Tu veux boire quèque chose? C'est ma (**tour, tournée, turne**).

GRAMMAR I: POPULAR USAGE OF OBJECTIVE CASE PERSONAL PRONOUNS AND ÇA

A. The student of French has no doubt learned how to emphasize the subject of a sentence with the use of personal pronouns *moi, toi, lui, elle, nous, vous, eux,* and *elles,* and the demonstrative pronoun *ça.*

> J'm'appelle David.
> **Moi, j'm'appele David.**

> T'es très amusant.
> **Toi, t'es très amusant.**

> C'est fantastique!
> **Ça, c'est fantastique!**

However, in colloquial French, these pronouns finish the statement. This construction is *extremely* popular:

> J'm'appele David, **moi.**
> T'es très amusant, **toi.**
> C'est fantastique, **ça.**

B. Further popular use of *ça*

The demonstrative pronoun **ça** is frequently used to emphasize the interrogative pronouns **combien, comment, où, pourquoi, quand, quel(le), qui,** and **quoi.** This is a *very* common usage of **ça:**

> Regarde qui s'approche de nous!
> **Qui ça?**; Who's that?

> J'vais y aller à midi.
> **Où ça?**; Where's that?

EXERCISES

A. Emphasize the subject by *simply* adding the appropriate personal or demonstrative pronoun to the sentence.

Example:

T'es en retard.
T'es en retard, **toi.**

1. J'suis fatigué _____ .
2. Y est grand _____ .
3. E court vite _____ .
4. Tu joues bien du piano _____ .
5. Vous arrivez toujours en retard _____ .
6. Pourquoi tu pleures _____ ?
7. J'ai gagné l'grand prix _____ !
8. Y est bizarre _____ .
9. E parle trois langues _____ .
10. C'est bien _____ .
11. Nous voilà arrivés _____ !
12. C'est parfait _____ !

B. Respond to each statement by using an interrogative pronoun (*combien, comment, où, pourquoi, quand, quel(le), qui, quoi*) followed by *ça.*

Example:

Y schlingue, lui!   J'pars maintenant.
(qui) **Qui ça?**   (pourquoi) **Pourquoi ça?**

1. La nana, è s'fait d'la bile.
    (**pourquoi**) _____ ?
2. Ça coûte cher c'tord-boyaux.
    (**combien**) _____ ?
3. J'vais la brancher facilement.
    (**comment**) _____ ?
4. J'dois grenouiller ce soir.
    (**pourquoi**) _____ ?
5. Y fume ses clopes l'une après l'autre.
    (**qui**) _____ ?
6. J'vais y aller demain, mon vieux.
    (**où**) _____ ?
7. Mais y déjante, lui. Tu sais c'qu'y a dit?
    (**quoi**) _____ ?

8. J'te l'tape.
   (**quand**) _____ ?
9. J'en pince pour elle.
   (**qui**) _____ ?
10. J'me nippe toujours bien l'soir.
    (**pourquoi**) _____ ?
11. Elle y était ronde comme une queue d'pelle.
    (**où**) _____ ?
12. Y t'a dit c'qu'y a biglé à la soirée?
    (**quoi**) _____ ?

ANSWERS TO LESSONS 1–5

LESSON 1

Practice the Vocabulary

A.
1. D
2. H
3. C
4. B
5. E
6. I
7. G
8. A
9. F
10. J
11. K

B.
1. dingue
2. caille
3. poisse
4. cloche
5. bouffe
6. fric
7. carrément
8. boudin

C.
1. B
2. E
3. D
4. H
5. J
6. I
7. A
8. C
9. F
10. G

Grammar I: Exercises

A.
1. T'as
2. J'te
3. J'comprends, c'que
4. J'vais, l'voir
5. T'entends pas
6. J'veux, prend'
7. J'dois
8. J'peux, prend', l'métro, j'me (or je m')
9. J'vais, mett'
10. J'pars, d'suite, êt'
11. J'ai pas
12. J'peux pas, l'faire

B. Aujourd'hui, jɇ vais mɇ lever dɇ bonne heure pour passer la journée en ville. Jɇ dois arriver vers midi pour prendrɇ lɇ déjeuner avec mes amis Irène et Jacques à notrɇ café préféré. J'aime bien cɇ café parcɇ que les prix n¢ sont pas astronomiques! Après, on va aller au parc pour prendr¢ d¢ la glace comme dessert! Si on a l¢ temps, on s¢ promènera dans l¢ jardin d¢ Versailles.

Grammar II: Exercises

A. 1. c't'un
    2. y a
    3. c'ui-là
    4. faut
    5. pis
    6. quèques
    7. pu
    8. c't'une
    9. y avait
   10. è

B. 1. Faut que, j'ui
    2. Y, pace, y, s'tirer
    3. C't'un
    4. Y a, d'
    5. m', s'te plaît
    6. Z'ont
    7. J'crois, è, m', d'
    8. J'ai, pu
    9. J'sais, c'qu'y, m'
   10. Y, pisqu'y

LESSON 2

Practice the Vocabulary

A. 1. b   6. a
   2. b   7. b
   3. c   8. b
   4. c   9. c
   5. a   10. a

B. 1. lèche les babines   7. barman
   2. bourré   8. boutanche
   3. douloureuse   9. faire figaro
   4. bidoche   10. ouais
   5. pépie   11. moussante
   6. caouah   12. s'goinfrer

C. 1. Ouais, j'vais laisser un pourliche.
   2. Ouais, j'aime le brouille-ménage.
   3. Ouais, j'connais c'resto.
   4. Ouais, j'veux d'la flotte.
   5. Ouais, j'veux piquer un dessert.
   6. Ouais, j'désire un apéro.
   7. Ouais, j'trouve l'café d'première bourre.
   8. Ouais, c't'un boui-boui.
   9. Ouais, c't'une maison nickel.
  10. Ouais, j'ai les crocs.

Grammar I: Practice Asking a Question

A. 1. Qui tu vas aider?
   2. Quand tu veux partir?
   3. Quelle heure il est?
   4. Pourquoi t'aimes pas ça?
   5. Comment y va aller au cinéma?
   6. T'écris quoi?
   7. Y vient d'où?
   8. Combien t'en as, des pantalons?
   9. Tu désires m'accompagner?
  10. Tu prends l'autobus?
  11. Tu sais conduire?
  12. T'aimes ça?

B. 1. A qui tu vas parler du boui-boui?
   2. E regarde quoi?
   3. Pourquoi tu vas acheter d'la moussante?
   4. Quelle boutanche d'vin tu vas commander?
   5. Qui tu vas inviter à la soirée?
   6. Comment t'es devenu rupin?
   7. Combien elle en a, des maisons?
   8. Où y va aller s'goinfrer?
   9. Avec qui è va picoler?
   10. Quel guindal y va laver?

LESSON 3

Practice the Vocabulary

A. 1. agrafer
   2. lourde
   3. écopé
   4. baraque
   5. flanqué
   6. salut
   7. flicaille
   8. plumard
   9. balader
   10. placard
   11. bousillé
   12. planquer

B. 1. lessivé
   2. cuisiné
   3. vanterne
   4. charivari
   5. radiner
   6. piges
   7. fissa
   8. s'est carapaté
   9. bigophone
   10. duraille

C. 1. Y a piqué l'vélo.
   2. J'veux regarder la téloche.
   3. J'ai bousillé mon examen.
   4. Voilà l'casseur!
   5. Tu veux encarrer?
   6. Tu connais c'mec?
   7. On pourrait toujours l'mettre au clou!
   8. A quelle heure elle a radiné?
   9. Tu veux t'balader après l'dîner?
   10. J'suis lessivé!

Grammar I: Exercises

A. 1. a. C'gâteau, y est délicieux.
      b. Y est délicieux, c'gâteau.
   2. a. Suzanne, elle est très jolie.
      b. Elle est très jolie, Suzanne.
   3. a. L'dîner, y est ruiné.
      b. Y est ruiné, l'dîner.
   4. a. Cette robe, è m'va comme un gant.
      b. E m'va comme un gant, cette robe.
   5. a. Le film, y était fantastique.
      b. Y était fantastique, le film.
   6. a. Ma mère, è m'appelle.
      b. E m'appelle, ma mère.

7. a. Les jours, y passent vite.
   b. Y passent vite, les jours.
8. a. Cette voiture, elle est toute neuve.
   b. Elle est toute neuve, cette voiture.
9. a. Mon p'tit frère, y est très grand.
   b. Y est très grand, mon p'tit frère.
10. a. Serge, y t'demande au téléphone.
    b. Y t'demande au téléphone, Serge.

B. 1. Tu fais c'charivari pourquoi?
   2. T'as bousillé quoi?
   3. Tu vas acheter quelle baraque?
   4. Y a volé ta montre quand?
   5. T'essaies d'planquer qui?
   6. Tu manges fissa pourquoi?
   7. Y va parler au flic quand?
   8. T'en as combien des téloches?
   9. Elle a radiné avec qui?
   10. Tu vas t'balader où?
   11. T'es lessivé pourquoi?

LESSON 4

Practice the Vocabulary

A.				B.			
1.	K	8.	I	1.	a	7.	a
2.	H	9.	L	2.	c	8.	c
3.	A	10.	E	3.	c	9.	a
4.	J	11.	F	4.	b	10.	b
5.	M	12.	G	5.	b	11.	a
6.	C	13.	D	6.	a	12.	a
7.	B						

C. See the "Family Tree" on page 31

Grammar I: Practice *c'te, un peu, ben,* and *alors*

A. 1. Ecoute un peu cette musique!
   2. Ecoute c'te musique!
   3. Ecoute un peu c'te musique!
   4. Ben écoute!
   5. Ecoute alors!
   6. Ben oui!
   7. Oui alors!
   8. Ben oui alors!
   9. Regarde c't'architecture!
   10. Regarde un peu ce livre!

11. Regarde un peu c'te livre!
12. Cours alors!
13. Ben viens alors!
14. Ben regarde un peu c'te bâtiment-là!

B. 1. c'te
2. alors
3. Ben
4. Ben
5. un peu
6. Ben, alors
7. c'te
8. Ben, un peu
9. c'te
10. Ben, un peu, c'te, alors

LESSON 5

Practice the Vocabulary

A. 1. clope
2. ficelé
3. nana, brancher
4. boule
5. marrant
6. trouille
7. bigle
8. schlingue
9. déjantes
10. Mate
11. boum

B. 1. E
2. F
3. H
4. K
5. A
6. D
7. I
8. C
9. J
10. G
11. B
12. L

C. 1. bile
2. jeter
3. boyaux
4. rond
5. amygdales
6. clope
7. pommes
8. brancher
9. pince
10. trouille
11. draguer
12. marrant
13. tournée

Grammar I: Exercises

A. 1. moi
2. lui
3. elle
4. toi
5. vous
6. toi
7. moi
8. lui
9. elle
10. ça
11. nous
12. ça

B. 1. Pourquoi ça?
2. Combien ça?
3. Comment ça?
4. Pourquoi ça?
5. Qui ça?
6. Où ça?
7. Quoi ça?
8. Quand ça?
9. Qui ça?
10. Pourquoi ça?
11. Où ça?
12. Quoi ça?

REVIEW EXAM
FOR LESSONS 1–5

[Answers to Review, p. 53]

A. Underline the word(s) that fall into the same category as the words to the left.

1. **eat**
   - a. se goinfrer
   - b. tomber des cordes
   - c. bouffer
   - d. se taper la cloche

2. **drunk**
   - a. soûlard
   - b. rond comme une queue de pelle
   - c. nana
   - d. bourré

3. **rain**
   - a. filer
   - b. tomber des cordes
   - c. saucée
   - d. lancequiner

4. **look**
   - a. mater
   - b. dégringoler
   - c. bigler
   - d. brancher

5. **family**
   - a. boui-boui
   - b. frangin
   - c. fric
   - d. frangine

6. **leave**
   - a. planquer
   - b. encarrer
   - c. se carapater
   - d. se tirer

7. **fight**
   - a. s'engueuler
   - b. se bouffer le nez
   - c. bagarre
   - d. boum

8. **to drink**
   a. s'en jeter un derrière la cravate
   b. s'humecter les amygdales
   c. lancequiner
   d. picoler

9. **food**
   a. bidoche
   b. bouffe
   c. boustifaille
   d. bled

10. **to arrive**
    a. piquer
    b. se pointer
    c. cailler
    d. radiner

11. **alcohol**
    a. tord-boyaux
    b. nickel
    c. moussante
    d. brouille-ménage

12. **money**
    a. schlingue
    b. rupin
    c. fric
    d. balle

B. Complete the following phrases by choosing the appropriate word(s) from the list below. Give the correct form of the verb.

cailler	dégringoler	dingue
filer	baraque	mauvais poil
moutards	clope	trouille
schlinguer	nana	marrant

1. Quelle odeur affreuse! Que ça _____ ici!
2. J'ai envie d'fumer. Passe-moi une _____ .
3. Y sait pas c'qu'y fait, lui. Mais y est _____ .
4. Elle est jolie, c'te _____ .
5. Y fait froid aujourd'hui. J'commence à _____ .
6. J'veux êt'papa pasque j'adore les _____ .
7. Daniel, y m'fait toujours rire. Qu'y est _____ .
8. Avant qu'y prenne son café, y est d'_____ .
9. T'as une _____ parfaite pour une grande soirée.
10. Elle a _____ l'escalier.
11. Quand j'ai vu l'voleur, j'avais la _____ .
12. Hé! C'est l'mien! _____ -moi ça tout d'suite!

C. Match the French with the English translation.

1. ___ Demain, j'signe un bail.
2. ___ Tu rigoles!
3. ___ Tu l'a branchée?
4. ___ Y est tombé dans les pommes.
5. ___ T'es pas mal ficelé, toi.
6. ___ J'veux rester au plumard.

A. I don't have any money on me.
B. You wanna take a walk?
C. You're not badly dressed.
D. Tomorrow, I'm getting married.
E. I want to stay in bed.
F. I'm fed up!

7. ___ Tu connais c'mec?
8. ___ J'aime bien c'bled.
9. ___ Tu veux t'balader?
10. ___ J'en ai marre!
11. ___ J'ai pas d'fric sur moi.
12. ___ Quelle poisse alors!

G. You're kidding!
H. What bad luck!
I. You talked to her?
J. I like this area.
K. He fainted.
L. You know that guy?

D. Underline the word in parentheses that best completes the phrase.

1. Y pleut! J'dois chercher mon (**pébroc, caouah, piaf**).
2. J'ai pas d'argent. Tu peux m'prêter cent (**bleds, moussantes, balles**)?
3. J'peux pas manger dans c'te restaurant. C'est (**rupin, cradingue, pige**)!
4. Pourquoi tu (**chiales, radines, bigophones**)? T'es pas content?
5. Y fait chaud aujourd'hui. J'commence à (**cailler, cramer, déjanter**).
6. C't'un fou! Y a perdu la (**lourde, téloche, boule**).
7. Ce (**charivari, salut, paluche**), y m'rend sourd!
8. Quelle jolie robe. T'es bien (**nippée, fissa, lessivée**) ce soir.
9. Qui a (**bourré, bousillé, lancequiné**) ma nouvelle montre?
10. Y fait qu'pleuvoir ici. Encore un pique-nique qui s'en est allé en eau d' (**boui-boui, barman, boudin**).
11. Elle est fantastique, c'te fille. J'en (**poisse, pince, dingue**) pour elle.
12. J'viens d'(**fusiller, lancequiner, ramer**) tout mon argent!

ANSWERS TO REVIEW (LESSONS 1–5)

A.
1. a, c, d
2. a, b, d
3. b, c, d
4. a, c
5. b, d
6. c, d
7. a, b, c
8. a, b, d
9. a, b, c
10. b, d
11. a, c, d
12. b, c, d

B.
1. schlingue
2. clope
3. dingue
4. nana
5. cailler
6. moutards
7. marrant
8. mauvais poil
9. baraque
10. dégringolé
11. trouille
12. File

C.
1. D
2. G
3. I
4. K
5. C
6. E
7. L
8. J
9. B
10. F
11. A
12. H

D.
1. pébroc
2. balles
3. cradingue
4. chiales
5. cramer
6. boule
7. charivari
8. nippée
9. bousillé
10. boudin
11. pince
12. fusiller

Leçon Six

A L'ECOLE...

DIALOGUE

André et Eric viennent de quitter leur cours de biologie.

André: Oh, **la vache**! Le **paquet** d'devoirs qu'è **fiche** aux **potaches**, c'te **prof**...c'est pas croyable!

Eric: J'ai même pas l'temps d'les faire pasque j'dois **bosser** ce soir. J'comptais même **sécher l'cours** demain!

André: Mais tu t'es **fait étendre** au dernier **exam**, toi, et y en aura un aut'vendredi!

Eric: J'sais bien! Et si j'le **potasse** pas, j'suis **frit**!

André: E doit êt'**cinglée** d'penser qu'on peut **ligoter** tous ces **bouquins** en deux journailles! J'crois qu'elle aime nous voir souffrir.

Eric: Ben, ouais! Sachant qu'j'suis pas **calé** en **maths**, è m'pose toujours des **colles** et m'fait **plancher d'vant** toute la **galerie**. E m'**casse les pieds**, elle!

André: Mais t'as **r'marqué** qu'son **chouchou**, y semble toujours **cartonner** aux exams? Y reçoit qu'des **méganotes**!

Eric: J'peux pas l'**blairer**, c'te **gonze**! Y est **moche à caler les roues d'corbillard**. Y a un œil qui joue au billard et l'aut'qui compte les points!

André: Et t'as **zieuté** un peu ses **tifs**? A chaque fois qu'y s'fait **déboiser la colline**, le **merlan**, y fait d'sa tête un **melon déplumé**.

54

AT SCHOOL. . . .

DIALOGUE

André and Eric have just left their biology class.

André: Holy cow! The stack of work this teacher piles on students is unreal!

Eric: I don't even have time to do it 'cause I have to work tonight. I was even planning on skipping class tomorrow!

André: But you bombed out on the last test and there's another one on Friday!

Eric: I know! And if I don't cram for it, I'm done for!

André: She must be out of her mind to think we can read all these books in two days! I think she likes to see us suffer.

Eric: I'll say! Knowing that I stink in math, she always puts these impossible questions to me and grills me at the board in front of everyone! She burns my butt!

André: But did you notice that her "pet" always seems to ace the tests? All he ever does is get high grades!

Eric: I can't stand that dude! He's ugly enough to stop a clock. He's so cross-eyed that it looks like one eye is playing billiards and the other is off counting the points!

André: And did you get a load of his hair? Every time he gets his hair lopped off, the barber makes him look like a plucked melon!

VOCABULARY

blairer v. to stand or tolerate someone / (lit); to smell / **J'peux pas l'blairer;** I can't stand him / This is said of someone who is so intolerable that just smelling him would be too much to bear / *Note:* **blair** m. nose; "schnoz" / **Jimmy Durante était connu pour son grand blair;** Jimmy Durante was known for his big schnozola.

bosser v. to work hard.

bouquin m.   book / *Note 1:* The word **bouquin** used to mean only "*old* book" but has now also become a popular slang synonym for "book" in general / *Note 2:* **bouquiner** v. to read / (lit); to go through old books.

calé(e) (être) adj. to be very smart.

cartonner v. to ace a test / **J'ai cartonné à l'exam;** I aced the test. / *Note:* This comes from the noun **carton** meaning "cardboard." The verb **cartonner** literally means "to hit a target." It refers to the cardboard targets that are found in shooting ranges or amusement parks.

casser les pieds à quelqu'un exp. to annoy someone greatly / (lit); to break one's feet / **Tu m'casses les pieds!;** You "burn my butt!" / *Note:* **casse-pieds** m. an annoying individual.

chouchou(te) n. teacher's pet / *Note:* **chouchouter** v. to spoil someone.

cinglé(e) (être) adj. to be cracked, off one's rocker.

colle f. a difficult question to answer / **poser une colle;** (lit); to pose a sticky question / *Note:* **colle** f. glue.

déboiser la colline (se faire) exp. to get a haircut / (lit); to deforest or untimber the hill.

d'vant prep. a commonly heard contraction of **devant**.

étendre (se faire) v. to flunk, fail, blow (a test) / (lit); to get oneself stretched out.

exam m. abbreviation of **examen**.

fiche v. (1) to give: **Fiche-moi ça!;** Give me that! (2) to put: **Fiche-le sur la table;** Put it on the table. (3) to do: **Tu fiches quoi ici?;** What are you doing here? / *Note:* Oddly enough, this *is* a verb although it does not have a traditional ending. The verb **fiche** has replaced its old form **ficher**.

frit(e) (être) adj. to be done for / (lit); to be fried.

galerie f. public (in general).

gonze m. guy; "dude" / *Note:* **gonzesse** f. girl, "chick."

"la vache!" exclam. (*extremely popular*) **Oh, la vache!;** Wow! / (lit); the cow / *Note:* Used as an exclamation, **Oh, la vache!** has nothing to do with "cow" although this is the literal translation. It is used in much the same way as the English expression, "Holy cow!"

ligoter v. to read / (lit); to tie up (a person, a package, etc.).

maths m.pl.   abbreviation of "mathematics"; math / *Note:* In colloquial French, many academic subjects may be abbreviated: **bio** f. biology; **géo** f. geography; **gym** f. gymnastics; **philo** f. philosophy.

méganote f. a high grade / (lit); a mega-grade.

melon déplumé (avoir le) humorous exp. to be completely bald / (lit); to have a plucked melon.

merlan m. barber / (lit); whiting (fish).

moche à caler les roues de corbillard (être) humorous exp. (lit); to be ugly enough to stop the wheels of a hearse.

paquet m. a lot; "a pile" / (lit); a package.

plancher v. to be called to the blackboard for questioning / *Note:* This comes from the word **planche** f. board.

potache m. student.

potasser v. to study hard; to bone up.

prof m.   and f.   teacher, professor / *Note:* The word **professeur** is a masculine noun. However, its abbreviation, **prof**, is both masculine *and* feminine.

r'marquer v. a commonly heard contraction of **remarquer**.

sécher v. to miss something voluntarily / **Y a séché l'cours pour aller au cinéma;** He skipped class to go to the movies.

tifs m.pl. hair.

un œil qui joue au billard et l'autre qui compte les points (avoir) humorous exp. said of someone who is cross-eyed / (lit); to have one eye that's playing billiards and the other off counting the points.

zieuter v. to look; to see / (lit); to eye / *Note:* The verb **zieuter** comes from **les yeux (z'yeux)** meaning "eyes."

PRACTICE THE VOCABULARY

[Answers to Lesson 6, pp. 92–93]

A.   Complete the phrases by choosing the appropriate word(s) from the list. Give the correct form of the verb.

merlan	tifs	zieuter
étendre	déboiser	casser
moche	calé	blairer
bosser	bouquin	la vache

1.   J'peux pas y aller pasque j'dois _____ ce soir.
2.   Y est pas populaire, c'te prof. Personne peut l' _____ .

3. J'peux rien _____ sans lunettes.
4. J'ai lu tout un _____ en deux heures.
5. Mais arrête d'me _____ les pieds!
6. Oh, _____ ! Elle est vachement belle!
7. Y est _____ à caler les roues d'corbillard.
8. J'suis _____ en maths.
9. Tu t'es fait _____ à l'examen?
10. Y sont longs tes _____ ! Pourquoi tu vas pas chez l' _____ pour t'faire _____ la colline?

B. Underline the word in parentheses that best completes the phrase.

1. T'as fusillé tout ton argent? T'es (**cinglé, lessivé, peinard**), non?
2. J'dois (**piquer, potasser, gueuletoner**) c't'exam pasque j'veux pas m'faire (**ligoter, figaro, étendre**).
3. Pour mon cours d'bio, j'ai une très bonne (**idée, prof, promenade**).
4. Y s'est fait (**déguiser, déboiser, délayer**) la colline et maintenant on dirait qu'y a l'(**fruit, abricot, melon**) déplumé.
5. Y nous (**fiche, pique, cuisine**) toujours un (**fiston, fromage, paquet**) d'devoirs.
6. Le prof, y m'a fait (**draguer, plancher, casser**) d'vant toute la (**voiture, baraque, galerie**).
7. C'est l'(**chouchou, chat, charbon**) du prof.
8. Y a une trentaine d' (**pots, porcs, potaches**) dans mon cours d'musique.
9. Ma sœur, elle est pas (**au courant, calée, amusante**) en (**livre, maths, bouffe**).
10. Alors, l'exam, y s'est bien passé? Ouais! J'ai reçu une (**notation, mininote, méganote**)!
11. J'l'ai pas vu en classe aujourd'hui. P't'êt'qu'y a (**mouillé, séché, nettoyé**) l'cours!

C. Underline the synonym:

1. **blairer**   a. sentir   b. courir   c. sourire
2. **moche**   a. gentil   b. amusant   c. laid
3. **cinglé**   a. fou   b. intelligent   c. malade
4. **ligoter**   a. rire   b. lire   c. donner

5. **bouquin**	a. porte	b. maison	c. livre
6. **bosser**	a. parler	b. travailler	c. donner
7. **fiche**	a. courir	b. donner	c. s'évanouir
8. **paquet**	a. beaucoup	b. peu	c. grand
9. **potasser**	a. partir	b. se fâcher	c. étudier
10. **zieuter**	a. regarder	b. tomber	c. travailler
11. **gonze**	a. restaurant	b. individu	c. clé
12. **cartonner**	a. marcher	b. dormir	c. réussir

GRAMMAR I: SLANG OBJECTIVE CASE PERSONAL PRONOUNS

A. Due to the extreme casualness of slang personal pronouns, they should only be used with friends or other speakers of slang. These slang personal pronouns add an almost "cool" or "tough guy" feeling to a statement. Since there are no English equivalents with which to compare them, a literal translation would be impossible. However, to loosely translate:

> **Alors, ça va tézigue?**
> So, how ya doin' Dude?

As you can see from the example, this style of communication would definitely be unacceptable in certain social situations.

SLANG OBJECTIVE CASE PERSONAL PRONOUNS

	SINGULAR	PLURAL
(1st person)	mézigue *(me)*	nozigues *(us)*
	mézigo	nozigos
	mécolle	nos poires
	ma pomme	
	ma poire	
	bibi	

	SINGULAR	PLURAL—cont'd.
(2nd person)	tézigue *(you)*	vozigues *(you)*
	tézigo	vozigos
	técolle	vos gniasses
	ta pomme	vos poires
	ta poire	
(3rd person)	cézigue *(him)*	leurzigues *(them)*
	cézigo	leurzigos
	sécolle	leurs poires
	sa pomme	cézigos
	sa poire	
	son gniasse	
	césarine *(her)*	
	sézigue *(one)*	

PRACTICE THE SLANG PERSONAL PRONOUNS

A. Match the two columns.

1. __ moi
2. __ toi
3. __ lui
4. __ elle
5. __ soi
6. __ nous
7. __ vous
8. __ eux

A. cézigue
B. leurzigos
C. mécolle
D. césarine
E. técolle
F. vozigos
G. nozigos
H. sézigue

B. Replace the word in parentheses with the appropriate slang objective case personal pronoun listed below.

mézigue	césarine	cézigue
nozigues	vozigues	sézigue
tézigue	leurzigues	

1. Y m'fait toujours plancher, (lui) _____ .
2. Elle est cinglée, (elle) _____ .

3. T'es potache, (toi) _____ ?
4. On est bien chez (soi) _____ quand y a pas d'devoirs à fiche!
5. Oh, la vache! Y sont riches, (eux) _____ .
6. J'suis pas calé en maths, (moi) _____ .
7. Vous devez bosser ce soir, (vous) _____ ?
8. Elle a acheté c'bouquin pour (nous) _____ .

Leçon Sept

LES VACANCES. . .

DIALOGUE

Georges et Antoine parlent de leurs vacances.

Georges: Salut, Antoine! T'as passé d'bonnes vacances?

Antoine: Oh, z'étaient **terribles**! J'aurai du mal à **reprend'l'collier**, crois-moi. J'**enfilais des perles** pendant un **marquet** . . . un vrai **cossard**, mézigue!

Georges: En général, moi **itou**. J'**en fiche pas une rame** quand j'**roule ma bosse**. Mais cette fois-ci, j'étais un peu **crispé** pasque mon p'tit **frelot**, y m'**tapait sur les nerfs** sans arrêt! Mais y était **collant**!

Antoine: J'me rappelle qu'tu m'a dit qu'y **a la frite** aussi! T'aurais dû essayer d'le **semer**.

Georges: Eh ben, enfin j'ui ai **balancé** du **pognon** pour l'**cinoche** pour qu'y **s'éclipse** pour quèques **plombes**. C't'ait du **gâteau**!

Antoine: **Chapeau**! Faut dire qu't'es **roublard**.

Georges: Bon, **revenons à nos moutons** . . . t'as **pioncé à la belle étoile** comme tu voulais?

Antoine: Non, on a décidé d'rester dans un hôtel spécial qui comprenait la **crèche** et la **becquetance**!

Georges: J'espère qu'tu t'es pas fait **rouler**!

Antoine: Que non! L'prix, y était pas **salé**. Franchement, j'**en reste baba** qu'j'sois pas complètement **fauché** comme d'habitude après les vacances!

Lesson Seven

THE VACATION...

DIALOGUE

Georges and Antoine talk about their vacations.

Georges: Hi, Antoine! Did you have a good vacation?

Antoine: Oh, it was great! I'm gonna have trouble getting back to the grind, believe me. I didn't do a thing for a month . . . a real lazy bum!

Georges: Usually, so am I. I don't do a thing when I'm on vacation. But this time, I was sort of uptight 'cause my little brother kept getting on my nerves! He's so clingy!

Antoine: I remember you telling me that he's always hyped up, too! You should have tried to ditch 'm!

Georges: Well, finally I threw some money at 'm for the movies so he'd disappear for a few hours. It was easy!

Antoine: Bravo! I must say you are sneaky.

Georges: Anyway, getting back to what we were talking about . . . did you sleep under the stars like you wanted?

Antoine: No, we decided to stay in a special hotel that included room and board!

Georges: I hope you didn't get ripped off!

Antoine: Oh, no! The price wasn't outrageous. Frankly, I'm shocked that I'm not totally broke as usual after a vacation!

VOCABULARY

balancer v. to give; to throw / (lit); to balance / **J'l'ai balancé dehors**; I threw him outside. / *Also:* **s'en balancer** exp. not to care / **J'm'en balance!**; I don't care!

becquetance f. food; grub / *Note:* **becqueter** v. to eat.

chapeau! exclam. bravo!; congratulations!; my hat's off to you! / (lit); hat.

cinoche m. cinema.

collant(e) (être) adj. said of someone who is hard to get rid of / (lit); to be sticky.

cossard m. a lazy individual / *Note:* **avoir la cosse;** to be lazy.

crèche f. room or bedroom / (lit); manger, crib / *Note:* **crécher** v. to live, stay.

crispé(e) (être) adj. to be uptight, on edge.

éclipser (s') v. to leave quickly; to vanish / (lit); to eclipse oneself.

enfiler des perles exp. to laze around and do nothing / (lit); to string pearls / **J'suis pas venu pour enfiler des perles!**; I didn't come here to just sit around!

fauché(e) (être) adj. to be broke / (lit); to be reaped / *Note:* The verb **faucher** (lit); to mow, cut, reap (a field) means "to steal" in French slang / **Qui a fauché mon portefeuille?;** Who stole my wallet?

fiche une rame (ne pas en) exp. to do absolutely nothing.

frelot m. brother.

frite (avoir la) exp. to be hyperactive; hyped up / *Note:* This comes from the verb **frire** meaning "to fry." The expression is said of one who is always moving around like the bubbles in a pan when something is being fried.

gâteau (c'est du) exp. said of something easy; it's a piece of cake / (lit); it's cake.

itou adj. also, same / **moi itou;** me too.

marquet m. month.

pioncer à la belle étoile exp. to sleep outside / *Note 1:* **pioncer** v. to sleep; *Note 2:* **à la belle étoile;** outside / (lit); by the pretty star.

plombe f. hour / *Note:* This comes from the word **plomb** m. lead. The word **plombe** conjures up a picture of an old lead chime being struck every hour.

pognon m. money; loot; dough.

reprendre le collier exp. to get back to work or school / (lit); to get back into the harness.

rester baba (en) exp. to be so stunned with amazement or surprise that the sound "bah-bah" is all that can be uttered.

revenons à nos moutons exp. let's get back to what we were talking about / (lit); let's get back to our sheep.

roublard(e) (être) adj. to be sneaky or clever.

rouler v. to rip off, cheat someone / **Y m'a roulé!;** He ripped me off / *Also:* **se faire rouler;** to get oneself ripped off / (lit); to roll (someone).

rouler sa bosse exp. to travel / (lit); to roll one's hump.

salé(e) (être) adj. to be expensive / (lit); to be salted.

semer v. to ditch someone / (lit); to sow (seed).

taper sur les nerfs à quelqu'un exp. to get on one's nerves.

terrible! exclam. (*extremely popular*) fantastic, wonderful / *Note:* Used in context, this exclamation has the opposite meaning of its traditional connotation. It could be compared to the old American exclamation, "bad!" actually meaning "good!"

PRACTICE THE VOCABULARY

[Answers to Lesson 7, pp. 93–94]

A. Replace the word in parentheses with its slang synonym from the second column. Make all necessary changes.

1. Y est (fantastique) _____ c'film!	A. frelot
2. Tu peux m'prêter d'l'(argent) _____ ?	B. gâteau
3. Tu veux aller au (cinéma) _____ avec mézigue?	C. salé
4. Y est (cher) _____ c'restaurant!	D. chapeau
5. J'ai (jeté) _____ mon bouquin sur la table.	E. terrible
6. J'dois (partir) _____ .	F. m'éclipser
7. C'est (facile) _____ .	G. rouler
8. Je m'suis fait (voler) _____ !	H. plombes
9. Elle arrivera dans trois (heures) _____ .	I. cinoche
10. (Félicitations) _____ !	J. marquet
11. Y a un (mois) _____ que j'bosse ici.	K. balancé
12. Tu connais mon (frère) _____ ?	L. pognon

B. Write the letter of the appropriate fill-in.

1. J'enfilais ___ tout l'après midi!
   a. **des diamants**   b. **des perles**   c. **des rubis**
2. C't'hôtel, y comprend la ___ et la ___ .
   a. **entrée, sortie**   b. **aller, retour**   c. **crèche, becquetance**
3. J'aime faire du camping pasqu'ça m'plaît d'pioncer ___ .
   a. **à la belle étoile**   b. **au beau jour**   c. **à la belle fille**
4. J'peux pas croire c'que tu m'dis! J'en ___ .
   a. **reste baba**   b. **lave les mains**   c. **lèche les babines**
5. Quel chauffeur horrible! J'étais ___ dans sa voiture.
   a. **heureux**   b. **lessivé**   c. **crispé**
6. Y en fiche pas une ___ à l'école, mon frère.
   a. **reine**   b. **rame**   c. **bosse**

7. Demain, j'dois reprend'l' __ .
    a. **collier**   b. **coin**   c. **mur**
8. J'vais en Europe souvent, mézigue. J'adore __ .
    a. **grenouiller**   b. **me faire rouler**   c. **roûler ma bosse**
9. Laisse-moi tranquille! Tu commences à m' __ .
    a. **taper sur les nerfs**   b. **lancequiner**   c. **brancher**
10. Moi __ , j'habite à Paris!
    a. **mézigue**   b. **piaf**   c. **itou**
11. Ma sœur, è m'suit partout. Elle est très __ .
    a. **petite**   b. **collante**   c. **rapide**
12. J'sais pas où y est pasque j'l'ai __ .
    a. **engueulé**   b. **fusillé**   c. **semé**

C. Underline the synonym.

1. **revenons à nos moutons**	a. revenons à l'école	b. revenons au sujet
2. **fauché**	a. sans argent	b. fatigué
3. **en rester baba**	a. être nerveux	b. être stupéfait
4. **avoir la frite**	a. avoir de l'énergie	b. avoir de l'argent
5. **félicitations**	a. bonnet	b. chapeau
6. **terrible!**	a. marrant	b. fantastique
7. **enfiler des perles**	a. ne rien faire	b. travailler
8. **s'éclipser**	a. partir vite	b. arriver vite
9. **cossard**	a. paresseux	b. mec
10. **roublard**	a. malin	b. stupide
11. **plombe**	a. lent	b. heure

GRAMMAR I: FURTHER USE OF PERSONAL PRONOUNS

A. Personal pronoun *moi*

In colloquial French, the personal pronoun **moi** is often used to add emphasis to a command or an imperative *only* when the statement involves the senses or personal perception. It is used in much the same way as "just" is used in English to add emphasis to the verb that it modifies:

Regarde ça!; Look at that!
Regarde-moi ça!; Just look at that!

Goûte ça!; Taste that!
Goûte-moi ça!; Just taste that!

B. Using objective case personal pronouns to add emphasis

In colloquial French, objective case personal pronouns (**moi, toi, lui, elle, nous, vous, eux** and **elles**) are used to (1) emphasize the object of a statement and (2) emphasize possession.

1. To Emphasize the Object of Statement

The object may be emphasized by simply repeating it at the end of the statement in the form of an objective case personal pronoun.

> J'peux la soulever, **elle**; I can lift her up!
> J'te vois, **toi**; I see you!

Note that the preposition **à** is not used before the objective case personal pronoun even when the object of the statement is indirect:

> J'te parle, **toi**; I'm talking **to** you!

2. To Emphasize Possession

Possessive adjectives are used to indicate possession:

> C'est **ma** montre; It's **my** watch.
> C'est **son** chien; It's his dog. etc . . .

In spoken French, the possessive adjective is reemphasized by adding the preposition **à** + the appropriate **objective case personal pronoun** to the statement:

> C'est **ma** montre **à moi**!; It's **my** watch!
> C'est **son** chien **à lui**; It's **his** dog!

Another common way to emphasize possession is simply to reverse the order of the subject and the objective case personal pronoun. *However*, with this construction, the possessive adjective is replaced by the definite article **le, la, l'**, or **les**:

> C't'**à moi**, la montre!; It's **my** watch!
> C't'**à lui**, l'chien!; It's **his** dog!

EXERCISES

A. Emphasize the verb using the personal pronoun *moi*.

1. Regarde ça!
   _____ !

2. Ecoute c'te musique!
   _____ !

3. Sens c'te gâteau!
   _____ !

4. Goûte c'te chocolat!
    _____ !

5. Touche c't'étoffe!
    _____ !

B. Emphasize the object of the statement according to the example.

Example:

> J'te vois.
> **J'te vois, toi.**

1. Tu l'as trouvé?
    _____ ?

2. J't'aime bien.
    _____ .

3. Mais, j't'ai remboursé!
    _____ !

4. Y vous l'a déjà expliqué.
    _____ .

5. E m'l'a promis.
    _____ .

6. Y nous a donné un cadeau.
    _____ .

7. J't'ai étonné?
    _____ ?

8. Tu l'as invitée?
    _____ ?

9. E nous a accompagnés.
    _____ ?

10. Y m'a beaucoup aidé.
    _____ ?

C. Add emphasis to the possessor according to the example.

Example:

> C'est sa télévision. **(lui)**
> **C'est sa télévision à lui.**
> **C't'à lui, la télévision.**

1. C'est son tricot. **(lui)**
    _____ .
    _____ .

2. C'est ton chien?
    _____ .
    _____ .

3. C'est sa voiture. **(elle)**

   _____ .

   _____ .

4. C'est leur appartement. **(eux)**

   _____ .

   _____ .

5. C'est son fauteuil. **(lui)**

   _____ .

   _____ .

6. C'est not'maison.

   _____ .

   _____ .

7. C'est votre enfant?

   _____ ?

   _____ ?

8. C'est mon pantalon.

   _____ .

   _____ .

9. C'est ta moto?

   _____ ?

   _____ ?

10. C'est son livre? **(elle)**

   _____ ?

   _____ ?

EN VOITURE...

DIALOGUE

Raoul et Henri font une promenade en voiture.

Raoul: Elle est **au poil**, ta **bagnole**! E t'a **coûté les yeux d'la tête**?

Henri: **Penses-tu**! Mon **daron**, y m'a **refilé** sa vieille **tire** pasqu'elle était toujours **patraque** et y **en avait plein les bottes**. Alors, j'ai mis d'nouveaux **boudins** pour qu'elle ait l'air **toute flambant neuve**.

Raoul: Mais ça **bâfre** beaucoup d'**jus**?

Henri: Presque **lape**!

Raoul: T'as d'la **veine**, **tézigue**! Moi, j'dois **béquiller** partout pasque j'sais même pas **driver**.

Henri: Tu sais, c'est la première fois qu'j'fais une **virée** dans c'**machin**. J'ai **les jetons** qu'on m'**rent'dedans**!

Raoul: **Allez**! T'as qu'à **faire gaffe** de n'pas **griller** les feux rouges. D'ailleurs, tu veux pas d'**contredanse**!

Henri: J'dois surtout essayer d'**couper** aux **chauffards** pasque... ben, tu vois, j'arrive à appuyer sur l'**champignon** mais l'**patin**, y s'coince tout l'temps!

Lesson Eight

IN THE CAR. . .

DIALOGUE

Raoul and Henri take a ride in the car.

Raoul: This car's really great! Did it cost you an arm and a leg?

Henri: Get outta here! My dad unloaded his old clinker on me because it was falling apart and he was fed up. So I put some new tires on it to make it look good as new.

Raoul: But does it guzzle up a lot of gas?

Henri: Almost nothing!

Raoul: You're really lucky! I have to walk everywhere 'cause I don't even know how to drive.

Henri: You know, this is the first time I've taken a spin in this thing. I'm kind of nervous that I'm gonna get bashed!

Raoul: Oh, come on! Just be careful not to run any red lights. Besides, you don't want to get a ticket!

Henri: I really have to try to avoid lousy drivers because . . . well, you see, I can step on the gas okay but the brake pedal keeps sticking!

71

VOCABULARY

allez! exclam. stop exaggerating!; come on! / *Note:* Although **allez** is commonly used as the second person plural of the verb **aller** meaning "to go," it may also be used when speaking to only *one* person when used in this context.

au poil exp. terrific; first-rate.

bâfrer v. to eat a lot; "to pork out."

bagnole f. car (*extremely popular*).

béquiller v. to walk / (lit); to walk on crutches / *Note:* Although **béquille** actually means "crutch," in French its slang connotation is that of "leg." Therefore, in slang **béquiller** might be loosely translated as "to leg it."

boudin m. tire / (lit); stuffed blood sausage / *Note:* **boudin** has two other distinct meanings in slang: (1) fat pudgy finger, (2) very fat woman (derogatory).

champignon m. gas pedal / (lit); mushroom / *Note:* This is probably because older cars used to have a round floor starter that resembled the shape of a mushroom.

chauffard m. bad driver.

contredanse f. ticket (issued by a policeman).

couper à v. to avoid / **couper à la conscription**; to avoid the draft.

coûter les yeux de la tête exp. to cost an arm and a leg / (lit); to cost the eyes from the head.

daron m. father.

driver v. to drive / *Note:* (See Unit II; English Words That Are Used in Spoken French).

gaffe (faire) exp. to pay attention; be careful / *Note:* **gaffer** v. to watch carefully.

griller v. to run a red light / (lit); to grill.

jetons (avoir les) exp. to have the jitters / (lit); to have the tokens / *Note 1:* This conjures up a picture of someone who is so jittery, that the sound of the tokens in his pocket can be heard clanging together. / *Note 2:* **jeton(s)** is commonly pronounced "shton."

jus m. gasoline / (lit); juice.

lape adv. nothing.

machin m. thing / *Also:* **machin-chose** m. thing; thing-a-magig / *Note:* **machin** is *not* the same as **machine** f. (lit); machine.

patin m. brake pedal / (lit); skate.

patraque adj. broken-down; worn out / *Note:* This may also be used to describe a sick person: **Y est patraque**; He is sick.

penses-tu! exp. the idea!; how could you think of such a thing?!

plein les bottes (en avoir) exp. to be fed up / (lit); to have had a boot-full.

refiler v. to give something away that one no longer wants; to palm something off on someone / *Note:* When **refiler** does not begin a statement, it is commonly pronounced "r'filer."

rentrer dedans v. to crash into something / (lit); to "reenter inside" / *Also:* **rentrer dans le décor**; to crash / (lit); to reenter in the decor (scenery).

tire f. old car / (lit); puller / *Note:* This comes from **tirer** v. to pull.

toute flambant neuve adj. brand spankin' new / (lit); all flaming new / **Son pantalon, y est tout flambant neuf**; His pants are brand new.

veine (avoir de la) exp. to be very lucky.

virée (faire une) exp. to take a spin; a quick jaunt / *Note:* **virer** v. to turn; to sweep round.

PRACTICE THE VOCABULARY

[Answers to Lesson 8, pp. 94–95]

A. Replace the word(s) in parentheses with the appropriate slang synonym from the right column.

1. Oh, (arrête d'exagérer) _____ !
2. T'as d'la (chance) _____ , tézigue!
3. J'sais pas très bien (conduire) _____ .
4. Elle est chouette ta nouvelle (voiture) _____ !
5. C'est trop loin pour y (marcher) _____ .
6. C'est quoi c'te (chose) _____ ?
7. (Attention) _____ de n'pas tomber!
8. Tu veux faire une (promenade) _____ en voiture?
9. C'est mon (père) _____ qui m'l'a donnée.
10. Appuie sur l'(frein) _____ !

A. **daron**
B. **veine**
C. **fais gaffe**
D. **allez**
E. **patin**
F. **driver**
G. **bagnole**
H. **béquiller**
I. **virée**
J. **machin**

B. Underline the word in parentheses that best completes the phrase.

1. Le flic, y m'a donné une (**voiture, danse, contredanse**).
2. Y essaie toujours d'couper (**de, à, en**) ses devoirs.
3. (**Penses, Trouves, Vois**)-tu! Certainement que non!
4. Attention! Tu vas (**courir, marcher, griller**) l'feu rouge!
5. Mais, ça coûte les yeux d'la (**tête, jambe, patate**).
6. E m'a (**bouffé, coupé, refilé**) sa vieille robe.
7. C'te chemise, elle a coûté cher? Non, presque (**lame, lape, léger**).
8. Y a (**bâfré, bougé, dansé**) tout son dîner en trois minutes!
9. J'peux plus l'supporter! J'en ai plein les (**bras, chaussettes, bottes**)!
10. Y sait pas conduire, c'te (**fric, resto, chauffard**).
11. Elle est (**patraque, soûlarde, marrante**), c'te vieille voiture!
12. Elle est toute (**flambant, flambé, fluorescente**) neuve!

C. Match the two columns.

1.	___ avoir les jetons	A.	a quick spin
2.	___ au poil	B.	nothing
3.	___ béquiller	C.	terrific
4.	___ daron	D.	to be jittery
5.	___ tire	E.	to crash
6.	___ bâfrer	F.	to walk
7.	___ machin	G.	father
8.	___ patin	H.	brake pedal
9.	___ rentrer dedans	I.	gasoline
10.	___ virée	J.	to eat a lot
11.	___ jus	K.	thing
12.	___ lape	L.	old car

GRAMMAR I: THE RELATIVE PRONOUN *QUOI*

A. To give an opinion

Often we are asked to give our opinion about something of a personal nature such as the clothes someone is wearing, an accomplishment, an idea, etc. If we feel that our honest opinion might hurt or insult the person, we try to answer in a positive yet noncommittal way. There is usually a slight pause as we search for just the right word to use. For example: (The actual thoughts of the speaker are shown in parentheses)

(What an ugly dress!)
I love your dress! It's so ... different!

(What a horrible actor!)
As an actor, you are really ... unbelievable!

The same pause may also occur if the speaker is simply overcome with emotion:

(I've never seen a more amazing show!)
I think that the show was absolutely ... fantastic!

(I think I'm going to cry!)
What you did for me was just so ... sweet!

In French, once the speaker has found the exact word to use, the relative pronoun **quoi** will follow. This is an *extremely* popular usage of **quoi**. The following are the French translations of the preceding examples:

(Quelle robe affreuse!)
J'adore vot'robe! Elle est tellement . . . différente, quoi!

(Quel acteur horrible!)
Comme acteur, vous êtes . . . incroyable, quoi!

(J'ai jamais vu un spectacle aussi stupéfiant!)
Le spectacle, y était absolument . . . fantastique, quoi!

(J'crois qu'j'vais pleurer)
C'que vous avez fait pour moi était si . . . gentil, quoi!

B. "It's alright . . . "

Quoi is also used at the end of a statement when the speaker simply has nothing further to say usually due to a lack of genuine enthusiasm. In the following examples, **quoi** is being used to mean, "It's alright, but nothing to get really excited about." Again, this is an *extremely* popular and frequent usage of **quoi**.

Comment tu trouves cette maison? Elle est jolie, quoi.
How do you like this house? It's alright . . .

Comment tu trouves cette pâtisserie? Elle est bonne, quoi.
How do you like this pastry? It's alright . . .

PRACTICE *QUOI*

A. Translate the phrases into French using the relative pronoun *quoi*. **The actual thoughts of the speaker are in parentheses. (This exercise practices the usage of** *quoi* **when the speaker is noncommittal or overcome with emotion)**

Example:

(What an awful dinner!)
The dinner was . . . interesting!
Le dîner, y était . . . intéressant, quoi!

1. **(I can't stand your dog!)**
Your dog has a lot of . . . personality!
_____ !

2. **(What an ugly shirt!)**
    Your shirt is so . . . bright!
    _____ !

3. **(What a terrible artist!)**
    That painting you made looks very . . . modern!
    _____ !

4. **(What a wonderful house!)**
    I love your house! It's so . . . warm!
    _____ !

5. **(What delicious food!)**
    The dinner was absolutely . . . delicious!
    _____ !

6. **(Your daughter has no talent!)**
    Your daughter dances so . . . well!
    _____ !

7. **(What a beautiful wedding!)**
    The ceremony was extremely . . . moving!
    _____ !

8. **(What a charming girl!)**
    Her sense of humor is . . . sensational!
    _____ !

B.   Continue the above exercise using *quoi* to mean, "It's alright, but nothing to get really excited about."

Example:

> This house is nice (but nothing to get really excited about).
> **Cette maison, elle est bien, quoi.**

1. Your shirt is nice (but nothing to get really excited about).
    _____ .

2. Your friend is cute (but nothing to get really excited about).
    _____ .

3. His apartment is comfortable (but nothing to get really excited about).
    _____ .

4. I'm feeling better (but nothing to get really excited about).
    _____ .

5. The dinner was good (but nothing to get really excited about).
    _____ .

6. The music is pretty (but nothing to get really excited about).
   _____ .

7. The actor is funny (but nothing to get really excited about).
   _____ .

8. He is very nice (but nothing to get really excited about).
   _____ .

A L'AEROPORT...

DIALOGUE

Paul rencontre Anne à l'aéroport.

Anne: Paul! J'avais du mal à t'**repérer** dans c'te **bousculade**. J'espère qu'tu devais pas **poireauter** trop longtemps.

Paul: Mais non! Alors, **ça carbure**? T'as pas l'air **dans ton assiette**.

Anne: Tu vas pas croire ma **déveine**. D'abord, j'pensais qu'j'avais **paumé** mon **tickson** en route!

Paul: Ah, non! Et c'est pas comme à Paris où on peut **brûler l'dur**.

Anne: **M'enfin**, j'l'ai **deniché** après avoir **farfouillé** dans mes **bagos**. J'ai failli m'**casser la gueule** essayant de n'pas être **à la bourre**. J'ai dû m'**magner l'derche** pasqu'mon **zinc**, y allait **s'barrer** dans **juste** dix **broquilles**!

Paul: Après tout ça, t'es arrivée à **pioncer** un peu?

Anne: Pas possible pasqu'y avait un drôle d'**type** à côté d'moi qui a dû **êt'vacciné avec une aiguille de phono**.

Paul: Oh, **arrête ton char**!

Anne: Mais, c'est pas du **baratin**! Y m'**cassait les oreilles** avec ses **tartines**!

Paul: J'ui aurais dit d'y **mettre un bouchon**.

Anne: **T'uses ta salive**! Y t'aurait pas **esgourdé**.

Paul: Eh ben, **bon débarras**!

Lesson Nine

IN THE AIRPORT. . .

DIALOGUE

Paul is meeting Anne at the airport.

Anne: Paul! I had trouble spotting you in this mess. I hope you didn't have to wait too long.

Paul: Not at all! So, how's it going? You seem a little out of it.

Anne: You're not going to believe my lousy luck. For openers, I thought I lost my ticket on the way here!

Paul: Oh, no! And it's not like in Paris where you can sneak a free ride in the subway without a ticket.

Anne: But finally I found it after rummaging through my baggage. I almost broke my neck trying not to be late. I had to haul buns 'cause my plane was leaving in just ten minutes!

Paul: After all that, did you manage to nod off a little?

Anne: No way, 'cause there was this weird guy next to me who must have been vaccinated with a phonograph needle.

Paul: Oh, stop exaggerating!

Anne: It's no bull! He totally wore me out with his endless stories!

Paul: I would've told him to can it.

Anne: You're wasting your breath. He wouldn't have listened to you.

Paul: Well, good riddance!

VOCABULARY

bagos m.pl. abbreviation of "bagages."

baratin m. lie; nonsense; "bull" / *Note:* **baratiner** v. to b.s.

barrer (se) v. to leave / Note: **barrer** v. (lit); to strike out; cross out a word.

bon débarras! exp. good riddance! / *Note:* **débarrasser** v. (lit); to rid.

bourre (être à la) exp. late / *Note:* As learned in Chapter 2, **bourre**, which literally means "flock for stuffing or padding," is also used in the expression **de première bourre** meaning "first-rate; the best."

bousculade f. hustling and jostling crowd / *Note:* This comes from the verb **bousculer** meaning "to push and shove."

broquille f. minute / *Note:* Because this word is an invention of slang, there is no literal translation.

brûler le dur exp. to ride the train without a ticket / *Note:* When used as an adjective, **dur** literally means "hard." However, when used as a noun, it takes on the slang connotation of "train." Therefore, the literal translation of this expression is "to burn the train" or better "to burn the system."

carburer v. to be going very well / (lit); to function well (said of a carburetor).

casser la gueule (se) exp. to break one's "neck" / (lit); to break one's mouth or face / *Note 1:* **gueule** is a derogatory slang synonym for either "mouth" or "face" / (lit); the mouth of an animal / *Note 2:* **casser la gueule à q.** means to hit someone in the face / **J'vais t'casser la gueule!**; I'm gonna belt you in the mouth!

casser les oreilles à q. exp. to tire one's ears due to excessive talking / (lit); to break one's ears.

char m. exaggeration / *Note 1:* This comes from the slang verb **charrier** meaning, "to exaggerate" / *Note 2:* The noun **char** also has the literal meaning of "chariot." / *Note 3:* **Arrête ton char!** is commonly used to mean "stop your exaggerating" but since it also means "stop your chariot," the French decided to play up this double meaning by inventing the expression: **Arrête ton char, Ben Hur!**; Stop you chariot, Ben Hur! (The French pronounce **Ben** the same way as in English, and the **h** in **Hur** is silent: "Benur") This play on words is perhaps one of the most famous in the French repertoire.

dans son assiette (ne pas être) exp. to be out of it; out of sorts / (lit); not to be in one's plate.

dénicher v. to find something (from where it was hiding) / (lit); to "de-niche" something.

déveine (avoir la) f. to have bad luck / *Note:* **avoir de la veine** f. to have good luck / Note that the **de** is dropped in the expression **avoir la déveine** but remains in **avoir de la veine**.

esgourder v. to listen / *Note:* **esgourde** f.pl. ear.

farfouiller v. to rummage (without taking much care).

juste adv. just / *Note:* In colloquial French, **juste** replaces the adverb **seule-ment** and is used in the same way as is "only" in English: **Y va rester chez nous juste trois jours;** He's going to stay at our house just three days.

magner le derche (se) exp. to "move one's buns" / (lit); to manipulate or direct one's "derrière" / *Note:* **derche** m. is slang for **derrière.**

m'enfin exp. This is an extremely popular contraction of **mais enfin.**

mettre un bouchon (y) exp. to shut up / (lit); to put a cork on it.

paumer v. to lose/ **J'suis paumé';** I'm lost.

poireauter v. to wait; "to take root" / *Note:* This comes from the noun **poireau** m. "leek." Therefore, **poireauter** might be translated as "to take root like a leek" (since leeks have a very dense network of roots) / *Also:* **faire le poireau.**

pioncer v. to sleep; snooze.

repérer v. to spot someone / (lit); to locate (with artillery).

tartine f. endless speech / (lit); a slice of bread with a condiment spread on top (e.g., butter, jam, etc.) / *Note:* The connotation of **tartine** becomes clear when we think of it as "something that is spread out" / *Note:* **tartiner** v. to make a long-winded speech / (lit); to spread (out).

tickson m. ticket (other than that issued by a policeman).

type m. guy; "dude" / (lit); type / *Note:* **typesse** f. girl, "chick."

user sa salive exp. to waste one's breath / (lit); to use (up) one's saliva.

vacciné(e) avec une aiguille de phono (être) exp. humorous expression for one who talks a lot / (lit); to be vaccinated with a phonograph needle.

zinc m. (1) airplane; (2) counter or bar / (lit); zinc.

PRACTICE THE VOCABULARY

[Answers to Lesson 9, pp. 95–96]

A. Complete the phrase by choosing the appropriate word from the list. Give the correct form of the verb.

poireauter	dénicher	tartine
pioncer	déveine	tickson
repérer	bousculades	salive
débarras	farfouiller	paumer

1. Le casseur, y a _____ dans mes affaires!
2. Arrête d'user ta _____ . Y t'écoute pas.
3. J'ai _____ ma bague! J'pensais qu'j'l'avais _____ !
4. J'ai du mal à _____ la nuit.
5. Y est cher c' _____ d'avion.
6. Mais, ça fait deux heures qu'j' _____ ici!
7. E pouvait pas m' _____ dans la foule.

8. Y fait d'une petite histoire une longue _____ .
9. Quelle _____ ! J'gagne jamais!
10. J'veux plus t'revoir! Bon _____ !
11. E sort pas pasqu'elle aime pas les _____ .

B. Circle the correct synonym.

1. **baratin**   a. mensonge   b. homme

2. **à la bourre**   a. de bonne heure   b. en retard

3. **char**   a. exagération   b. vérité

4. **zinc**   a. avion   b. voiture

5. **broquille**   a. heure   b. minute

6. **type**   a. femme   b. homme

7. **esgourder**   a. parler   b. écouter

8. **se barrer**   a. partir   b. arriver

9. **ça carbure**   a. ça va mal   b. ça va bien

10. **y mettre un   a. se taire   b. parler
    bouchon**

C. Match the two columns

1. __ ne pas être dans son assiette   A. to hurry
2. __ brûler le dur   B. exaggeration
3. __ bagos   C. to be "out of it"
4. __ casser la gueule à q.   D. to be very talkative
5. __ se magner le derche   E. just
6. __ juste   F. to annoy someone
7. __ vacciné avec une aiguille de phono   with chatter
8. __ char   G. to ride without a
9. __ casser les oreilles à q.   ticket
                                             H. baggage
                                             I. to hit someone

GRAMMAR I: THE MANY COLLOQUIAL USES OF *BON*

A. To begin a conversation or wrap up a thought

Bon is frequently used as a way either to begin a conversation or to wrap up one thought before beginning another. It is used in the same way as "okay" is in English:

Bon. Tu tournes à gauche au coin d'la rue, pis tu continues tout droit...
Okay. You turn left at the corner, then you continue straight ahead...

Enfin, après avoir cherché un hôtel pendant trois heures, j'en un trouvé un au cent'd'la ville. Bon. Tout allait très bien jusqu'à c'que...
Finally, after having looked for a hotel for three hours, I found one
in the center of town. Okay. Everything was going just fine until...

B.   To express anger

Bon is also used to express anger or resentment. In this case, it would be equivalent to the English word "fine" when used in anger.

> **Vouz allez pas m'augmenter? Bon! J'vous quitte!**
> You're not going to give me a raise? Fine! I quit!

> **Tu vas pas m'répondre? Bon!**
> You're not going to answer me? Fine!

C.   *Bon* + *ben* = *Bon ben...*

Often, **Bon ben** is used in the beginning of a statement while the speaker searches for the right words to use. It could be loosely translated as "Well, um...." For this reason, the sound of **ben** is usually held out in the same manner as its English equivalent "um":

> **–T'en penses quoi?**
> **–Bon ben... J'pense qu'son patron, y a eu tort d'le mettre à la porte.**
> –What do you think about it?
> –Well, um... I think his boss was wrong to fire him.

> **–Pourquoi t'as pris la poupée d'ta sœur?**
> **–Bon ben... C'était l'chien qui l'a prise!**
> –Why did you take your sister's doll?
> –Well, um... It was the dog that took it!

D.   *Ah* + *bon* = *Ah, bon?*

When used as a question, **bon** takes on the meaning of "really" when preceded by "Ah":

> **–La semaine prochaine, j'vais aller en France.**
> **–Ah, bon?**
> –Next week, I'm going to go to France.
> –Really?

Note:

When used in question form, **Ah, bon** does *not* mean "Ah, good," although this is indeed its literal translation. Therefore, it is quite correct to use **Ah, bon** upon receiving *bad* news:

> –Mon père, y est très malade.
> –Ah, bon?
> –My father is very sick.
> –Really?

E. *Pour de bon*

Although this expression literally translates as "for good," it does not always mean "forever" as it does in English. Its closest colloquial translation is "for real":

> –J'ai trouvé un billet d'vingt francs!
> –Pour d'bon?
> –I found a twenty-franc bill!
> –For real?

Note:

Pour d'bon and **Ah, bon** are very similar and can certainly be used interchangeably.

PRACTICE THE COLLOQUIAL USES OF *BON*

A. Choose the appropriate definition:

1.	___ **Ah, bon?**	A.	It may replace "Ah, bon?"
2.	___ **Bon.**	B.	It is used to express anger.
3.	___ **Bon ben...**	C.	It may be used either to begin a conversation or to wrap up one thought before beginning another (e.g., "okay").
4.	___ **Bon!**		
5.	___ **Pour d'bon?**	D.	When used as a question, it means "really?"
		E.	It is used in the beginning of a statement while the speaker searches for what to say.

B. Replace the word(s) in parentheses with the appropriate use of *bon*. Use GRAMMAR I, A–E as a reference:

A. *Bon.*   B. *Bon!*   C. *Bon ben*   D. *Ah, bon*   F. *Pour d'bon*

1. (Okay) _____ . J'dois m'barrer.
2. Comment tu l'trouves? (Well ...) _____ _____ , y semble très gentil, c'type.

3. J'ai repéré une grande vedette dans la foule! (Really?)
   _____ _____ ?
4. Tu vas pas m'laisser pioncer?! (Fine!) _____ !
5. (Okay) _____ . J't'appelle demain.
6. J'ai paumé mon portefeuille! (For real?) _____ _____ _____ ?
7. T'as utilisé mon tickson?! (Fine!) _____ !
8. Alors, ça carbure? (Well...) _____ _____ , j'suis pas vraiment dans mon assiette.
9. Y a essayé d'me casser la gueule! (Really?) _____ _____ ?

AU MARCHE AUX PUCES...

DIALOGUE

Simone et Yvonne sont au marché aux puces.

Simone:	Tu vas **attriquer** c'te **galure**? Y est vraiment **grisole**.
Yvonne:	Que non! Dix mille balles, c'est trop d'**grisbi** à **affurer** sur un **truc** qui est **tarte** d'ailleurs. J'veux pas **m'faire écorcher** tout d'suite!
Simone:	Mais, tu dois essayer d'**dégotter** des **baths affures**. Tiens, **mire** un peu ces **fringues**. T'as besoin d'**fumantes** ou d'**tirants**?
Yvonne:	Non, j'cherche un bel **oignon** pour mon mari.
Simone:	Mais, fais gaffe au **toc**, hein! Y en a **pas mal** ici!
Yvonne:	C'est sûr! Tu sais, la semaine dernière y avait deux **bonnes femmes** ici qui **s'crêpaient l'chignon** à cause d'une **roupane** et des **pompes**! J'voulais **m'bidonner**! Mais, z'étaient **à cran**! Heureusement qu'on **bazarde** pas des **opinels** ici!
Simone:	**T'en fais pas.** Si tu vois quèque chose d'**badour**, j'te **donnerai pas du fil à retordre**! Au fait, on accepte des chèques ici?
Yvonne:	Non, faut **payer cash**!

Lesson Ten

AT THE FLEA MARKET...

DIALOGUE

Simone and Yvonne are at the flea market.

Simone: You're gonna buy that hat? It's really expensive.

Yvonne: No way! One hundred francs is too much money to spend on a thing that's ugly as well. I don't want to get myself ripped off right away!

Simone: But you have to hunt for good bargains. Hey, just look at these clothes. You need any socks or stockings?

Yvonne: No, I'm looking for a nice watch for my husband.

Simone: But watch out for junk! There's a pile of it here!

Yvonne: That's for sure! You know, last week there were two women here who were having a huge chick-fight over a dress and some shoes! I wanted to bust up laughing. They were so ticked off! Luckily they don't sell knives here!

Simone: Don't worry. If you see something neat, I won't give you any trouble! By the way, do they accept checks here?

Yvonne: No, you have to pay cash!

VOCABULARY

à cran (être) adj. to be on the verge of getting angry / *Note:* **cran** m. notch.

affurer v. to spend.

attriquer v. to buy.

badour(e) adj. very pretty or handsome / **Y est badour, elle est badoure;** He's handsome, she's pretty.

bath affure f. good bargain; great buy / *Note 1:* **bath** adj. terrific; great / *Note 2:* **affure** f. comes from the slang verb **affurer** meaning "to spend" / You'll notice that in the dialogue the indefinite article **des** was used before the adjective **bath**. Although the academic practice is to use **de** when followed by an adjective, in colloquial French **des** is commonly used.

bazarder v. to sell / *Note:* Although **bazarder** literally means "to sell something quickly in order to turn it into money," it is commonly used to mean "to sell" in general.

bidonner (se) v. to laugh hard; to belly-laugh / (lit); to shake one's belly / *Note:* **bidon** m. belly / *Also:* **bidonnant** adj. funny.

bonne femme f. (*extremely popular yet pejorative*) woman / (lit); good woman / *Note:* **bonne femme** is commonly used for "woman" whereas **nana** is used for "girl" or "chick."

crêper l'chignon (se) exp. humorous expression said of two women who are having a fight / (lit); to crimp each other's chignon or bun.

dégotter v. to find, discover.

donner du fil à retordre exp. to cause someone difficulty / (lit); to give someone wire to untangle.

écorcher (se faire) v. to get oneself ripped off; taken / (lit); to get oneself skinned.

faire (s'en) v. to worry; to get worked up over something / *Note:* This is usually heard only in the imperative form: **T'en fais pas!;** Don't worry!

fringues f.pl. clothes / *Note:* **se fringuer** v. to get dressed.

fumantes f.pl. socks / (lit); smokers.

galure m. hat.

grisbi m. money; dough.

grisole adj. expensive.

mirer v. to look / (lit); to aim at something / *Note:* **mirettes** f.pl. eyes.

oignon m. watch / (lit); onion / *Note:* This has become a popular synonym since the old-fashioned pocket watches had the stem on the top resembling the shape of an onion.

opinel m. pocketknife / *Note:* This is in fact the brand name of a pocketknife that has become accepted as its actual name, like "Kleenex."

pas mal adv. a lot; many / **Y a pas mal d'gens à la soirée;** There are a lot of people at the party.

payer cash exp. to pay cash / *Note:* The French use the word **cash** in the same manner as in English: **C'est cent francs cash**; It's one hundred francs cash. (See Unit II; English Words That Are Used in Spoken French.)

pompes f.pl. shoes / (lit); pumps.

roupane f. dress.

tarte adj. ugly / *Also:* **tartignolle**.

tirants m.pl. stockings / (lit); pullers.

toc m. junk / **C'est du toc**; It's junk. / *Also:* **tocard**.

truc m. thing / **C'est quoi c'truc?**; What is this thing?

PRACTICE THE VOCABULARY

[Answers to Lesson 10, pp. 96-97]

A. Write the letter of the word that best completes the phrase.

1. J'adore c'te chemise! J'vais l' _____ .
   a. brancher   b. balader   c. attriquer

2. Mon père, y était à _____ pasqu'on 'ui a donné une contredanse.
   a. crâne   b. cran   c. craquer

3. Elle est bizarre c'te bonne _____ .
   a. dame   b. fille   c. femme

4. Y est vraiment _____ , c't'enfant. Y est loin d'êt'beau!
   a. tourte   b. tarte   c. gâteau

5. T'en _____ pas! Y arrive!
   a. fabriques   b. béquilles   c. fais

6. T'as vu c'qu'y a _____ dans son garage?
   a. dégotté   b. piqué   c. fusillé

7. Y a pas _____ d'gens dans c'te théâtre.
   a. mauvais   b. mal   c. bien

8. Tu peux m'prêter du _____ ?
   a. grain   b. grisole   c. grisbi

9. Mes pieds, y sont trop grands pour ces _____ -là.
   a. guindals   b. pompes   c. pompiers

10. Elle est _____ , c'te bagnole! Quelle beauté!
    a. badoure   b. roupane   c. grisbi

11. Un _____ , y s'porte sur la tête.
    a. boui-boui   b. guindal   c. galure

12. Un _____ , c'est pour couper.
    a. opinel   b. pin   c. sapin

B.   Match the English with the French.

1. __ Y est grisole c'te galure.
2. __ J'ai affuré tout mon grisbi.
3. __ C'est quoi c'truc?
4. __ J'crois qu'è t'mire.
5. __ E sont tartes ses fringues.
6. __ Y porte jamais d'fumantes.
7. __ J'ai déchiré mes tirants.
8. __ Quel bel onion.
9. __ T'es toujours à cran.
10. __ T'as payé cash?
11. __ C'est du toc, ça.
12. __ T'as vu la bonne femme?

A . Did you pay cash?
B . I think she's looking at you.
C . That's junk.
D . That hat's expensive.
E . Did you see that woman?
F . What is this thing?
G . I spent all my money.
H . You're always mad.
I . His clothes are ugly.
J . What a pretty watch.
K . He never wears socks.
L . I ripped my stockings.

C.   Replace the word(s) in parentheses with the appropriate slang synonym from the list below. Give the correct form of the verb.

baths affures	roupane	pompes
s'bidonner	dégotter	badour
bazarder	grisbi	donner du fil à retordre
attriquer	mirer	s'crêper l'chignon

1. Les deux filles, è (s'battent) _____ tout l'temps.
2. Ma mère, elle a (vendu) _____ sa bagnole.
3. J'ai du mal à béquiller dans ces (chaussures) _____ .
4. Y viennent d'(acheter) _____ une nouvelle baraque.
5. Y a volé tout mon (argent) _____ !
6. E porte que des (robes) _____ super courtes!
7. J'(riais) _____ pendant tout l'film.
8. Y m'(pose des problèmes) _____ .
9. (Regarde) _____ pas la téloche d'si près!
10. J'ai (trouvé) _____ , des (bonnes occasions) _____ .
11. Y est (beau) _____ , c'type.

GRAMMAR I: COLLOQUIAL USE OF *ON* AND ADJECTIVES

A.   Colloquial use of personal pronoun *on*

The personal pronoun **on** traditionally falls under the heading of third person singular and is translated as meaning "one" or "they":

On sait jamais.
One never knows.

On dit qu'y va pleuvoir.
They say it's going to rain.

However, in colloquial French, **on** is frequently used to replace the first person plural **nous**:

<table>
<tr><td>**On y va?**</td><td>**On devrait s'dépêcher!**</td></tr>
<tr><td>Shall we go?</td><td>We should hurry!</td></tr>
</table>

Note 1:

This is an extremely popular usage of **on** and may be used with anyone.

Note 2:

On y va? is one of the most popular ways of saying, "Shall we go?"

EXERCISES

A. Rewrite the sentences using the personal pronoun *on*.

1. Nous l'avons pas vue.

    _____ .

2. Nous devrions signaler l'accident à la police.

    _____ .

3. Si nous allions à la plage?

    _____ ?

4. Nous nous voyons tout l'temps.

    _____ .

5. J'crois qu'nous nous sommes rencontrés avant.

    _____ .

6. Nous arrivons!

    _____ !

7. Nous pourrons aller au cinéma si tu veux.

    _____ .

8. Nous nous amusons ici.

    _____ .

9. J'espère qu'nous trouverons une belle maison.

    _____ .

10. Nous y allons?

    _____ ?

ANSWERS TO LESSONS 6–10

LESSON 6

Practice the Vocabulary

A. 1. bosser
    2. blairer
    3. zieuter
    4. bouquin
    5. casser
    6. la vache
    7. moche
    8. calé
    9. étendre
    10. tifs, merlan, déboiser
    11. séché

B. 1. cinglé
    2. potasser, étendre
    3. prof
    4. déboiser, melon
    5. fiche, paquet
    6. plancher, galerie
    7. chouchou

    8. potaches
    9. calée, maths
  10. méganote
  11. séché

C. 1. a   7. b
   2. c   8. a
   3. a   9. c
   4. b   10. a
   5. c   11. b
   6. b   12. c

Grammar I: Practice the Slang Personal Pronouns

A. 1. C   B. 1. cézigue
   2. E   2. césarine
   3. A   3. tézigue
   4. D   4. sézigue
   5. H   5. leurzigues
   6. G   6. mézigue
   7. F   7. vozigues
   8. B   8. nozigues

LESSON 7

Practice the Vocabulary

A. 1. E   B. 1. b
    2. L   2. c
    3. I   3. a
    4. C   4. a
    5. K   5. c
    6. F   6. b
    7. B   7. a
    8. G   8. c
    9. H   9. a
  10. D   10. c
  11. J   11. b
  12. A   12. c

C. 1. b   7. a
   2. a   8. a
   3. b   9. a
   4. a   10. b
   5. b   11. a
   6. b

Grammar I: Exercises

A. 1. Regarde-moi ça!
   2. Ecoute-moi c'te musique!
   3. Sens-moi c'te gâteau!
   4. Goûte-moi c'te chocolat!
   5. Touche-moi c't'étoffe!

B. 1. Tu l'as trouvé, lui?
   2. J't'aime bien, toi.
   3. Mais, j't'ai remboursé, toi!
   4. Y vous l'a déjà expliqué, vous.
   5. E m'l'a promis, moi.
   6. Y nous a donné un cadeau, nous.
   7. J't'ai étonné, toi?
   8. Tu l'as invitée, elle?
   9. E nous a accompagnés, nous.
   10. Y m'a beaucoup aidé, moi

C. 1. C'est son tricot à lui; C't'à lui l'tricot.
   2. C'est ton chien à toi?; C't'à toi l'chien?
   3. C'est sa voiture à elle; C't'à elle la voiture.
   4. C'est leur appartement à eux; C't'à eux l'appartement.
   5. C'est son fauteuil à lui; C't'à lui l'fauteuil.
   6. C'est not'maison à nous; C't'à nous la maison.
   7. C'est votre enfant à vous?; C't'à vous l'enfant?
   8. C'est mon pantalon à moi; C't'à moi l'pantalon.
   9. C'est ma moto à moi; C't'à moi la moto.
   10. C'est son livre à elle?; C't'à elle l'livre?

LESSON 8

Practice the Vocabulary

A. 1. D   6. J
   2. B   7. C
   3. F   8. I
   4. G   9. A
   5. H   10. E

B. 1. contredanse   7. lape
   2. à   8. bâfré
   3. Penses   9. bottes
   4. griller   10. chauffard
   5. tête   11. patraque
   6. refilé   12. flambant

C. 1. D   7. K
   2. C   8. H
   3. F   9. E
   4. G   10. A
   5. L   11. I
   6. J   12. B

Grammar I: Practice *Quoi*

A. 1. Ton chien, y a beaucoup de. . .personalité, quoi!
   2. Ta chemise, elle est tellement. . .brillante, quoi!
   3. La peinture qu't'as faite, elle a l'air très. . .moderne, quoi!
   4. J'adore ta maison! Elle est tellement. . .chaleureuse, quoi!
   5. Le dîner, y était absolument. . .délicieux, quoi!
   6. Ta fille, è danse tellement. . .bien, quoi!
   7. La cérémonie, elle était extrêmement. . .émouvante, quoi!
   8. Son sens d'humour, y est. . .sensationnel, quoi!

B. 1. Ta chemise, elle est bien, quoi.
   2. Ton ami, y est mignon, quoi.
   3. Son appartement, y est confortable, quoi.
   4. Je m'sens mieux, quoi.
   5. Le dîner, y était bon, quoi.
   6. La musique, elle est jolie, quoi.
   7. L'acteur, y est marrant, quoi.
   8. Y est très gentil, quoi.

LESSON 9

Practice the Vocabulary

A. 1. farfouillé   B. 1. a
   2. salive   2. b
   3. déniché, paumée   3. a
   4. pioncer   4. a
   5. tickson   5. b
   6. poireaute   6. b
   7. repérer   7. b
   8. tartine   8. a
   9. déveine   9. b
  10. débarras   10. a
  11. bousculades

C. 1. C   6. E
   2. G   7. D
   3. H   8. B
   4. I   9. F
   5. A

Grammar I: Practice the Colloquial Uses of *Bon*

A. 1. D
   2. C
   3. E
   4. B
   5. A

B. 1. Bon.   6. Pour d'bon?
   2. Bon ben...   7. Bon!
   3. Ah, bon?   8. Bon ben...
   4. Bon!   9. Ah, bon?
   5. Bon.

LESSON 10

Practice the Vocabulary

A. 1. c   7. b
   2. b   8. c
   3. c   9. b
   4. b   10. a
   5. c   11. c
   6. a   12. a

B. 1. D   7. L
   2. G   8. J
   3. F   9. H
   4. B   10. A
   5. I   11. C
   6. K   12. E

C. 1. s'crêpent l'chignon
   2. bazardé
   3. pompes
   4. attriquer
   5. grisbi
   6. roupanes
   7. me bidonnais
   8. donne du fil à retordre
   9. Mire
   10. dégotté, baths affures
   11. badour

Grammar I: Exercises

A. 1. On l'a pas vue.
   2. On devrait signaler l'accident à la police.
   3. Si on allait à la plage?

4. On s'voit tout l'temps.
5. J'crois qu'on s'est rencontré avant.
6. On arrive!
7. On pourra aller au cinéma si tu veux.
8. On s'amuse ici.
9. J'espère qu'on trouvera une belle maison.
10. On y va?

REVIEW EXAM
FOR LESSONS 6–10

[Answers to Review, p. 101]

A. Underline the word(s) that fall into the same category as the word(s) to the left.

1. **regarder**
   - a. zieuter
   - b. béquiller
   - c. mirer
   - d. pioncer

2. **trouver**
   - a. s'en faire
   - b. dégotter
   - c. dénicher
   - d. paumer

3. **se faire voler**
   - a. s'faire rouler
   - b. s'faire écorcher
   - c. s'en faire
   - d. s'faire d'la bile

4. **argent**
   - a. machin
   - b. paquet
   - c. grisbi
   - d. pognon

5. **ennuyer**
   - a. s'casser
   - b. casser les pieds
   - c. casser les verres
   - d. casser les oreilles

6. **cher**
   - a. grisbi
   - b. grisole
   - c. salé
   - d. fauché

7. **famille**
   - a. frelot
   - b. patin
   - c. daron
   - d. badour

8. **voiture**
   - a. oignon
   - b. opinel
   - c. tire
   - d. bagnole

9. **laid**   a. collant   b. moche
                             c. potache   d. tarte

10. **partir**   a. s'barrer   b. s'éclipser
                             c. bosser   d. griller

11. **exagération**   a. galure   b. char
                             c. "Allez!"   d. la vache

12. **coiffeur**   a. merlan   b. chauffard
                             c. tifs   d. patin

B. Complete the phrases by choosing the appropriate words from the list. Make all necessary changes to the verbs.

pas mal	bidonner	tartine
plombe	poireauter	contredanse
déveine	paumer	ligoter
bazarder	type	fringues

1. Y m'a raconté une longue _____ .
2. C'est qui c'te _____ ?
3. J'ai _____ ma moto pasque j'la voulais plus.
4. E m'a fait _____ ici pendant trois heures.
5. Ce comédien, y m'fait _____ .
6. Le flic, y m'a filé une _____ .
7. Y est mal ficelé, lui. Mais regarde un peu ses _____ !
8. Y a _____ d'gens sur l'autoroute.
9. J'dois _____ tout c'bouquin en une _____ .
10. J'ai _____ mon portefeuille! Quelle _____ !

C. Match the two columns.

1. ___ à cran   A. late
2. ___ broquille   B. shoes
3. ___ pompes   C. ticket
4. ___ potasser   D. to hurry
5. ___ cinglé   E. minute
6. ___ marquet   F. angry
7. ___ du gâteau   G. crazy
8. ___ béquiller   H. bad driver
9. ___ chauffard   I. month
10. ___ tickson   J. to walk
11. ___ à la bourre   K. to study
12. ___ s'magner l'derche L. easy

D. Underline the appropriate word.

1. Y est (**mou, moche, mousse**) à caler les roues d'corbillard.
2. Tu vas t'marier? (**Bonnet, Chapeau, Casque**)!
3. On est en retard! Faut s'(**casser, rouler, magner**) l'derche.
4. Regarde un peu ces filles! E s'(**peignent, brossent, crêpent**) l'chignon.
5. J'ai (**dégotté, poireauté, bossé**) c'te vieux livre dans l'grenier.
6. Mais j'en ai plein les (**bouteilles, bottes, chaussures**)!
7. Appuie sur l'(**champignon, champs, citron**)!
8. Pourquoi t'as acheté c'(**badour, tarte, truc**)? C'est du (**jus, toc, opinel**).
9. J'peux pas y aller à pied pasque j'ai du mal à (**pioncer, béquiller, mirer**).
10. Y était tellement étonné qu'y en restait (**baba, bébé, badour**).
11. T'uses ta (**salle, salé, salive**). Y t'écoute pas.
12. Mais y est (**cinoche, collant, chouchou**), c'te (**type, pompe, tartine**)!

ANSWERS TO REVIEW (LESSONS 6–10)

A. 1. a, c
   2. b, c
   3. a, b
   4. c, d
   5. b, d
   6. b, c
   7. a, c
   8. c, d
   9. b, d
   10. a, b
   11. b, c
   12. a, c

B. 1. tartine
   2. type
   3. bazardé
   4. poireauter
   5. bidonner
   6. contredanse
   7. fringues
   8. pas mal
   9. ligoter, plombe
   10. paumé, déveine

C. 1. F
   2. E
   3. B
   4. K
   5. G
   6. I
   7. L
   8. J
   9. H
   10. C
   11. A
   12. D

D. 1. moche
   2. chapeau
   3. magner
   4. crêpent
   5. dégotté
   6. bottes
   7. champignon
   8. truc, toc
   9. béquiller
   10. baba
   11. salive
   12. collant, type

Leçon Onze

AU TELEPHONE...

DIALOGUE

Hélène et Edith, è **taillent une bavette** au **cornichon**.

Hélène: Ben alors? E t'a **bonit** quoi cette fois-ci?

Edith: Oh, tu la **connobres**, la **crâneuse**. C'est toujours la même **rengaine**. E pense qu'à devenir fameuse vedette! E m'**dégoisait** pendant toute une **plombe** disant qu'elle est **goualeuse impec, et patati et patata!**

Hélène: Franchement, **j'm'en fiche comme d'ma première chaussette!** E s'ra fameuse **quand les poules auront des dents!**

Edith: Elle a pas **la bosse** du chant.... C'est carrément pas **dans ses cordes.**

Hélène: D'ailleurs, è manque des attributs les plus importants.... Elle est **pas bien roulée** et **ça saute aux yeux** qu'y a **pas d'monde au balcon!**

Edith: Ben, **ça j'te dis!** Quand même, è continue à **en faire tout un plat!**

Hélène: Elle a **la comprenette dure**, c'est tout.

Edith: T'es trop **sympa**. C'est qu'elle est **bête à bouffer du foin**, voilà! T'essaies d'raisonner et è fait semblant d'**entraver que t'chi.**

Hélène: Le **pépin**, c'est qu'è veut pas **batt'le pavé** et c't'une carrière qui **s'fait pas sur une jambe.**

Edith: Ben, elle **a un poil dans la main**. J'te jure... **un d'ces mat'**, j'vais finir par 'ui **dire ses quat'vérités**. P't'êt'qu'ça la fera **déchanter** un peu!

ON THE PHONE...

DIALOGUE

Hélène and Edith are chatting on the phone.

Hélène: So? What did she spout off about this time?

Edith: Oh, you know her, the conceited wonder. It's always the same old story. She only thinks about becoming a big star! She went on and on for a whole hour saying that she's a great singer, etc., etc.

Hélène: Frankly, I couldn't care less! She'll be famous when chicken have teeth!

Edith: She doesn't have the knack for singing. . . . It's just not up her alley.

Hélène: Besides, she's missing the most important attributes. . . . Her body's lousy and it's obvious that she doesn't have much up front!

Edith: Boy, I'll give you that! Anyway, she keeps on making a big deal about it!

Hélène: She's just dense, that's all.

Edith: You're too kind. She's just big-time stupid! You try reasoning and she pretends that she doesn't understand a thing.

Hélène: The problem is that she doesn't want to pound the pavement and it's a career that just doesn't happen by itself.

Edith: Well, she's lazy. I swear to you . . . one of these days, I'm going to end up telling her just what I think. Maybe that'll make her come down a peg or two.

VOCABULARY

battre le pavé exp. (lit); to pound the pavement (in search of a job).

bête à bouffer du foin (être) exp. to be very stupid; to be dumb as an ox / (lit); to be stupid enough to eat hay.

bien roulé(e) (être) adj. to have a good body / (lit); to be rolled (together) well.

bonir v. to tell, to recount / **Y m'a bonit une longue histoire;** He told me a long story.

bosse de qqc. (avoir la) exp. to be gifted for something / (lit); to have the bump for something / **Elle a la bosse du piano;** She has a knack for piano.

ça j'te dis! exp. of agreement / "I'm telling you!"; "You're not kidding!" / (lit); "That I'm telling you!"

ça saute aux yeux exp. said of something that is obvious / (lit); it jumps to the eyes.

comprenette dure (avoir la) exp. to be dense; slow / *Note:* This comes from the verb **comprendre** meaning "to understand."

connobrer v. to know / *Note:* This is used the same way as the verb **connaître** meaning "to know."

cornichon m. telephone / (lit); pickle / *Note:* A telephone is commonly called a **cornichon** since the receiver somewhat resembles the shape of a pickle.

crâneuse f. conceited woman or girl / *Note 1:* This comes from the verb **crâner** meaning "to act conceited"; "to boast" / *Note 2:* **crâneur** m. conceited man or boy.

dans ses cordes (être) exp. to be up one's alley / **C'est pas dans mes cordes;** It's not up my alley. / (lit); to be in one's ropes.

déchanter v. to come down a peg or two; to sing a different tune / *Note:* This comes from the verb **chanter** meaning "to sing."

dégoiser v. to talk a lot; to spout off.

dire ses quatre vérités à q. exp. to tell one's true feelings about someone; to tell someone off / (lit); to tell someone their four truths (of inadequacy).

entraver v. to understand / **J'entrave pas c'qu'y m'bonit;** I don't understand what he's talking about.

et patati et patata onom. "and so on and so forth"; "etc., etc."

faire sur une jambe (se) exp. said of something easy to do / (lit); to happen on one leg.

faire tout un plat (en) exp. to make a big deal about something / (lit); to make a whole main dish out of something.

fiche comme de sa première chaussette (s'en) exp. not to care at all / (lit); to care about something as much as one's first sock.

goualeuse f. female singer / *Note 1:* This comes from the slang verb **goualer** meaning "to sing" / *Note 2:* **goualeur** m. male singer.

il y a du monde au balcon exp. said of a woman with large breasts / (lit); there are a lot of people on the balcony.

impec adj. abbreviation of "impeccable."

pépin m. trouble; complication / **Voilà l'pépin!**; There's the problem!

poil dans la main (avoir un) exp. said of a person who is very lazy / (lit); to have a hair in the hand.

quand les poules auront des dents humorous exp. never; "when donkeys fly" / (lit); when chicken have teeth.

que t'chi adv. nothing; "zip."

rengaine f. repetitious story / **C'est toujours la même rengaine**; It's always the same old story.

s'ra v. a commonly heard contraction of **sera** (third person singular of the verb **être** / *Note:* The **e** may also be muted in all forms of the future and conditional tense of the verb **être**, e.g., j's'rai, tu s'ras, nous s'rons, vous s'rez, ils/elles s'ront / *Exception:* The **e** is *not* muted when the first person plural is in the conditional tense, e.g., nous **serions** *not* nous **s'rions**.

sympa (être) adj. nice / *Note:* This is a commonly heard abbreviation of **sympathique**. It may also be used to refer to clothes as well as people: **Cette robe, elle est très sympa**; That dress is very nice.

tailler une bavette exp. to chat / (lit) to trim a bib.

un de ces mat; exp. one of those days, / (lit); one of these mornings / *Note:* **mat'** is an abbreviation of "matin."

PRACTICE THE VOCABULARY

[Answers to Lesson 11, pp. 148–149]

A.   Match the slang word to the left with its correct synonym.

1. **cornichon**	a. homme	b. téléphone	c. livre
2. **que t'chi**	a. rien	b. beaucoup	c. un peu
3. **pépin**	a. difficulté	b. maison	c. porte
4. **goualeuse**	a. de l'argent	b. pantalon	c. chanteuse
5. **bonir**	a. marcher	b. raconter	c. courir
6. **déchanter**	a. chanter mal	b. changer de ton	c. partir
7. **connobrer**	a. être fou	b. parler	c. connaître
8. **entraver**	a. manger	b. comprendre	c. écouter

B.   Underline the appropriate word that best completes the phrase.

1.   Elle est bien (**trouille, roulée**), c'te fille!
2.   Y est bête à bouffer du (**fric, foin**).

3. Z'ont taillé (**une bavette, un blair**) pendant trois heures!
4. J'aime bien c'te mec. Y est très (**sympa, soûlard**).
5. Mais, y fait (**que t'chi, quèque chose**) toute la journée! Faut dire qu'y a (**une poire, un poil**) dans la main.
6. J'arrive pas à faire ça. C'est pas dans mes (**cordes, clopes**).
7. C'te prof, y nous (**draguait, dégoisait**) pendant toute une heure!
8. Regarde un peu c'te poitrine! Y a (**du monde au balcon, des gens à l'intérieur**)!
9. C'te bagnole, elle est (**moche, impec**)! J'la veux!
10. E changera d'attitude quand (**les poules, les oiseaux**) auront des dents.
11. J'm'en fiche comme d'ma première (**chaussette, chaussure**).

C. **Choose the letter of the appropriate English translation.**

1. ___ Y a la bosse du piano.
2. ___ Ben, ça saute aux yeux.
3. ___ Mais, ça s'fait pas sur une jambe.
4. ___ J'vais 'ui dire ses quat'vérités.
5. ___ C'est toujours la même rengaine.
6. ___ Un d'ces mat', j'le ferai.
7. ___ J'en ai marre d'batt'le pavé.
8. ___ Ah, ouais . . . ça j'te dis.
9. ___ C't'une vraie crâneuse.
10. ___ . . . et patati et patata.
11. ___ Y a la comprenette dure, lui.
12. ___ Elle en a fait tout un plat.

A. I'm going to tell him just what I think.
B. I'm tired of pounding the pavement.
C. It's always the same old story.
D. It just doesn't happen by itself.
E. One of these days, I'll do it.
F. She made a big deal about it.
G. He has a knack for piano.
H. She's a real show-off.
I. Well, it's obvious.
J. He's so dense.
K. Oh, yeah, . . . I'll say.
L. . . . etc., etc.

GRAMMAR I: THE OMISSION OF THE POSSESSIVE ADJECTIVE

A. In an imperative or command

In French, possessive adjectives (**mon, ma, mes, ton, ta, tes, son, sa, ses, notre, nos, votre, vos, leur** and **leurs**) are used to modify the noun they precede:

Voici ma mère.
This is my mother.

Regarde ma nouvelle voiture!
Look at my new car!

In colloquial French, when the noun is a physical attribute (head, back, arm, etc), the possessive adjective may be dropped in an imperative or command under one condition: *only* if an action is being taken on that physical attribute. For example, in the following, action is *not* being taken on the physical attribute; therefore, the possessive adjective remains:

Regarde mon dos.
Look at my back.

Remarque mes cheveux.
Notice my hair.

In the following, an action *is* being taken on the physical attribute:

Masse-moi l'dos.
Massage my back.

Coupe-moi les cheveux.
Cut my hair.

The possessive adjective is simply replaced by a personal pronoun and a definite article:

VERB	POSSESSIVE ADJECTIVE	NOUN
Masse	mon	dos.
Coupe	mes	cheveux.

=

VERB		PERSONAL PRONOUN	DEFINITE ARTICLE	NOUN
Masse	–	moi	le	dos.
Coupe	–	moi	les	cheveux.

B. In a statement

The possessive adjective may also be dropped in a statement *only* if an action is being taken on the physical attribute. In the following, an action is *not* being taken:

Je regarde son dos.
I'm looking at his/her back.

Elle remarque ses cheveux.
She's noticing his/her hair.

In the following, an action *is* being taken on the physical attribute:

J'ui masse le dos.
I'm massaging his/her back.

Elle m'coupe les cheveux.
She's cutting my hair.

The possessive adjective takes the form of the appropriate personal pronoun and is placed before the verb, and a definite article is placed before the object:

SUBJECT	VERB	POSSESSIVE ADJECTIVE	OBJECT
Je	masse	son	dos.
Elle	coupe	mes	cheveux.

=

SUBJECT	PERSONAL PRONOUN	VERB	DEFINITE ARTICLE	OBJECT
Je	lui	masse	le	dos.
Elle	me	coupe	les	cheveux.

Note:

This construction is also used when asking a question:

Tu m'masses le dos, s'te plaît?
Will you massage my back please?

E va t'couper les cheveux?
She's going to cut your hair?

C. In the past tense *(passé composé)*

In the past tense, the personal pronoun is placed after the subject just as it is in the present tense. However, this time it is placed between the subject and the auxiliary verb **avoir** or **être**:

SUBJECT	PERSONAL PRONOUN	**VERB**	DEFINITE ARTICLE	OBJECT
Je	lui	masse	le	dos.
Elle	me	coupe	les	cheveux.

=

SUBJECT	PERSONAL PRONOUN	**AVOIR**	**PAST PARTICIPLE**	DEFINITE ARTICLE	OBJECT
Je	lui	ai	massé	le	dos
Elle	m'	a	coupé	les	cheveux.

PRACTICE THE OMISSION OF THE POSSESSIVE ARTICLE

A. Rewrite the imperatives, omitting the underlined possessive article.

1. Gratte son cou. (Scratch his neck)

   _____ .

2. Masse mon dos. (Massage my back)

   _____ .

3. Brosse tes cheveux. (Brush my hair)

   _____ .

4. Arrache ma dent. (Pull my tooth)

   _____ .

5. Touche son épaule. (Touch his shoulder)

   _____ .

6. Tiens mon bras. (Hold my arm)

   _____ .

7. Serre ma main. (Shake my hand)

   _____ .

8. Lave sa figure. (Wash his face)

   _____ .

B. Rewrite the statement, omitting the underlined possessive article.

1. Y touche mon épaule. (He's touching my shoulder)

   _____ .

2. J'ai gratté son cou. (I scratched his neck)

   _____ .

3. J'ai cassé son bras. (I broke his arm)

   _____ .

4.   Elle a frappé <u>mon</u> nez. (She hit my nose)
————————————————— .

5.   J'peigne <u>ses</u> cheveux. (I'm combing his hair)
————————————————— .

6.   Le dentiste, y a arraché <u>ses</u> dents. (The dentist pulled out his/her teeth)
————————————————— .

7.   Elle a giflé <u>ma</u> figure. (She slapped my face)
————————————————— .

8.   Que ça fend <u>mon</u> cœur. (That just breaks my heart)
————————————————— .

9.   J'brosse <u>mes</u> dents. (I'm brushing my teeth)
————————————————— .

10. E maquille <u>ses</u> yeux. (She's making up her [own] eyes)
————————————————— .

11. E maquille <u>ses</u> yeux. (She's making-up her [someone else's] eyes)
————————————————— .

12. Y a chuchoté dans <u>son</u> oreille. (He whispered in his/her ear)
————————————————— .

GRAMMAR II: PERSONAL PRONOUNS WHEN OFFERING AND ASKING FOR FAVORS

A. In an imperative or command

A construction similar to that shown in GRAMMAR I (Part A) also holds true when the imperative or command is in reference to a favor or service, e.g., "Hold this for me," "Carry this suitcase for me," etc. In this case, the object and personal pronoun change places and **pour** is omitted since it is built into the construction:

VERB	OBJECT	POUR	PERSONAL PRONOUN
Tiens	ça	pour	moi.
Porte	la valise	pour	moi.

=

VERB		PERSONAL PRONOUN	OBJECT
Tiens	–	moi	ça.
Porte	–	moi	la valise.

B. In a statement

When a statement is in reference to a favor or service, the personal pronoun is placed before the verb and **pour** is once again omitted since it is built into the construction. This is similar to the construction in GRAMMAR I (Part B):

SUBJECT	VERB	OBJECT	POUR	PERSONAL PRONOUN
Je	tiens	la porte	pour	toi.
Je	porterai	la valise	pour	toi.

=

SUBJECT	PERSONAL PRONOUN	VERB	OBJECT
Je	te	tiens	la porte.
Je	te	porterai	la valise.

Note:

This construction is also used when asking a question:

J'te tiens la porte?
May I hold the door for you?

J'te porte la valise?
May I carry the suitcase for you?

C. In the past tense *(passé composé)*

In the past tense, the personal pronoun is placed after the subject, just as it is in the present tense. However, this time it is placed between the subject and the auxiliary verb **avoir** or **être**:

SUBJECT	PERSONAL PRONOUN	VERB	OBJECT
Je	te	tiens	la porte.
Je	te	porterai	la valise.

=

SUBJECT	PERSONAL PRONOUN	AVOIR	PAST PARTICIPLE	OBJECT
Je	t'	ai	tenu	la porte.
Je	t'	ai	porté	la valise.

PRACTICE OFFERING AND ASKING FOR FAVORS

A. Rewrite the imperative according to the example

Example:

Tiens la porte pour moi.
Tiens-moi la porte.

1. Tiens ça pour moi. (Hold this for me.)
    _____ .

2. Porte c'manteau pour lui. (Carry this coat for him.)
    _____ .

3. Ouv'la porte pour moi. (Open the door for me.)
    _____ .

4. Soulève c'te valise pour moi. (Lift this suitcase for me.)
    _____ .

5. Vérifie c'te liste pour lui. (Verify this list for him.)
    _____ .

6. Coupe c'te ficelle pour moi. (Cut this string for me.)
    _____ .

7. Lave c'te tasse pour moi. (Wash this cup for me.)
    _____ .

8. Change c't'ampoule pour moi. (Change this bulb for me.)
    _____ .

9. Ferme la fenêt'pour moi. (Close the window for me.)
    _____ .

10. Répare la voiture pour moi. (Fix the car for me.)
    _____ .

B. Rewrite the sentence according to the example.

Example:

Y a peint la maison pour moi. (He painted the house for me.)
Y m'a peint la maison.

1. J'tiens les livres pour toi? (May I hold the books for you?)
    _____ ?

2. Y a porté l'manteau pour moi. (He carried my coat for me.)
    _____ .

3. Y a ouvert la porte pour moi. (He opened the door for me.)
    _____ .

4. J'soulève la chaise pour toi? (May I lift the chair for you.)
    _____ ?

5. J'ai vérifié la liste pour lui. (I verified the list for him.)

   _____ .

6. J'coupe la ficelle pour toi? (May I cut the string for you.)

   _____ ?

7. J'ai lavé la tasse pour toi. (I washed the cup for you.)

   _____ .

8. Y a changé l'ampoule pour moi. (He changed the bulb for me.)

   _____ .

9. Elle a fermé la fenêt'pour moi. (She closed the window for me.)

   _____ .

10. Y a réparé la voiture pour moi. (He fixed the car for me.)

    _____ .

TOUJOURS MALADE. . .

DIALOGUE

Marie attend que Robert et Thomas arrivent chez elle. Enfin. . .

Marie: Salut Robert. Ben, où y est, Thomas?

Robert: Oh, y a **attrapé la crève**. Mais, y s'croit toujours **mal fichu**, c'ui-là!

Marie: Y s'croit toujours **à l'article d'la mort**. La semaine dernière, y pensait qu'y allait **clamser** d'une crise d'**battant**!

Robert: A l'**hosto**, tous les **canulards**, y doivent **prend'la tangente** en l'voyant **débarquer**! Il y est tout l'temps pour s'faire **piquouser** pour une raison ou une autre.

Marie: J'parie qu'y a un **pageot** permanent pour sa pomme avec son **blaze** dessus!

Robert: Franchement, c'qui **tourne pas rond** c'est qu'y **graillonne** constamment mais arrête pas d'**bombarder**. Pis, y en fait **toute une salade** pasqu'y a mal aux **éponges** et s'en met **martel en tête** jusqu'au point où y va s'faire une **belle corbuche**. Mais, **ça va pas non**?

Marie: **Un d'ces quat'**, un **tranche-lard**, y va 'ui dire d'**passer sur l'billard**. J'suis sûre qu'y **remontera la pente** en **moins de deux**!

ALWAYS SICK. . .

DIALOGUE

Marie is waiting for Robert and Thomas to arrive at her house. Finally. . .

Marie: Hi Robert. So where's Thomas?

Robert: Oh, he caught a cold. That guy always thinks he's sick!

Marie: He always thinks he's on death's door. Last week, he thought he was gonna croak from a heart attack! The dough he forks out on doctors is unreal!

Robert: At the hospital, all the orderlies must run and hide when they see him show up! He's always there getting shots for one reason or another.

Marie: I bet they have a permanent bed for him with his name on it!

Robert: Frankly, what just doesn't add up is that he coughs and gags constantly but doesn't stop smoking. Then he makes a big deal about how his lungs hurt and drives himself crazy until he ends up with one hell of an ulcer. That doesn't make any sense, does it?

Marie: One of these days, a surgeon is going to tell him to get up on the operating table. I'm sure that'll make him jump back on his feet in no time flat!

VOCABULARY

à l'article de la mort (être) exp. to be at death's door / (lit); to be at the critical point of death.

bagatelle f. small sum of money; a trifle / **Mille balles? C't'une bagatelle, ça!**; A thousand francs? That's a mere drop in the bucket!

battant m. heart / *Note:* This comes from the verb **battre** meaning "to beat."

beau/belle adj. considerable, "one big . . . " / **Tu vas t'faire une belle hernie si tu soulèves ça**; You're gonna give yourself one big hernia if you lift that.

blaze m. name / *Also:* (1) **surblaze** m. nickname; (2) **blazer/surblazer** v. to be named/nicknamed / **Y est surblazé Bobby**; He's nicknamed Bobby.

bombarder v. to smoke / (lit); to bombard (with smoke).

canulard m. orderly, hospital worker / (lit); syringe carrier / *Note:* This comes from the noun **canule** f. meaning "the nozzle of a syringe."

ça tourne pas rond exp. said of something that just doesn't add up or is "fishy" / (lit); it doesn't turn round.

ça va pas non? exp. it doesn't make any sense; one just doesn't do that / **T'as pris ma bagnole sans m'demander? Mais, ça va pas non?**; You took my car without asking me? You just don't go around doing that!

clamser v. to die; "to croak."

corbuche f. ulcer

crève f. bad cold; "one's death" / **attraper la crève** (lit); to catch one's death / *Also:* **crever** v. to die.

débarquer v. to arrive without notice / (lit); to disembark.

éponges f.pl. lungs / (lit); sponges.

graillonner v. to cough hard; to hack.

hosto m. hospital / abbreviation of "hôpital."

mal fichu adj. sick / (lit); badly put together.

moins de deux (en) adv. quickly / (lit); in less than two (seconds).

martel en tête (se mettre) exp. to worry / (lit); to put a hammer in the head / *Note 1:* The expression conjures up an image of a person who is so worked up over something that he can hear his own pulse banging like a hammer in his head / *Note 2:* **martel** m. old term for hammer; current term is **marteau** m.

oseille f. money; "dough" / (lit); sorrel / *Note:* See the section on "Fruits and Vegetables in Slang" in this lesson.

pageot m. bed / *Note:* **se pageoter** v. to go to bed ≠ **se dépageoter** v. to get out of bed.

passer sur le billard exp. to undergo an operation / (lit); to proceed onto the billiard table / *Note:* **billard** m. operating table.

piquouser v. to inject / *Note:* This is simply a slang transformation of the verb **piquer** meaning "to inject."

prendre la tangente exp. to slip away without being seen / (lit); to take the tangent.

raquer v. to pay; to "fork out" / *Note 1:* This comes from the feminine noun **raquette** meaning "racket" (for tennis, etc.). The verb **raquer** might be loosely translated as "to give money out just as soon as it comes in as one would hit a ball with a racket." / *Note 2:* Don't be fooled by this common mistake. The verb **raquer** does *not* mean "to rake *in* money."

remonter la pente exp. to get better, to recuperate / (lit); to raise up the slope (from bad health).

salade (en faire toute une) exp. to make a big deal about something / (lit); to make a big salad over something.

toubib m. doctor / pronounced "tou-bibe."

tranche-lard m. surgeon / (lit); fat-slicer.

un de ces quat' exp. one of these days / (lit); one of these four (mornings) / *Note:* This is an abbreviation of the expression, **un de ces quatre matins**, which is much like the one in the previous chapter, **un d'ces mat'**.

PRACTICE THE VOCABULARY

[Answers to Lesson 12, pp. 149–150.]

A. Complete the phase by choosing the appropriate word(s) from the list. Give the correct form of the verb.

crève	à l'article	battant
oseille	raquer	beau
toubib	clamser	martel
billard	pente	éponges

1. Le malade, y a _____ hier soir.
2. Arrête d'fumer comme ça! Tu vas t'faire mal aux _____ !
3. Y est toujours _____ d'la mort.
4. Mais pourquoi tu t'mets _____ en tête?
5. Si t'es malade, tu devrais aller voir un _____ .
6. C't'un _____ menteur lui!
7. On a volé toute mon _____ .
8. Demain, j'vais à l'hôpital pour passer sur l' _____ .
9. C'est pas bon pour l' _____ d'bouffer trop d'cholestérol.
10. Y a _____ dix mille balles pour un pantalon.
11. E va pas à l'école pasqu'elle a attrapé la _____ .
12. Peu à peu, y commence à remonter la _____ .

B. Underline the synonym.

1. **bagatelle**   a. grand sac   b. maison   c. peu d'argent
2. **pageot**   a. homme   b. porte   c. lit

3. **blaze**	a. prénom	b. chemise	c. nez
4. **graillonner**	a. tousser	b. marcher	c. parler beaucoup
5. **bombarder**	a. arriver	b. fumer	c. parler beaucoup
6. **tranche-lard**	a. couteau	b. boucher	c. chirurgien
7. **en moins de deux**	a. rapidement	b. lentement	c. silencieusement
8. **débarquer**	a. arriver	b. partir	c. se déshabiller
9. **mal fichu**	a. stupide	b. malade	c. énergique
10. **corbuche**	a. femme	b. tête	c. ulcère

C. Underline the appropriate word(s) that best complete the phrase.

1. C'est bien bizarre, ça. Y a quèque chose ici qui (**tape, tourne** pas rond.)
2. Pourquoi tu m'as menti? Mais (**ça va pas, ça s'arrête pas**) non?!
3. C'est l'patron! On prend la (**tarte, tangente**)!
4. A chaque fois qu'y perd, y en fait toute une (**salle, salade**).
5. Y reste au (**pageot, paumer**) toute la journée!
6. Je m'suis fait (**piquouser, pioncer**) contre l'virus.
7. Un d'ces (**trois, quat'**), j'vais devenir grand chanteur!
8. Tu m'passes une clope? J'ai envie d'(**bomber, bombarder**).
9. Y est (**collant, canulard**), mon frère. Y travaille (**au resto, à l'hosto**).
10. J'm'appelle Robert, mais mon (**surblaze, soûlard**), c'est Bobby.
11. Tu (**graillonnes, grilles**) sans arrêt! Pourquoi tu vois pas un (**tord-boyaux, toubib**)?

GRAMMAR I: SURELY YOU GESTURE!

Most people think of the Italians as cornering the market on gestures and all the dramatics that go along with them. The French certainly hold their own in expressing themselves nonverbally and seem to include a great deal of slang in many of their gestures:

A. "That one's drunk!" (see figure at top of p. 119)

As learned earlier, the adjective **rond(e)**, whose meaning is literally "round," is commonly used in slang to mean "drunk." As well known as this slang adjective is the gesture to convey this condition:

• Make a fist.
• Hold it up against the tip of your nose with your little finger farthest away from you.
• Now twist your fist as if you were tightening the tip of your nose.

Y est rond c'ui-là!

B. "There's a screw loose somewhere!" (see figure below)

The expression **ça tourne pas rond** is also used to refer to one's brain in which the "wheels" aren't turning. The gesture for this is similar to the American gesture of "crazy" in which the index finger is held a few inches away from the ear then circles the outline of the ear several times. In French, it's a little more subtle:

- Holding your index finger straight, place the very tip of your finger against your temple.
- Make sure the pad of your finger is facing slightly forward.
- Now twist the pad of your finger down and slightly back.

Mais ça tourne pas rond!

C. "My eye!" (see figure at top of p. 120)

In English, when someone tries to pull the wool over our eyes by recounting something ludicrous, we commonly respond with the expression "My foot!" (although there are a few other colorful expressions that also come to mind). The French agreed that the "eye" would indeed serve as an adequate symbol of incredulity. **Mon œil!** is extremely popular in France as is its gesture:

- Put your index finger just underneath your lower eyelid.
- Now pull down slightly.

Mon œil!

D.   "What are you talking about?!" (see figure below)

This gesture may be used in place of the gesture for **Mon œil**; however, it *is* much more subtle. The gesture for **Mon œil** is used to let the other person know that what he has just said is absolutely and undeniably hogwash, whereas the gesture for "What are you talking about?" lets him know that if he doesn't clear up what he's talking about, he will be on the verge of getting a **Mon œil**:

- Simply cock your head to the left or right with an expression of "Oh brother!" on your face.

Mais qu'est-ce que tu racontes?!

E. "Beats me!" (see figure below)

A gesture that is constantly encountered in France, especially when asking for directions, is the one for "I dunno" or "Beats me!" It's a lovely little number that can be accessorized beautifully:

The basic gesture
• Protrude your lower lip slightly past your upper lip to form a *tight* pout.
• Make sure to hold the lips tightly together as you force out a quick "ppp" sound.

Add one or all of the following as you do the "ppp" sound:
• Lift your eyebrows.
• Push your head slightly forward.
• Lift your shoulders.

Now ... go for broke!
Doing all of the above at the same time is *extremely* common, which will probably be proven by the first person who can't give you directions once in Paris. However, occasionally you will encounter the **pièce de résistance** in which all the above ingredients will be mixed together along with one other:

• Hold the palms of your hands facing upward and level to the outside of your shoulders.
• Now, as you make the "ppp" sound, lift your eyebrows, push your head slightly forward, and lift your shoulders and simply push the palms of your hands upward slightly.

J'sais pas!

F. "Nothing!"(see figure below)

The next gesture is a common one in Italy where its meaning is loosely translated as "Go get stuffed!" However, in French this gesture simply means "Absolutely nothing!" For example, if someone asks you what you got for your birthday and your reply is "Absolutely nothing!" this gesture would come in quite handy:

• Make a fist holding your thumb on the side of your index finger.
• Place the nail of your thumb behind your front teeth.
• Now quickly force the thumb forward making a clicking sound.

Y m'a donné que t'chi!

G. Count with your fingers like the French (see figure below)

"Holding up two fingers to indicate that I want two of a certain item couldn't be easier. Then why do I keep getting three?!" Simple . . . your thumb is being counted as well! In France and almost all of Europe, the thumb starts off the countdown and the little finger ends it:

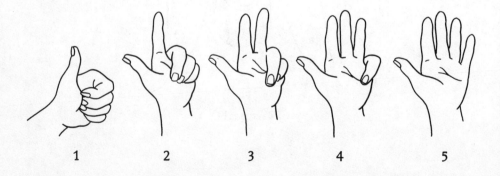

1   2   3   4   5

PRACTICE YOUR GESTURES

A.   Write down what each gesture represents under the illustration.

1. _____   2. _____

3. _____   4. _____

5. _____   6. _____

7. _____

B. Trying not to look at the illustrations, do the gesture for:

1. drunk (**rond**)
2. my eye! (**mon œil!**)
3. crazy (**ça tourne pas rond**)
4. I dunno
5. nothing!
6. count from one to five

GRAMMAR II: FRUITS AND VEGETABLES IN SLANG

It's commonly known that the French do not eat to live but LIVE TO EAT! So it's only natural that food should creep into slang and make its own mark. For some reason, fruits and vegetables are among the most commonly used in slang:

A *blow to the face*	**pêche** (peach)
Bigwig	**grosse légume** (big vegetable)
Blood	**raisin** (grape)
Face	**cerise** (cherry)
	citrouille (pumpkin)
	fraise (strawberry)
	poire (pear)
	pomme (apple)
For nothing	**pour des prunes** (for plums)
Gas pedal	**champignon** (mushroom)
Head	**citron** (lemon)
It's none of your business	**c'est pas tes oignons** (it's not your onions)

Money	**oseille** (sorrel)
My sweetheart	**mon chou** (my cabbage)
Nose	**betterave**--red nose (beet)
	patate--big nose (potato)
Tall and thin person	**asperge** (asparagus)
Telephone	**cornichon** (pickle)
To be stone broke	**n'avoir plus un radis** (to be without a single radish)
To wait	**faire le poireau** (to do like a leek)

Therefore, the following sentences are not really about food at all!:

–Qu'est-ce qu'y a mon **chou**! T'as mal au **citron**?

–What's wrong my sweet? You've got a headache?

–Non, j'ai dit à la **grosse légume** qu'c't'ait **pas ses oignons** et y m'a filé une **pêche** en pleine **poire**!

–No, I told the bigwig that it was none of his business and he threw me a punch right in the face!

PRACTICE THE USE OF FRUITS AND VEGETABLES IN SLANG

A. Match the two columns.

1. __ Y m'a filé une pêche en pleine poire!
2. __ Comment tu vas mon chou?
3. __ On te demande au cornichon.
4. __ J'ai mal au citron.
5. __ Y travaille pour des prunes!
6. __ Appuie sur l'champignon!
7. __ J'ai plus un radis!
8. __ C't'une grosse légume, lui.
9. __ C'est pas tes oignons.
10. __ Quelle grosse patate!

A. I don't have a red cent.
B. It's none of your business.
C. He's a bigwig.
D. You're wanted on the phone.
E. How are you sweetheart?
F. He works for nothing!
G. He slugged me in the face!
H. What a fat nose!
I. I have a headache.
J. Step on the gas!

Leçon Treize

UNE PARTIE DE CARTES. . .

DIALOGUE

Nancy et David essayent d'organiser une partie de cartes entre amis.

David: Tu veux **jardiner** ce soir?

Nancy: Tu vas **prend'une culotte**, mon vieux!

David: Non, cette fois c'est moi qui vais t'**faire la pige**!

Nancy: Pas possible à moins qu'tu **maquilles** les **brèmes** ou m'**fasse un douze**!

David: Bon! On fait une partie d'**poke**? On invite Charles? C't'un très bon **flambeur**!

Nancy: **J'en parlerai à mon cheval**! Y est pas **fair-play** et j'te dis à **brûle-pourpoint** qu'c't'un beau **graisseur**! En plus, y met jamais que t'chi dans la **cagnotte**! Tu ferais mieux d'inviter Cécile et son ami l'**pharmaco**.

David: Le **rouquin** à la **barbouze**? T'as **déraillé**, non? Quand y sont ensemble, y font que s'**bécoter** . . . et d'ailleurs, c't'un **sacré baragouineur**, lui!

Nancy: Bon! On invite Michelle alors!

David: Celle qui porte un kilo d'**badigeon** sur l'**portrait**?! Mais **tu veux rire**! J'peux pas la voir en peinture! C't'un vrai **remède cont'l'amour**, césarine! On peut toujours demander à Léon d'nous rejoindre . . .

Nancy: Oh, quel **cave** c'ui-là! Tu sais, à l'**attrape-pognon**, y met **l'paquet** sans savoir c'qu'y fait . . . et y gagne! Quelle **embellie**!

David: Bon! Si on faisait une **partie d'sœurs** juste nous deux?

Nancy: Au poil!

Lesson Thirteen

A GAME OF CARDS. . .

DIALOGUE

Nancy and David try to organize a card game between friends.

David: Wanna play cards tonight?

Nancy: You'll lose your shirt, pal.

David: Nope, this time I'm gonna cream you!

Nancy: No way unless you mark the cards or trick me!

David: OK! How 'bout a game of poker? Should we invite Charles? He's a real good player!

Nancy: Baloney! He doesn't play fair and I'm telling you point-blank that he's a cheater! Not only that, he never puts money in the kitty! You'd be better off inviting Cecily and her friend the pharmacist.

David: The redhead with the beard? Have you lost your mind? When they're together, all they do is neck . . . and besides, he's a friggin' blabbermouth!

Nancy: OK! Then let's invite Michelle!

David: The one who wears pounds of makeup on her face?! You've gotta be kidding! I can't stand her! She's a real cure for love, that one! We could always ask Leon to join us. . . .

Nancy: Oh, that guy's such a nitwit! You know, at the casino he always bets the whole wad without knowing what he's doing . . . and wins! What unbelievable luck!

David: OK! Suppose we play some checkers just the two of us?

Nancy: Perfect!

VOCABULARY

à brûle-pourpoint adv. point-blank, bluntly.

attrape-pognon m. casino / (lit); money-trap.

badigeon m. makeup / (lit); (color-)wash; distemper (for walls, etc.) / *Also:* **se badigeonner** v. to put on makeup.

baragouineur, euse n. one who jabbers / *Note:* **baragouiner** v. to jabber.

bécoter v. to kiss; to "neck" / *Note:* **bécot** m. a kiss.

brème f. playing card / (lit); a freshwater fish that is long and flat called a "bream."

cagnotte f. (of games, etc.) kitty, pot.

cave m. a real "sucker"; one who lets himself be easily duped.

dérailler v. to go crazy; "to lose it" / (lit); to derail.

embellie f. stroke of luck / (lit); clearing (in the weather); smooth (in the sea).

faire la pige exp. to surpass someone; to "beat."

faire un douze exp. to trick the adversary / (lit); to make a twelve.

fair-play (être) adj. said of one who plays fair / (See Unit II; English Words That Are Used in Spoken French).

flambeur, euse n. (of games) player / (lit); one who flames or "cooks" at something / *Note 1:* **flambe** f. game / *Note 2:* **flamber** v. to play a game / (lit); to flame.

graisseur, euse n. cheater / (lit); one who greases (the cards, etc.).

jardiner v. to play cards, etc. / (lit); to garden / *Note:* This comes from playing cards and shooting craps on the green felt that is commonly used in casinos.

j'en parlerai à mon cheval exp. nonsense; "bull" / (lit); I'll talk to my horse about it.

maquiller v. to cheat; to cover up / (lit); to put on makeup / **maquiller les brèmes**; to mark cards.

mettre le paquet exp. to shoot the wad of money; to put it all down / (lit); to put down the package (of money).

partie de soeurs f. checkers / (lit); game of sisters / *Note:* In French, checkers is called **les dames**. Here, **sœurs** is replacing **dames**.

pharmaco m. a slang variant of **pharmacien** meaning "pharmacist".

poke m. an abbreviation of **poker** meaning "poker."

portrait m. face / (lit); portrait / *Also:* **C'est l'portrait d'son père**; He's the image of his father.

pouvoir voir q. en peinture (ne pas) exp. to be unable to stand someone / (lit); to be unable (even) to see a picture of someone.

prendre une culotte exp. to lose heavily (at cards) / (lit); to take a pair of trousers / *Note:* In its contracted form, **prend'une culotte**, the d is silent.

remède contre l'amour (un) exp. said of an ugly person / (lit); a remedy for love.

rouquin(e) adj. & n. red; redhead / *Also:* **Un verre d'rouquin;** A glass of red wine.

sacré(e) adj. big (when placed before a noun); "blessed" / **sacré menteur;** blessed liar / (lit); sacred.

tu veux rire! exp. you've got to be kidding! / (lit); you want to laugh.

PRACTICE THE VOCABULARY

[Answers to Lesson 13, p. 150]

A. Underline the appropriate word(s) that best completes the phrase.

1. E porte un kilo d'(**babines, badigeon**) sur (**l'portrait, la porte**).
2. J'aime pas (**jardiner, jurer**) avec lui pasqu'y essaie toujours d'me faire un (**onze, douze**).
3. On va aller à Las Vegas pour voir les (**avant-gardes, attrapes-pognon**).
4. J'peux pas la voir en (**porcelaine, peinture**)!
5. Comme t'es riche, pourquoi pas mett'le (**paquet, palmier**)?
6. J'ai gagné l'premier prix! Quelle (**abeille, embellie**)!
7. Y croit tout c'qu'on 'ui balance! Mais quel (**cheval, cave**)!
8. Arrête d'(**baragouiner, balader**)! Tu m'casses les oreilles!
9. Cette fois-ci, j'vais t'faire (**la pige, l'pigeon**)!
10. J'veux t'parler à brûle-(**pourlèche, pourpoint**).

B. Replace the word(s) in parentheses with the slang synonym from the right column. Make all other necessary changes.

1. Tu veux faire un (jeu de dames) _____ ?
2. Y a (perdu) _____ .
3. C't'un (grand) _____ menteur.
4. On fait une partie d'(poker) _____ ?
5. C't'un très bon (joueur) _____ .
6. Y font qu's'(embrasser) _____ .
7. Tu connais ce (type aux cheveux rouges) _____ ?
8. Mais quel (tricheur) _____ !
9. Y est (pharmacien) _____ , c'ui-là.
10. Le Père Noël, y a une (barbe) _____ blanche.
11. T'(es devenu fou) _____ , non?
12. Où t'as acheté ces (cartes) _____ ?

A. dérailler
B. brèmes
C. prend'une culotte
D. pharmaco
E. sacré
F. rouquin
G. graisseur
H. barbouze
I. partie d'sœurs
J. poke
K. bécoter
L. flambeur

C. Fill in the blanks by choosing the appropriate word(s) from the list below.

faire la pige	mon cheval	maquiller
rire	embellie	portrait
badigeon	flambeur	graisseur
sacré	baragouineur	fair-play

1. C't'un _____ idiot, c'ui-là!
2. J'aime bien jouer aux cartes avec lui pasqu'y est très _____ .
3. C'que tu racontes est carrément ridicule! J'en parlerai à _____ !
4. E porte un kilo d' _____ sur l' _____ !
5. J'aime pas jouer avec lui pasque c't'un _____ !
6. Attention! T'as _____ les brèmes!
7. Z'ont trouvé la maison idéale! Quelle _____ !
8. Y m'fatigue les oreilles, c'ui-là. Quel _____ !
9. C'est pas possible c'que tu m'racontes! Tu veux _____ , non?
10. J'aime pas jouer aux cartes pasque j'suis mauvais _____ .
11. Cette fois-ci, j'vais pas perdre. C'est moi qui vais t' _____ !

GRAMMAR I: THE LANGUAGE OF *VERLAN*

Slang was originally thought up as a way for crooks to make themselves unintelligible to the police. However, it didn't take long for this "secret" language to become unmasked. Something else had to be done. Thus emerged **verlan**. By the way, this is how pig-latin got its start! However, it must be stressed that, unlike pig-latin, **verlan** (as well as **largonji** and **javanais**, discussed in the following chapters) is an actively spoken slang "language."

It merely consists of turning around the most important word (*usually* a slang word) in the sentence. For instance, the slang word **falzar** meaning "pants" would become **zarfal**. In the heading itself, **verlan** is actually the reverse of **l'envers** meaning "the reverse." It has become even more popular since the rise of the French slang singer Renaud and his popular song, "Laisse béton," which is **verlan** for "Laisse tomber" or "Let it drop." The existence of **verlan** takes slang one step further and makes it that much more interesting and fun. After having learned slang, you will find it easier and easier to recognize **verlan**. The following are a few well-known **verlan** transformations:

balpeau adv. nothing; "zip" / (lit); skin of the ball / *Note:* This is verlan for **peau de balle.**

barjot adj. stupid gullible person / *Note:* This is verlan for the slang word **jobard.**

brelica m. revolver / *Note:* This is verlan for the slang word **calibre.**

être au funpar exp. to be up to date / (lit); to be in the perfume / *Note:* This is verlan for **être au parfum.**

être dans le tarcol exp. to be exhausted / *Note:* This is verlan for **être dans le coltar.**

lépou m. policeman; "cop" / (lit); chicken. / *Note:* This is verlan for **poulet.**

meffe f. woman; wife / (lit); woman / *Note:* This is verlan for **femme.**

péclot f. cigarette / *Note:* This is verlan for the slang word **clope.**

quèm m. guy; "dude" / *Note 1:* This is verlan for **mec** / *Note 2:* An *accent grave* is used in order to retain the sound of the **e** in the word **mec.**

raquebar f. house / (lit); barracks / *Note:* This is verlan for **baraque.**

zesgon f. girl; "chick" / *Note:* This is verlan for **gonzesse.**

PRACTICE VERLAN

A. Below is a list of words transformed into verlan. (1) Put each word back into its "non-verlan" state and (2) write down its English translation.

Example:

> balpeau
> **peau de balle**
> **nothing**

1. brelica

   _____

   _____

2. être au funpar

   _____

   _____

3. lépou

   _____

   _____

4. péclot

   _____

   _____

5. quèm

   _____

   _____

6. zesgon

   _____

   _____

7. raquebar

   _____

   _____

8. être dans le tarcol

   _____

9. zarfal

   _____

   _____

10. meffe

    _____

    _____

11. barjot

    _____

    _____

B. Fill in the blank with the appropriate word from the list below.

brelica	raquebar	quèm
zesgon	meffe	balpeau
lépou	péclot	funpar
tarcol	barjot	zarfal

1. J'ai acheté une nouvelle _____ .
2. Pour mon anniversaire, y m'a donné _____ !
3. Tu savais pas qu'y est mort? T'es pas au _____ ?
4. Y a pris l' _____ et l'a tué!
5. Voleur! Appelle un _____ !
6. Y est très sympa, c' _____ .

7. J'te présente ma _____ .
8. J'vais m'coucher. J'suis dans l' _____ .
9. Tu m'passes une _____ ? J'ai envie d'fumer.
10. Elle est bien roulée, c'te _____ !
11. Y est _____ , c'mec!
12. Mon _____ , y est trop long!

Leçon Quatorze

AU THEATRE...

DIALOGUE

Jeanette et Suzanne attendent que la pièce commence.

Jeanette: Mais j'en ai **basta** d'**moisir** comme ça! Quand on va lever l'**torchon**?!

Suzanne: Sois contente qu'on ait pu **entifler** ici **à l'œil**! Mais pourquoi t'es tellement **mal vissée**?

Jeanette: J'ai la **frousse** que l'gérant découvre qu'on a **resquillé** et qu'on s'fourre dans l'**pétrin**!

Suzanne: **La barbe!** Tu veux **éventer la mèche**? Bon! On **change de disques d'acc**?

Jeanette: D'acc. J'suppose qu'on pourrait au moins **châsser** l'programme pour **s'rencarder** un peu d'quoi y s'agit, c'truc. Tu connobres c't'acteur... Serge Leblond?

Suzanne: Ah, ouais! C't'un acteur **à tout casser**! Y est **archi-rigolard**, c'te **zigue**! J'me **fend la pipe** à tous ses films!

Jeanette: Oh, j'me rappelle maintenant. Y **brûle les planches** mais y en a qui pensent qu'c't'un vrai **cabot**. Quand même, y arrive à **casser la baraque** chaque soir!

Suzanne: **Vingt-deux!** C'est l'gérant qui **s'amène**! On est **cuites**!

Jeanette: On **met les bouts**!

Suzanne: Voilà le **décambutage**! **Grouille-toi**!

Lesson Fourteen

AT THE THEATER. . .

DIALOGUE

Jeanette and Suzanne are waiting for the play to start.

Jeanette: I've really had it with waiting like this! When are they gonna lift the curtain?

Suzanne: Be glad we were able to get in here for free! What are you so worked up for?

Jeanette: I'm nervous that the manager is gonna find out that we snuck in and that we're gonna get ourselves into a mess!

Suzanne: Shut up! You wanna spill the beans? Alright! Let's change subjects, ok?

Jeanette: OK. I suppose we could at least look at the program to find out what this thing's about. You know this actor . . . Serge Leblond?

Suzanne: Oh, yeah! He's one helluv'an actor! That guy's so funny! I crack up at all of his films!

Jeanette: Oh, I remember now. He acts with unbelievable energy, but some people think he's a real ham. Anyway, he manages to bring the house down every night!

Suzanne: Watch out! The manager is coming!

Jeanette: We're done for!

Suzanne: Let's scram! There's the exit! Haul!

VOCABULARY

à l'œil exp. free; "for nothing" / (lit); at the eye / *Note:* This expression means "nothing" since the "eye" is the same shape as O / **On est entré à l'œil**; We got in for nothing.

amener (s') v. to arrive / (lit); to bring oneself.

archi- prefix. very, really / *Note:* This prefix may be attached to any adjective to intensify its meaning / **Y est archibête, lui!**; He's really stupid!

à tout casser adj. the best, "that beats all" / (lit); to break everything / *Note:* This expression was originally used with **attaque à tout casser** meaning an "out-and-out attack" or literally an "attack to break everything." It is now used with nouns to express that they are the best in their category. / **Une histoire à tout casser!**; A story that beats all!

basta adv. enough / *Note:* This word is borrowed from Italian.

brûler les planches exp. said of an actor who performs with great energy / (lit); to burn the boards / *Note:* **planches** f.pl. the stage.

cabot m. bad actor; ham actor / *Also:* **cabot** m. dog.

casser la baraque exp. to bring the house down / (lit); to break the house / *Note:* **baraque** f. house.

changer de disques exp. to change topics / (lit); to change records.

châsser v. to look, "to eye something" / *Note 1:* This comes from **châsse** f. frame (for glasses) / *Note 2:* **châsse** f. slang for "eye."

cuit(e) (être) adj. to be done for / (lit); to be cooked / *Note:* Notice that in the dialogue, the adjective **cuites** is in the plural form. This is because **on** is used to replace the first person plural **nous**.

d'acc abbreviation of **d'accord** meaning "okay."

décambutage m. exit / *Note:* **décambuter** v. to exit.

entifler v. to enter.

éventer la mèche exp. to "spill the beans"; "let the cat out of the bag" / (lit); to air out the plot / *Also:* **être de mèche avec q.**; to be in cahoots with someone.

fendre la pipe (se) exp. to laugh hard / (lit); to split one's pipe.

frousse (avoir la) f. to be frightened / *Note:* **froussard(e)** n. scardy-cat.

grouiller (se) v. to hurry, "to haul"; to look alive / (lit); to swarm; to be alive with / **La branche grouillait d'insectes**; The branch was alive with insects.

la barbe! exclam. shut up! / (lit); the beard / *Note:* Perhaps this exclamation came to be since it conjures up an image of someone getting his beard pulled as a way to make him shut up.

mal vissé(e) (être) adj. to be in a bad mood, to be all worked up / (lit); to be badly screwed together.

mettre les bouts exp. to leave quickly / (lit); to put the legs (to work) / *Note:* In this expression, **les bouts** refers to **les bouts de bois**, which means "legs" in slang. This expression can also be shortened to **les mettre** in which **les** refers to **les bouts: On les met?**; Shall we get out of here?

moisir v. to wait / (lit); to mold.

pétrin (se fourrer dans le) exp. to get into a mess / (lit); to throw oneself into the kneading-trough.

rencarder v. to inform / *Also:* **rencard** m. piece of information / **Où t'as eu c'rencard?**; Where did you get that bit of information?

resquiller v. to enter without paying or invitation, to crash (a party, etc.) / **Comment t'as pu resquiller la soirée?**; How were you able to crash the party? / *Also:* **resquilleur, euse** n. one who enters for free or without an invitation; party crasher.

rigolard adj. funny / *Note:* **rigoler** v. to laugh.

torchon m. the curtain of a theater / (lit); rag.

vingt-deux! exclam. watch out! / (lit); twenty-two / Note: perhaps this could be compared to the American 1920s expression, "twenty-three skiddoo!"

zigue m. guy, "dude."

PRACTICE THE VOCABULARY

[Answers to Lesson 14, p. 151]

A. Replace the word(s) in parentheses with the appropriate slang synonym to the right. Make all other necessary changes.

1. (Assez) _____ !	A. grouiller
2. Y m'a fait (attendre) _____ pendant une heure.	B. cabot
3. Quel (acteur prétentieux) _____ !	C. vingt-deux
4. Bon! J'dois (partir) _____ _____ .	D. rigolard
5. (Attention) _____ !	E. châsser
6. (Dépêche) _____ -toi!	F. pétrin
7. Quand y t'parle, y t'(regarde) _____ pas.	G. à l'œil
8. Quelle (situation difficile) _____ !	H. zigue
9. C'est (gratuit) _____ .	I. basta
10. J'ai (peur) _____ moi!	J. la frousse
11. Y est (amusant) _____ c'type!	K. moisir
12. Tu connais c'te (type) _____ ?	L. mettre les bouts

B. Underline the synonym.

1. **mal vissé**	a. mauvaise humeur	b. mal habillé	c. pas clair
2. **entifler**	a. partir	b. courir	c. entrer
3. **s'amener**	a. voler	b. arriver	c. partir
4. **à tout casser**	a. mauvais	b. formidable	c. fatigué
5. **fendre la pipe**	a. rire	b. pleurer	c. mourir
6. **torchon**	a. siège	b. rideau	c. homme
7. **moisir**	a. partir	b. attendre	c. parler

8. **basta**	a. assez	b. encore	c. chemise
9. **châsser**	a. regarder	b. dormir	c. marcher
10. **mettre les bouts**	a. arriver	b. battre	c. partir

C. Choose the correct English translation.

1.	__ La barbe!	A. Hurry!
2.	__ Change de disques!	B. She's super weird.
3.	__ Y casse la baraque!	C. Shut up!
4.	__ J'suis cuit!	D. Change the subject!
5.	__ Y brûle les planches.	E. It's free.
6.	__ Elle est archibizarre.	F. I'm done for!
7.	__ Y a éventé la mèche.	G. He spilled the beans.
8.	__ Regarde un peu qui s'amène.	H. Look who's coming.
9.	__ D'acc!	I. He acts with energy.
10.	__ Grouille-toi!	J. Okay!
11.	__ C't'à l'œil.	K. He brings the house down!

GRAMMAR I: THE LANGUAGE OF *LARGONJI*

Largonji is another interesting "language" that has produced many slang words in French. It consists of replacing the first letter of the word with the letter l and putting that first letter at the end of the word. Then the suffix **i, ic, é, èm, gue, ot, que,** or **uche** is generally attached. Therefore, you can start to see that the word **largonji** is merely the word **jargon** transformed by this formula. **Largonji** takes slang one step further in that it not only rearranges the word as does **verlan,** but it also adds an extra suffix to make the recognition of the word that much more difficult ... which is just what crooks wanted! The following are some common results of **largonji:**

à loilpé, à loilpuche (= **à poil**) adv. naked / (lit); (down) to the hair.
lacsé (= **sac**) m. 10 francs / (lit); sack.
lamefé (= **femme**) f. woman / Note the **a** in **lamefé.** This spelling change was made in order to retain the first **e** sound in **femme** (pronounced "fahme").
laranqué (= **quarante**) m. a 40-franc piece.
larteaumic (= **marteau**) m. crazy / (lit); hammer.
lateaubèm (= **bateau**) m. boat.
latrompèm (= **patron**) m boss.
laubé, laubiche (= **beau**) adj. handsome.
lerche, lerchot, lerchèm (= **cher**) adj. expensive.
leurrebèm (= **beurre**) m. money / (lit); butter.
linvé (= **vingt**) m. a 20-franc piece.
listrobèm (= **bistrot**) m. café.
loinqué (= **coin**) m. corner.
loubé (= **bout**) m. end.

loucedoc (= en **douce**) adv. quietly.
loucherbèm (= **boucher**) m. butcher.
louf, loufoque, louftingue (= **fou**) adj. crazy.

PRACTICE *LARGONJI*

A. Below is a list of words transformed into largonji. (1) Put each word back into its "non-largonji" state and (2) write down its English translation.

Example:

> à loilpé
> **à poil**   naked

1. larteaumic
   _____
   _____

2. lamefé
   _____
   _____

3. laranqué
   _____
   _____

4. loubé
   _____
   _____

5. lateaubèm
   _____
   _____

6. laubiche
   _____
   _____

7. lerche
   _____
   _____

8. leurrebèm
   _____
   _____

9. linvé
   _____
   _____

10. listrobèm
    _____
    _____

B. Fill in the blank with the appropriate word from the list below:

loinqué	lacsé	loucedoc
loucherbèm	loufoque	listrobèm
lerche	lamefé	laubiche

1. Regarde c'te nana...è s'parle! Mais elle est _____ !
2. Y est _____ c't'acteur!
3. J'habite au _____ d'la rue.
4. Mais si, y s'est marié! Voilà sa _____ !
5. J'veux pas qu'y nous entende. Faut parler en _____ !
6. Son père, c't'un _____ .
7. J'ai soif, moi. Tu veux m'accompagner au _____ ?
8. Tu peux m'prêter un _____ ?
9. Mais, ça coûte _____ , c'te truc!

Leçon Quinze

AU TRAVAIL...

DIALOGUE

Anne raconte ses nouvelles à Margot.

Anne: Tu sais qu'Alain, y a **rendu ses clous**?

Margot: Oh, c'est du **réchauffé**, ça! Mais, **entre quat'z'yeux**, y s'est fait **mett'sur les roses**.

Anne: Mais, j'avais toujours pensé qu'y **s'décarcassait**, lui!

Margot: T'es pas **à la coule**? La semaine dernière, ça a **bardé**! Y s'est fait **moucher** par l'**singe** pasque c't'un sacré **cafouilleur**. En plus, j'veux pas colporter des **cancans**, mais on dit qu'y **rapplique** souvent au **boulot brindezingue à zéro**! Pis, y **en écrase** pendant une plombe pour **cuver son vin**!

Anne: Ah, c'est pour ça qu'y a toujours des **châsses en capote d'fiacre**!

Margot: Oh, c't'un beau **picoleur**, c'te **mironton**!

Anne: Y doit **avoir la G.D.B.** presque sans arrêt!

Margot: Alors, l'singe, y 'ui a dit d'**fiche le camp** et Alain, y **s'est mis en boule** et 'ui a flanqué un **marron** en pleine **bouille**! Tu devrais voir un peu l'**coquard** qu'y porte maintenant!

Anne: Mais, pisqu'y est **sur l'carreau**, comment y va pouvoir **s'défendre**? Le **chômedu**, c'est pas marrant!

Margot: Y a pas à **t'faire du mauvais sang** pour cézig. Y arrive toujours à dénicher des bons **fromages**.

AT WORK...

DIALOGUE

Anne is telling Margot about her news.

Anne: Did you know Alain quit?

Margot: Oh, that's old news! But between you and me, he got himself axed.

Anne: But I always thought that he worked his butt off!

Margot: You don't know what happened? Last week, things got hot! He got himself chewed out by the big cheese because he's such a screw-up. Not only that, I don't want to spread rumors, but they say he often shows up to work blitzed out of his mind! Then he crashes for an hour to sleep it off!

Anne: Ah, then that's why his eyes are always swollen!

Margot: Oh, that guy's a real drinker!

Anne: He must have a constant hangover!

Margot: So the boss told him to beat it, and Alain got all ticked off and threw him a punch right in the face! You should see the shiner he's wearing now!

Anne: But since he's out of a job, how's he gonna get by? Unemployment isn't fun!

Margot: You don't have to worry about him. He always manages to find good cushy jobs.

VOCABULARY

à la coule (être) exp. to be up-to-date on something / (lit); to be in the flow.

à zéro exp. completely and absolutely / (lit); to zero.

barder v. to turn to violence, to get "heated up" (lit); to arm for attack.

bouille f. face, "kisser"; head / **Elle a une bonne bouille**; She's cute.

boule (se mettre en) exp. to get very angry / (lit); to get oneself into a ball.

boulot m. (*extremely popular*) work / *Note:* **boulonner** ("to work") is the verb that comes from **boulot**—*not* **boulotter** ("to eat") as one would think.

brindezingue (être) adj. to be drunk, "bombed."

cafouilleur adj. & n. one who works in an unsure manner and makes a lot of mistakes / *Note:* **cafouiller** v. to go about things in an unsure manner.

cancans m.pl. rumors / **colporter des cancans sur q.**; to spread rumors about someone / *Also:* **cancaner** v. to spread rumors.

châsses en capote de fiacre (avoir les) exp. to have swollen eyes / (lit); to have eyes like the top of a horse-drawn carriage / *Note:* **châsse** f. slang for "eye."

chômedu m. unemployment / *Note:* This is a slang variant of **chômage** meaning "unemployment."

coquard m. black eye / *Note:* This is a slang variant of **coquelicot** meaning "red poppy" but also used in slang to mean "black eye" / *Also:* **coquelique** m. another slang variant.

cuver son vin exp. to sleep off one's booze / (lit); to ferment one's wine / *Note:* **cuver le vin** is said of wine that is in its vat (**cuve**) fermenting.

décarcasser (se) v. to work one's butt off / (lit); to "decarcass" oneself.

défendre (se) v. to get by / (lit); to defend oneself / **Y s'défend bien**; He gets by well.

écraser (en) v. to sleep; "to crash" / (lit); to crush some / *Note:* This expression probably came to be because of the "crushing" sound that one makes when snoring.

entre quat'z'yeux exp. between you and me / (lit); between four eyes.

fiche le camp exp. to leave quickly; to "beat it" / (lit); to "make like the camp" or better "to decamp" / **Fiche le camp!**; Beat it!

fromage m. a cushy job (that's soft like cheese) / (lit); cheese.

G.D.B. (avoir la) exp. to have a hangover / *Note:* This is actually a slang version of another slang expression. **Avoir la gueule de bois** literally means "to have the mouth of wood" or "to have a hangover." The abbreviation of **gueule de bois** (pronounced **jé, dé, bé**) is commonly used in its place.

marron m. punch to the face / (lit); chestnut.

mauvais sang (se faire du) exp. to worry, to get all worked up / (lit); to make oneself bad blood.

mettre sur les roses exp. to fire one from office / (lit); to place on the roses.

mironton m. individual, "dude."

moucher (se faire) v. to get oneself severely reprimanded / *Note:* The verb **moucher** by itself means "to snuff out (a candle, etc.)" Perhaps a loose translation of this might be "to get oneself snuffed out by someone's yelling."

picoleur m. one who drinks a great deal / *Note:* **picoler** v. to drink.

rappliquer v. to show up; to come back.

réchauffé m. old news, "news that has been heated up again" / (lit); reheated leftovers / *Note:* **réchauffer** v. to bring up old news again.

rendre ses clous exp. to quit / (lit); to return one's nails / *Note:* **clous** m.pl. is slang for "tools."

singe m. boss, "big cheese" / (lit); monkey.

sur le carreau (être) exp. to be out of work / (lit); to be on the "tile floor" or sidewalk.

PRACTICE THE VOCABULARY

[Answers to Lesson 15, pp. 151–152]

A. Fill in the blank with the appropriate word(s) from the list below that goes with the definition.

en écraser	se décarcasser	se faire moucher
barder	fromage	se faire du mauvais sang
marron	être à la coule	se mettre en boule
cuver son vin	se défendre	mettre sur les roses

1. _____ exp. to sleep off one's booze
2. _____ exp. to be up-to-date on something.
3. _____ exp. to worry, to get all worked up.
4. _____ exp. to get very angry.
5. _____ v. to get oneself severely reprimanded.
6. _____ v. to work one's butt off.
7. _____ exp. to fire one from office.
8. _____ v. to get by.
9. _____ v. to sleep; "to crash".
10. _____ m. a cushy job (that's soft like cheese).
11. _____ m. punch to the face.
12. _____ v. to turn to violence, to get "heated up".

B. Underline the synonym.

1. **barder**	a. chauffer	b. refroidir	c. parler
2. **rappliquer**	a. s'habiller	b. arriver	c. partir
3. **picoleur**	a. buveur	b. travailleur	c. professeur
4. **mironton**	a. enfant	b. maison	c. individu
5. **brindezingue**	a. intelligent	b. énergique	c. ivre
6. **à zéro**	a. complètement	b. rien	c. petit
7. **singe**	a. grand	b. patron	c. père
8. **bouille**	a. figure	b. travail	c. voiture
9. **boulot**	a. montre	b. patron	c. travail
10. **chômedu**	a. chambre	b. chômage	c. chance

C. Underline the word(s) that best completes the phrase.

1. J'peux pas travailler pour lui! J'(**rends mes clous, rends mon fric**)!
2. Tu sais que Christophe, y a acheté une nouvelle bagnole? —Oh, c'est du (**refroidi, réchauffé**), ça!
3. (**Entre quat'z'yeux, Un d'ces quat'**), c't'un beau menteur!
4. Y s'est fait (**moucher, marron**) par l'(**chien, singe**).
5. J'veux pas qu'y travaille avec moi. C't'un (**cacahuète, cafouilleur**), c'ui-là!
6. Mais, comment tu peux croire c'qu'è t'bonit? Ce sont qu'des (**cancans, caves**)!
7. Y a les (**châsses, châssis**) en capote d'fiacre.
8. Parle pas trop fort. J'ai (**l'O.V.N.I., la G.D.B.**), moi.
9. Tu m'énerves! Fiche le (**camp, charivari**)!
10. Y m'a flanqué un (**marrant, marron**) en pleine (**bouille, boui-boui**).
11. Oh, c'te (**coquille, coquard**)! J'ai mal à l'œil!
12. Comme j'ai pu d'(**boulot, boume**), j'suis sur l'(**carré, carreau**).

GRAMMAR I: THE LANGUAGE OF *JAVANAIS*

Some of the most common users of **javanais** are students who don't want teachers to understand them! It consists of intertwining the letters **av** or **ag** (whichever the user desires) between each consonant and vowel as well as between each syllable. Usually, a person will throw in a word of **javanais** to add more color to a word or a little extra "oomph" to another slang word as a way to make it even harder to understand. The real aficionado of slang, however, may even construct an entire sentence using this formula! Since it is *absolutely* a "language" that only a native would know, any foreigner who demonstrates a command of **javanais** would surely leave mouths open in surprise. The following are a few examples of **javanais** using **av** and **ag**:

baveau (= **beau**) adj. handsome.
bavelle (= **belle**) adj. pretty.
gravos (= **gros**) adj. fat.
favouille (= **fouille**) adj. pocket / *Note:* This is slang for "pocket" since it
    comes from the verb **fouiller** meaning "to rummage."
javavanavais (= **javanais**).
javardavin (= **jardin**) m. garden.
magoustagache (= **moustache**) f. mustache.
sagœur (= **sœur**) f. sister / *Note:* This is also used to mean "girl" or "chick."
    / **Tu connais c'te sagœur?**; You know that chick?

PRACTICE *JAVANAIS*

A. **Write the following words in *javanais* (*av* or *ag*).**

1. beau (**av**)
    _____

2. gros (**av**)
    _____

3. sœur (**ag**)
    _____

4. bouche (**av**)
    _____

5. mec (**av**)
    _____

6, bouille (**av**)
    _____

7. singe (**ag**)
    _____

8. mironton (**av**)
    _____

9. belle (**av**)
    _____

10. jardin (**av**)
    _____

GRAMMAR II: COLLOQUIAL USAGE OF PRONOUN *EN*

A. To add emphasis to the verb

It is commonly taught in French classes that the pronoun **en** (translated
as "some" in this case) replaces the object of the phrase when preceded by a
partitive article (**de, des, de la,** and **du**) or indefinite article (**un, une**):

J'veux du vin. (I want some wine.)
J'en veux. (I want some.)

T'as une bonne bagnole. (You have a good car.)
T'en as une bonne. (You have a good one.)

In colloquial French, the pronoun **en** *and* the subject may be used together to emphasize the verb. In this case, **en** is translated as "do." Note that in English, the stress falls on the word "do"; whereas in French, it falls on the word just *after* **en**:

J'en veux du vin! (I *do* want some wine!)
T'en as une bonne bagnole! (You *do* have a good car!)

B. To emphasize quantity

The same construction is extremely popular when emphasizing the number of objects in question. Note that the stress is on the number:

J'ai deux bagnoles = J'en ai deux = **J'en ai deux des bagnoles**
J'ai trois enfants = J'en ai trois = **J'en ai trois des enfants**

PRACTICE THE COLLOQUIAL USAGE OF *EN*

A. Answer each question using *en* to add emphasis to the phrase.

Example:

Tu veux pas d'vin?   Tu veux pas d'enfants?
Si! J'en veux du vin!   **Si! J'en veux des enfants!**

1. Tu veux pas d'gâteau?
    Si! _____
2. Y a pas d'maison, lui?
    Si! _____
3. Elle a pas d'sœurs?
    Si! _____
4. Tu viens pas d'Paris?
    Si! _____
5. T'as pas d'idées sur l'sujet?
    Si! _____
6. T'as jamais conduit une bagnole?
    Si! _____
7. Y a jamais vu un coucher d'soleil?
    Si! _____
8. Elle a pas d'chance?
    Si! _____

9. Tu bois pas d'alcool?
   Si! _____

10. Y prend pas d'risques?
    Si! _____

B. Answer each question using *en* to emphasize the quantity.

Example:

T'en as combien des enfants?
(deux) J'en ai deux des enfants.

T'en as mangé combien des sandwiches?
(trois) J'en ai mangé trois des sandwiches.

1. T'en a combien des chemises?
   (huit) _____ .

2. Elle en a combien des enfants?
   (trois) _____ .

3. Y en a bu combien des bières?
   (quatre) _____ .

4. T'en as acheté combien des pantalons?
   (six) _____ .

5. Elle en a pris combien des aspirines?
   (cinq) _____ .

6. Y en a combien des chaussures?
   (quatre) _____ .

7. T'en as combien des frères?
   (cinq) _____ .

8. T'en comptes combien des spectateurs?
   (quarante) _____ .

9. T'en as rencontré combien des vedettes?
   (dix) _____ .

10. Elle en a brûlé combien des dîners cette semaine?
    (cinq) _____ .

11. T'en as trouvé combien des erreurs?
    (trois) _____ .

12. T'en veux combien des macarons au chocolat?
    (un millier) _____ .

ANSWERS TO LESSONS 11–15

LESSON 11

Practice the Vocabulary

A.
1. b
2. a
3. a
4. c
5. b
6. b
7. c
8. b

B.
1. roulée
2. foin
3. une bavette
4. sympa
5. que t'chi, un poil
6. cordes
7. dégoisait
8. du monde au balcon
9. impec
10. les poules
11. chaussette

C.
1. G
2. I
3. D
4. A
5. C
6. E
7. B
8. K
9. H
10. L
11. J
12. F

Grammar I: Practice the Omission of the Possessive Article

A.
1. Gratte-lui l'cou.
2. Masse-moi l'dos.
3. Brosse-toi les cheveux.
4. Arrache-moi la dent.

5. Touche-lui l'épaule.
6. Tiens-moi l'bras.
7. Serre-moi la main.
8. Lave-lui la figure.

B. 1. Y m'touche l'épaule.
   2. J'ui ai gratté l'cou.
   3. J'ui ai cassé l'bras.
   4. E m'a frappé l'nez.
   5. J'ui peigne les cheveux.
   6. Le dentiste, y 'ui a arraché les dents.
   7. E m'a giflé la figure.
   8. Que ça m'fend l'cœur.
   9. J'me brosse les dents.
   10. E s'maquille les yeux.
   11. E 'ui maquille les yeux.
   12. Y m'a chuchoté dans l'oreille.

Grammar II: Practice Offering and Asking for Favors

A. 1. Tiens-moi ça.
   2. Porte-lui c'manteau.
   3. Ouv'-moi la porte.
   4. Soulève-lui c'te valise.
   5. Vérifie-lui c'te liste.
   6. Coupe-moi c'te ficelle.
   7. Lave-moi c'te tasse.
   8. Change-moi c't'ampoule.
   9. Ferme-moi la fenêtre.
   10. Répare-moi la voiture.

B. 1. J'te tiens les livres?
   2. Y m'a porté l'manteau.
   3. Y m'a ouvert la porte.
   4. J'te soulève la chaise?
   5. J'ui ai vérifié la liste.
   6. J'te coupe la ficelle?
   7. J't'ai lavé la tasse.
   8. Y m'a changé l'ampoule.
   9. E m'a fermé la fenêtre.
   10. Y m'a réparé la voiture.

LESSON 12

Practice the Vocabulary

A. 1. clamsé
   2. éponges
   3. à l'article
   4. martel
   5. toubib
   6. beau
   7. oseille
   8. billard
   9. battant
   10. raqué
   11. crève
   12. pente

B. 1. c
   2. c
   3. a
   4. a
   5. b
   6. c
   7. a
   8. a
   9. b
   10. c

C. 1. tourne
   2. ça va pas
   3. tangente
   4. salade
   5. pageot
   6. piquouser
   7. quat'
   8. bombarder
   9. canulard, à l'hosto
   10. surblaze
   11. graillonnes, toubib

Grammar I: Practice Your Gestures

(See the illustrations beginning on page 118)

Grammar II: Practice the Use of Fruits and Vegetables in Slang

A. 1. G
   2. E
   3. D
   4. I
   5. F

6. J
7. A
8. C
9. B
10. H

LESSON 13

Practice the Vocabulary

A. 1. badigeon, portrait
2. jardiner, douze
3. attrapes-pognon
4. peinture
5. paquet
6. embellie
7. cave
8. baragouiner
9. la pige
10. pourpoint

B. 1. (une) partie d'soeurs
2. pris une culotte
3. sacré
4. poke
5. flambeur
6. bécoter
7. rouquin
8. graisseur
9. pharmaco
10. barbouze
11. as déraillé
12. brèmes

C. 1. sacré
2. fair-play
3. mon cheval
4. badigeon, portrait
5. graisseur
6. maquillé

7. embellie
8. baragouineur
9. rire
10. flambeur
11. faire la pige

Grammar I: Practice *Verlan*

A. 1. calibre; revolver
2. être au parfum; to be up-to-date
3. poulet; cop
4. clope; cigarette
5. mec; guy
6. gonzesse; girl
7. baraque; house
8. être dans le coltar; to be exhausted
9. falzar; pants
10. femme; woman, wife
11. jobard; stupid gullible person

B. 1. raquebar
2. balpeau
3. funpar
4. brelica
5. lépou
6. quèm
7. meffe
8. tarcol
9. péclot
10. zesgon
11. barjot
12. zarfal

LESSON 14

Practice the Vocabulary

A. 1. Basta
2. moisir
3. cabot
4. mettre les bouts
5. Vingt-deux
6. Grouille

7. châsse
8. Quel pétrin
9. à l'œil
10. la frousse
11. rigolard
12. zigue

B. 1. a
2. c
3. b
4. b
5. a

6. b
7. b
8. a
9. a
10. c

C. 1. C
2. D
3. K
4. F
5. I

6. B
7. G
8. H
9. J
10. A
11. E

Grammar I: The Language of *Largonji*

A. 1. marteau; crazy
2. femme; wife, woman
3. quarante; 40-franc piece
4. bout; end
5. bateau; boat
6. beau; handsome
7. cher; expensive
8. beurre; money
9. vingt; 20-franc piece
10. bistrot; café

B. 1. loufoque
2. laubiche
3. loinqué
4. lamefé
5. loucedoc
6. loucherbèm
7. listrobèm
8. lacsé
9. lerche

LESSON 15

Practice the Vocabulary

A. 1. cuver son vin
2. être à la coule
3. se faire du mauvais sang
4. se mettre en boule
5. se faire moucher
6. se décarcasser

7. mettre sur les roses
8. se défendre
9. en écraser
10. fromage
11. marron
12. barder

B. 1. a
2. b
3. a
4. c
5. c

6. a
7. b
8. a
9. c
10. b

C. 1. rends mes clous
   2. réchauffé
   3. Entre quat'z'yeux
   4. moucher, singe
   5. cafouilleur
   6. cancans
   7. châsses
   8. la G.D.B.
   9. camp
   10. marron, bouille
   11. coquard
   12. boulot, carreau

Grammar I: Practice *Javanais*

A. 1. baveau
   2. gravos
   3. sagœur
   4. bavouche
   5. mavec
   6. bavouille
   7. saguinge
   8. maviravontavon
   9. bavelle
   10. javardavin

Grammar II: Practice the Colloquial Usage of *en*

A. 1. J'en veux du gâteau!
   2. Y en a des maisons!
   3. Elle en a des sœurs!
   4. J'en viens d'Paris!
   5. J'en ai des idées sur l'sujet!
   6. J'en ai conduit des bagnoles!
   7. Y en a vu des couchers d'soleil!
   8. Elle en a d'la chance!
   9. J'en bois d'l'alcool!
   10. Y en prend des risques!

B. 1. J'en ai huit des chemises.
   2. Elle en a trois des enfants.
   3. Y en a bu quat'des bières.
   4. J'en ai acheté six des pantalons.
   5. Elle en a pris cinq des aspirines.
   6. Y en a quat'des chaussures.
   7. J'en ai cinq des frères.
   8. J'en compte quarante des spectateurs.
   9. J'en ai rencontré dix des vedettes.
   10. Elle en a brûlé cinq des dîners cette semaine.
   11. J'en ai trouvé trois des erreurs.
   12. J'en veux un millier des macarons au chocolat.

REVIEW EXAM FOR LESSONS 11–15

[Answers to Review, p. 156]

A. Underline the word(s) that fall into the same category as the word(s) to the left.

1. **figure**
   a. singe
   b. portrait
   c. bouille
   d. flambeur

2. **arriver**
   a. rappliquer
   b. s'amener
   c. débarquer
   d. cuver son vin

3. **avoir du talent**
   a. rendre ses clous
   b. avoir la bosse
   c. être dans ses cordes
   d. clamser

4. **mourir**
   a. clamser
   b. à l'article de la mort
   c. à la coule
   d. à l'œil

5. **partir**
   a. jardiner
   b. mettre les bouts
   c. déchanter
   d. prendre la tangente

6. **individu**
   a. zigue
   b. rengaine
   c. mironton
   d. bouille

7. **rire**
   a. fendre la pipe
   b. entraver
   c. battre le pavé
   d. rigolard

8. **hôpital**
   a. toubib
   b. canulard
   c. blaze
   d. hosto

9. **être malade**
   a. connobrer
   b. attraper la crève
   c. mal fichu
   d. bombarder

10. **rapidement**   a. en moins de deux   b. se grouiller
                            c. dégoiser   d. déraillé

11. **parler**   a. tailler une bavette   b. bonir
                            c. dégoiser   d. déchanter

12. **travail**   a. singe   b. à zéro
                            c. boulot   d. se décarcasser

B. Fill in the blank with the appropriate word(s) that best completes the phrase. Make all necessary changes to the verbs.

battre le pavé	du foin	comprenette dure
dégoiser	toubib	rouquin
la barbe	châsser	à tout casser
archi	fromage	boulot

1. _____ -moi c'te bagnole! Elle est chouette!
2. _____ ! Tu veux qu'y nous entende?!
3. C't'ait un film _____ !
4. Comme y travaille plus, y est obligé d' _____ .
5. Y est pas stupide, mais faut dire qu'y a la _____ .
6. Mais elle est _____ bête.
7. Tu connais c'type-là? Qui? Le _____ par là?
8. Mais, y est bête à bouffer _____ .
9. Le professeur, y nous _____ pendant une heure!
10. Si t'es malade, pourquoi tu vois pas un _____ ?
11. Enfin! J'ai trouvé un travail fantastique. C't'un vrai _____ .
12. Enfin! J'ai trouvé un _____ fantastique!

C. Match the French with the English.

1. __ se décarcasser   A. drinker
2. __ se mettre en boule   B. to enter
3. __ marron   C. telephone
4. __ en écraser   D. singer
5. __ brèmes   E. to sleep (to crash)
6. __ dérailler   F. cards
7. __ bécoter   G. name
8. __ moisir   H. to wait
9. __ à l'œil   I. to become angry
10. __ entifler   J. free
11. __ d'acc   K. okay
12. __ picoleur   L. to go crazy
13. __ cornichon   M. to work one's butt off

14. ___ goualeuse

15. ___ blaze

N. a punch

O. to kiss (to neck)

D. Underline the word(s) that best completes the phrase.

1. Tu (**connobres, clamses**) c'te mec?
2. J'(**entifle, entrave**) pas c'qu'y m'dit.
3. Cent francs? Mais c't'une (**bagatelle, crâneuse**), ça!
4. Y m'a dit (**à brûle-pourpoint, à tout casser**) qu'c't'un beau menteur.
5. Arrête d'parler comme ça. T'as (**déraillé, taillé une bavette**), non?
6. Mais, calme-toi! T'es vraiment (**à zéro, mal vissé**) aujourd'hui.
7. Faut pas l'faire! Sinon, tu vas t'fourrer dans un beau (**pétrin, fromage**)!
8. Y peut pas s'passer d'clopes pasqu'ça 'ui plaît d'(**piquouser, bombarder**).
9. J'ai trop bu hier soir. J'ai la (**G.D.B., cave**), moi!
10. J'suis dans l'coltar. J'vais en (**graillonner, écraser**).
11. Mais, j'le sais! C'est du (**réchauffé, chômedu**), ça!
12. Comment tu peux croire c'qu'è t'balance? Ce sont qu'des (**cabots, cancans**).
13. Quand j'ai appris la nouvelle, je m'suis mis en (**boule, attrape-pognon**)!
14. (**Vingt-deux, trente-deux**)! Les flics!
15. J'm'en fiche comme de ma première (**chaussure, chaussette**)!

ANSWERS TO REVIEW (LESSONS 11–15)

A.
1. b, c		7. a,d
2. a, b, c		8. a, b, d
3. b, c		9. b, c
4. a, b		10. a, b
5. b, d		11. a, b, c
6. a, c		12. a, c, d

B.
1. Châsse	7. rouquin
2. La barbe	8. du foin
3. à tout casser	9. dégoisait
4. batt'le pavé	10. toubib
5. comprenette dure	11. fromage
6. archi	12. boulot

C.
1. M	9. J
2. I	10. B
3. N	11. K
4. E	12. A
5. F	13. C
6. L	14. D
7. O	15. G
8. H	

D.
1. connobres	9. G.D.B.
2. entrave	10. écraser
3. bagatelle	11. réchauffé
4. à brûle-pourpoint	12. cancans
5. déraillé	13. boule
6. mal vissé	14. Vingt-deux
7. pétrin	15. chaussette
8. bombarder	

UNIT TWO

ENGLISH WORDS THAT ARE COMMONLY USED IN COLLOQUIAL FRENCH

Often, as you speak French, you may find yourself having to stop in midstream because suddenly you've run into a word that you don't know how to interpret. It is quite possible that the word is the same in French as it is in English (yet still pronounced with a French accent). The following words should be pronounced the same as you would if they **were** French words. The noted exceptions are in quotes and should also be pronounced following the rules of French pronunciation.

baby-sitting m. (pronounced "bébi-sitting")

bacon m.

bank-note f.

bar m.

barmaid f. (pronounced "bar-maide").

barman m. (pronounced "bar mane").

base-ball m. (pronounced "bèz-bol").

basket-ball m. (pronounced "baskette-bol") / *Also* just called **basket**.

bestseller m. (pronounced "best-selleur").

betting m.

bikini m.

black-out m. (pronouned "blak-aoute").

blazer m. (pronounced "blazère").

blue-jean m. (pronounced "blou-djine").

blues m. (pronounced "blouz").

bluff m. (pronounced "blœf") / *Also:* **bluffer** m. (pronounced "blœfé").

bookmaker m. bookie / (pronounced "boukmékeur").

boss m.

bowling m. (pronounced "boling").

box-window m.

brain-trust m. (pronounced "brène-trœst").

breakfast m. (pronounced "brèkfast").

building m. (pronounced "bilding").

bulldozer m. (pronounced "bul-dozeur").

cake m. (pronounced "kèk").

call-girl f. (pronounced "kal-gœrl").

caméraman m. (pronounced "caméra-mane").

camping m.

campus m. (pronounced "cam-pusse").

caravane f.

cash m. *Also:* **payer cash**

chewing-gum m. (pronounced "shwing-goem").

chips m. (pronounced "shipsse").

clergyman m. (pronounced "clergy-mane").

clown m. (pronounced "cloune").

cocker m. (pronounced "cockère").

cocktail m. (pronounced "cock-tèl").

cold-cream m. (pronounced "kold-krime").

cool adj.

copyright m. (pronounced "kopi-raït").

corned-beef m. (pronounced "kornèd-bif").

cover-girl f. (pronounced "koveur-gœrl").

cow-boy m. (pronounced "ko-boï").

crash m.

crawl m. (of swimming) (pronounced "kraule").

curry m.

dog m.

drugstore m. (pronounced "drœg-stor").

dry adj. (pronounced "draï).

fading m.

fair-play adj.

far-west m.

ferry-boat m. (pronounced "fairi-bot").

flash m.

football m. soccer / *Also:* **foot** m.

footing m. jogging.

freezer m. (pronounced "frizeur").

gadget m. (pronounced "gadjette").
gag m.
gang m. (pronounced "gangue").
gangster m. (pronounced "gangue-staire").
gin m. (pronounced "dgin").
glass m. glass or drink
grill-room m. (pronounced "grile-roume").
groggy adj.

hand-ball m. (pronounced "ande-bol") / *Also:* **hand** m.
hold-up m. (pronounced "olde-op").
home m. (pronounced "aume").

iceberg m. (pronounced "aïcebœrg" or "isebèrgue").
interview m.

jeep m. (pronounced "djip").
jerk m. (the dance) / (pronounced "djèrk").
jersey m. (pronounced "jèrsè").
jet m. (pronounced "djette").
job m. (pronounced "djob").
jockey m. (pronounced "djokè").
joint m. (as in marijuana).
joker m. (pronounced "djokeur").

kleenex m. (pronounced "klinex").

leader m. (pronounced "lideur").
lob m. (in tennis) / *Also:* **lober** v.
    to lob / **balle lobée** f. lobbed ball.
lunch m. (pronounced "lœnch").

meeting m. (pronounced "miting").
melting-pot m. (pronounced "melting-pote").
music-hall m. (pronounced "musique-ol").

no man's land m. (pronounced "no-mann'z-lande).

offset m. (pronounced "of-sette").
okay interj. (pronounced "oké" or "oque").

parking m.
pickles m.pl. (pronounced "picœlz").
pickpocket m. (pronounced "peek-pokette").
pin-up f. (pronounced "pinope").
pipe-line m. (pronounced "pipline").
playback m. (pronounced "plaibak").
play-boy m. (pronounced "plaiboï").
pop-corn m.
pudding m. (pronounced "pouding").
pullover m. *Also:* **pull** m. pullover/ (pronounced "pule-auveur" or "pule-auvair").
punch m. (the drink) / pronounced "ponch").
puzzle m. (pronounced "pœzl").

racket m. a dishonest scheme / (pronounced "raquette").
remake m. (pronounced "rimèk").
rock or **rock n'roll** m. (pronounced "rok" or "rok-'n-rol").
rocking-chair m. (pronounced "roking-tchair").
rodeo m. (pronounced "rode-yo").
round m. (in boxing) / (pronounced "raounde").
rush m. (pronounced "rœsh") / **C'est l'grand rush vers la plage;** It's the big rush to the beach.

scooter m. (pronounced "sku-teur" or "sku-taire").
score m.
script m.
script-girl f. (pronounced "skript-gœrl").
self-made-man m. (pronounced "self-mèd-mane").
self-service m.
set m. (in tennis, ping-pong, volley-ball, etc.) / (pronounced "sete").

sex-appeal m. (pronounced "sex-apile").

shaker m. (used in making drinks) / (pronounced "shèkeur").

shampooing m. (pronounced "shampoin").

shocking m. (pronounced "shoking").

shoot m. (of basketball) (pronounced "shoute") / *Also:* **shooter** v. to shoot the ball.

short m. shorts / **J'ai acheté un nouveau short**; I bought new shorts.

shopping m.

show m. (pronounced "shau").

side-car m. (pronounced "saïde-kar").

sitting m. a sit-down strike / **faire un sitting**; to execute a sit-down strike.

skate-board m. (pronounced "skaite-borde").

sketch m.

slang m. (pronounced "slangue").

slow m. slow dance / (pronounced "slau").

smart adj. chic / *Note:* Interestingly enough, the French use the English word "smart," whereas, in the English language, the French word **chic** is used! / (pronounced "smarte").

smash m. (of tennis).

smoking m. tuxedo.

snack-bar m.

snob m.

snow-boot m. (pronounced "snau-boute").

soda m.

sofa m.

speaker m. (pronounced "spikeur") male public speaker / **speakerine** f. woman public speaker.

spot m. spotlight.

sprint m. (pronounced "spreente") / **Y a gagné au sprint**; He won the sprint.

sprinter m. (pronounced "sprine-teur") / *Also:* **sprinter** v. to sprint (pronounced "sprine-té").

standing m. status.

star m. movie-star.

starter m. (pronounced "startaire") (1) one who gives the signal, (2) choke (of car).

starting-block m.

starting-gate m. (pronounced "starting-gaite").

steak m. (pronounced "stèk").

steward m. (pronounced "stuwar").

stick m. riding whip.

stock m.

stock-car m.

stone adj. stoned (of drugs).

stop m. stop sign.

stress m.

strict adj.

strip-tease m. (pronounced "stripe-tiz").

surf m.

suspense m. (pronounced "suspèns").

sweater m. (pronounced "swèteur").

sweat-shirt m. (pronounced "swète-shœrt").

sweepstake m. (pronounced "swip-stèk").

swing m. (in music) / **C't'orchestre, y a du swing!**; This orchestra really swings!

tank m.

taxi m.

tempo m.

toast m. (pronounced "tauste") / (1) toast (grilled bread), (2) toast (to make a toast).

traffic m.

traveler chèque m. (**traveler** is pronounced "traveleur") / *Note:* Interestingly enough, the French do *not* say **chèque de voyageur**.

trench-coat m. (pronounced "trènch-kaute").

trust m. (as in cartel) / (pronounced "trœst").

t-shirt m. (pronounced "ti-shœrt").

tub m. (pronounced "tœb").

water-polo m. (pronounced "wataire-
    polo").
weekend m. (pronounced
    "wikènde").
western m.
whisky m.

yacht m. (pronounced the same as in
    English.)
yachting m. (pronounced "yating").

zigzag m. *Also:* **zigzaguer** v. to zigzag.

THESAURUS OF COLLOQUIAL FRENCH AND SLANG

GUIDE TO THESAURUS

THESAURUS

The following is a list of French slang synonyms for each English heading given with its standard translation in parentheses.

Note:

1. A literal translation will be given whenever possible to help give you a good idea of the weight of the term.
2. Any term that should not be be used in certain social situations will *always* be followed by a detailed explanation.

A

A LOT (beaucoup)

bésef/bézef adv. **Y en a bésef;** There's a lot.
flopée f. a bunch / **Elle a une flopée d'mômes;** She has a bunch of kids.
gogo (à) adv. **Elle en a à gogo;** She has a lot of 'em.
ribambelle f. a bunch / **Elle a une ribambelle d'mômes;** She has a bunch of kids.
tire-larigot (à) adv. **boire à tire-larigot;** to drink like a fish.
tripotée f. a bunch / **Elle a une tripotée d'mômes;** She has a bunch of kids.

AFRAID, to be (avoir peur)

chair de poule (avoir la) f. (lit); to have chicken skin or "goose bumps."
chocottes (avoir les) f.pl. to have the jitters, shakes / *Note:* **chocottes** is slang for "teeth" / **avoir les chocottes** might be loosely translated as "to have teeth (that chatter from fear)."
colique (avoir la) f. to have intense fear / (lit); to have diarrhea and cramps.

dans le ventre (ne rien avoir) exp. to have no guts / (lit); to have nothing in the stomach.

dégonfler (se) v. to lose one's courage / (lit); to deflate / *Note:* **dégonflard, dégonflé, dégonfleur** m. scaredy cat.

frousse (avoir la) f. to have the creeps.

grelots (avoir les) m. pl. (lit); to have the shakes / **Note: grelotter** v. to shake or tremble (from fear, cold, etc.).

grolles (avoir les) f.pl. to have the jitters, shakes / *Note:* **grolle** f. shoe / **avoir les grolles** might be loosely translated as "to have shoes that shake (from fear)"; "to shake in one's boots."

jetons (avoir les) m.pl. to have the jitters, shakes / *Note:* **jeton** m. small token that is used for public telephones / **avoir les jetons** might be loosely translated as "to have tokens (that are jingling because the possessor is shaking from fear)."

nerfs en pelote (avoir les) exp. (lit); to have one's nerves in a ball.

pétoche (avoir la) f. to have great fear / (lit); to have farts (out of intense fear) / *Note 1:* As you can see from the literal translation, this should be used with discretion / *Note 2:* The masculine noun **pet**, meaning "fart," comes from its infinitive **péter**. It is often the case in French slang that special slang suffixes are added to adjectives and nouns either to create a slang word or to make another slang word more colorful. Some of the slang suffixes are: **asse, ouche, ouille, ouse, ace,** etc.

pétouille (avoir la) f. slang variant of: **avoir la pétoche** / *Note:* This is vulgar and should be used with discretion.

trac (avoir la) f. to have stage fright

traquette (avoir la) f. to have the jitters / *Note:* **traquer** v. to hunt or track down / **la traquette** might be loosely translated as "the jittery and unsettled feeling that one might have if being pursued."

traquouse (avoir la) f. slang variant of **avoir la traquette** / *Note:* The common suffix **ette** has been changed to the slang suffix **ouse** to give this variant a heavier slang feeling.

tremblotte (avoir la) f. to have the jitters, shakes / (lit); to have the trembles.

trouille (avoir la) f. have intense fear / *Note:* **trouillard(e)** n. one who is terribly scared/ scaredy cat.

venette (avoir la) f. to have the jitters.

ALCOHOL (alcool)

bibine f. beer of poor quality.

brouille-ménage m. red wine (*Note:* **brouiller** v. to mix up; stir up / **ménage** m. household / This literally translates as "something that stirs up the household" since husbands and wives often get into fights after having too much to drink.

brutal m. ordinary wine / (lit); brutal.

casse-gueule m. very strong liquor / (lit); mouth-breaker / *Note:* **gueule** f. derogatory for "mouth" / (lit); mouth of animal.

casse-pattes m. very strong liquor / (lit); paw breaker / *Note:* **patte** f. limb / (lit); paw.

casse-poitrine m. very strong liquor / (lit); chest-breaker.

gniole f. brandy or alcohol in general.

gros rouge qui tache m. ordinary red wine / (lit); the fat red that stains.

gros rouge m. ordinary red wine / (lit); fat red.

moussante f. beer / *Note:* This comes from **mousse** f. (lit); foam.

pétrole m. brandy / (lit); petrol.

pictance f. alcohol in general / *Note:* **picter** v. to drink alcohol.

pousse-au-crime m. ordinary red wine / (lit); push-to-crime.

rouquin m. ordinary red wine / *Note:* **rouquin** n. & adj. red; redhead.

schnaps m. alcohol in general / *Note:* This is borrowed from German.

tord-boyaux m. very strong or poor quality brandy; rot gut / (lit); gut-twister.

vitriol m. low quality liquor / (lit); vitriol.

ANGRY, to be (être en colère)

à prendre avec des pincettes (ne pas être) exp. (lit); to be unable to be picked up with tweezers (because the person is so hot with anger).

baver (en) v. to foam at the mouth (lit); to drool over something.

bisquer v. to be very angry.

boule (se mettre en) exp. to be furious over something / (lit); to get oneself into a ball (because the muscles are so tight with anger).

caille (l'avoir à la) f. to be furious / (lit); to have it (one's blood) to the point of curdling.

cran (être à) adj. to be ready to explode with anger / (lit); **cran** m. notch.

crin (être comme un) exp. to be ready to explode with anger / (lit); to be like a horsehair.

emporter (s') v. to flare up with anger; to lose one's temper / (lit); to carry oneself away / **Calme-toi! Tu t'laisses emporter!**; Relax! You're letting yourself get carried away!

rogne (être en) adj. to be furious.

fâcher tout(e) rouge (se) exp. to be furious / (lit); to get red with anger.

fou/folle de rage (être) exp. (lit): to be crazy with rage.

fumer v. (lit); to smoke (with anger).

furibard(e) (être) adj. to be furious.

furibond(e) (être) adj. to be furious.

mal vissé(e) (être) adj. to be in a bad mood / (lit); to be badly screwed (together).

monter l'échelle exp. (lit); to go up the ladder / **Y m'fait monter l'échelle**; He makes me go right up the wall / *Also:* **grimper l'échelle**.

pester v. to be furious / (lit); to storm (with anger).

rager v. to be furious / (lit); to rage.

râler v. to be furious / (lit); to rile.

sauter v. to become suddenly angry / (lit); to jump.

tempêter v. (lit); to storm (with anger).

tête près du bonnet (avoir la) exp. to be in a bad mood / (lit); to have the head close to the bonnet.

voir rouge exp. to be furious / (lit); to see red.

ANNOY, to (ennuyer)

assommer v. to annoy greatly / (lit); to knock senseless.

barber v. to annoy greatly.

bassiner v. to annoy to the point of anger / (lit); to bathe (wound, etc.) with water or in this case with annoyance.

canuler v. to annoy little by little until it becomes too much / (lit); to inject with a syringe.

casser les oreilles à q. exp. to annoy and tire someone out by talking non-stop / (lit); to break one's ear.

casser les pieds à q. exp. to annoy greatly / (lit); to break one's feet / *Note:* **casse-pieds** m. annoying person / (lit); foot-breaker.

courir v. to pester constantly / (lit); to run.

cramponner v. to annoy by hanging around too much; to cramp one's style / (lit); to cramp.

embêter v. to annoy greatly / (lit); to cause to go crazy.

enquiquiner v. to annoy to the point of suffocation / *Note:* This comes from **quiqui** m. neck.

faire suer v. to annoy greatly / (lit); to make sweat.

raser v. to annoy by boredom or dullness / (lit); to shave / *Note:* **rasoir** m. a boring, dull person / (lit); razor.

taper sur les nerfs à q. exp. (lit); to tap on one's nerves.

tarabuster v. to pester.

tracasser v. to plague / **Cette idée, è m'tracasse!**; This idea is plaguing me!

ARREST, to (arrêter)

(See: **JAIL**)

Note:

se faire may be used in front of any of the words below to change the meaning from "to arrest" to "to get arrested":

Example:

> **se faire agrafer**; to get oneself arrested or nabbed

Exceptions:

1. **être bon** does not take **se faire** in front of it;
2. **être fait** becomes **se faire faire**

agrafer v. (lit); to staple.

arnaquer v. (lit); to sting.

ballonner v. (lit); to put into the **ballon** / (lit); **ballon** m. jail.

bon (être) adj. to be caught, to be done for / (lit); to be good.

choper au tournant exp. (lit); to catch at the bend of the road / *Note:* **choper** v. to catch.

coffrer v. to put into prison / (lit); to put in the trunk. / *Note:* **coffre** m. (lit); trunk

cravater v. (lit); to grab someone by the tie (or neck). / *Note:* **cravate** f. (lit); tie

cueillir v. (lit); to pick, gather, pluck.

cuit(e) (être) adj. (lit); to be cooked (as in one's goose).

emballer v. (lit); to wrap up.

épingler v. (lit); to pin. / *Note:* **épingle** f. (lit); pin

fabriquer v. (lit); to fabricate.

fait(e) (être) ajd. (lit); to be done (for).

fiche dedans v. (lit); to throw inside (the slammer) / *Note:* **fiche** v. to throw.

flanquer dedans v. same as **fiche dedans** / *Note:* **flanquer** v. to throw; chuck.

grouper v. (lit); to group or gather.

harponner v. (lit); to harpoon.

jeter dedans v. (lit); to throw inside (the slammer).

mettre à la boîte exp. (lit); to put in the box / *Note:* **boîte** f. prison.

mettre sous les verrous exp. (lit); to put under the locks.

pincer v. (lit); to pinch.

piper v. (lit); to lure, decoy

piquer v. (lit); to catch.

poisser v. (lit): to coat with a sticky wax.

prendre v. (lit); to take.

ramasser v. (lit); to gather.

sucrer v. (lit); to sweeten.

ARRIVE, to (arriver)

amener (s') v.(lit); to bring oneself along.

amener comme une fleur (s') exp. to drop in quickly, to breeze in / (lit); to bring oneself along like a flower.

amener sa graisse exp. (lit); to bring along one's fat / **Amène ta graisse!**; Get your butt over here!

amener sa viande exp. (lit); to bring along one's meat / *Note:* The slang word for meat, **bidoche**, may be used in place of **viande**.

arriver comme une flèche exp. to drop in quietly, to breeze in / (lit); to arrive like an arrow.

débarquer v. to arrive without notice / (lit); to disembark.

pointer (se) v. to show up / (lit); to point oneself.

radiner v. to run up; to show up.

ralléger v. to come; to arrive / **Tu rallèges?**; You comin'?

rappliquer v. to arrive; to turn up; to come back.

B

BAD LUCK, to have (avoir de la malchance)

(*See:* **LUCKY,** to be)

déveine (avoir la) f. **Quelle déveine!**; What rotten luck! / *Note:* Not "avoir <u>de la</u> déveine."

guignard(e) n. unlucky individual.

guigne (avoir la) f. to have bad luck.

main malheureuse (avoir la) f. (lit); to have a sad hand.

mal loti (être) adj. (lit); to be poorly provided for.

manque de bol m. (lit); lack of luck / *Note:* **bol** m. luck / **avoir du bol**; to be lucky.

manque de pot m. (lit); lack of luck / *Note:* **pot** m. luck / **avoir du pot**; to be lucky.

pas verni adj. (lit); badly varnished (with luck).

poissard(e) n. unlucky individual.

poisse (avoir la) f. to have bad luck.

série noire f. run of bad luck / (lit); black series.

tuile f. unexpected bad luck / (lit); tile / *Note:* The word **tuile** has taken on this slang connotation because "unexpected bad luck" can fall on a person as unexpectedly as a tile off a roof.

BALD (chauve)

billard m. (lit); billiard.

boule de billard f. (lit); billiard ball.

caillou m. (lit); pebble.

genou m. (lit); knee.

melon déplumé (avoir le) m. (lit); to have a featherless melon.

tête de veau f. (lit); head of veal.

BARBER (coiffeur)

figaro m. *Note:* This is from Beaumarchais' *Barber of Seville*.

merlan m. (lit); whiting (fish).

pommadin m. (lit); the one who puts **pommade** in your hair / *Note:* **pommade** f. ointment.

tiffier m. (lit); the one who works with the **tifs** / *Note:* **tifs** m.pl. hair.

BAWL SOMEONE OUT, to (réprimander)

(See: **FIGHT**, to / **THRASHING***)*

attraper v. to catch.

dire ses quatre vérités à q. exp. (lit); to tell someone his four truths / **J'vais 'ui dire ses quat'vérités**; I'm going to tell him just what I think of him!

dire son fait à q. exp. same as **dire ses quatre vérités à q.** / (lit); to tell someone his fact.

engueuler v. to yell at someone / *Note:* This comes from **gueule** f. derogatory for "mouth" / (lit); mouth of an animal / This might be loosely translated as "to mouth off at someone" / *Also:* **s'engueuler: Je m'suis engueulé avec la marchande**; I yelled at the saleswoman.

enguirlander v. to chew someone out.

laver la tête à q. v. (lit); to wash someone's head.

lessiver la tête à q. v. (lit); to soap up someone's head.

mettre les pieds dans le plat exp. to give someone a piece of one's mind / (lit); to put the feet in the platter / **J'en ai marre! J'finirai par mett'les pieds dans l'plat!**; I've had it! Now, I'm going to give him (her) a piece of my mind!

passer un savon à q. v. to give someone a bawling out / (lit); to give a soaping to someone.

rembarrer v. to chew someone out royally / **Y s'est fait vertement rembarrer!** He got himself royally bawled out!

remettre q. à sa place v. (lit); to put someone in his place.

savon m. a scolding / (lit); soap(-ing).

savonnage v. same as **savon.**

savonner la tête à q. v. (lit); to soap up someone's head.

BED (lit)

paddock m. (lit); paddock.

page m.

pageot/pajot m.

pieu m. (lit); stake; post.

plumard m.

plume m.

pucier m. (lit); flea-bag.

BED, to go to (se coucher)

(See: **SLEEP,** to)

aller au schloff v. to go to bed / **schloff** is borrowed from German.

bâcher (se) v. (lit); to sheet something over; to cover with a **bâche** f. cover.

mettre au page (se) v. (lit); to put oneself into the **page** m. bed.

paddocker (se) v. ≠ **se dépaddocker;** to get out of bed.

pageoter (se) v. ≠ **se dépageoter;** to get out of bed.

pager (se) v. ≠ **se dépager;** to get out of bed.

pagnoter (se) v. ≠ **se dépagnoter;** to get out of bed.

pieuter (se) v. ≠ **se dépieuter;** to get out of bed.

plumer (se) v. ≠ **se déplumer;** to get out of bed.

BEDROOM (chambre)

cambuse f. (lit); storeroom; poorly kept room.

carrée f. (lit); square.

piaule f.

turne f. **Quelle turne!;** What a hole!

BIG WHEEL (personnage éminent)

gros bonnet m. (lit); big bonnet.

grosse légume f. (lit); big vegetable.

huile f. big wheel / (lit); oil.

singe m. the boss / (lit); monkey.

BLABBERMOUTH, to be a (être bavard)

bagout (avoir du) m. to be talkative / *Note:* **bagouler** v. to talk a lot.

bavard(e) comme une pie (être) exp. (lit); to be talkative as a magpie / *Note:* **bavarder** v. to talk a lot.

gueulard(e) n. loud blabbermouth; one who uses his **gueule** a lot / *Note:* **gueule** f. derogatory for "mouth" / (lit); mouth of animal.

langue bien pendue (avoir la) exp. (lit); to have a well-hung tongue / *Also:* **l'avoir bien pendue (l'** referring to **la langue).**

langue dans sa poche (ne pas avoir la) exp. said of someone who is talkative / (lit); not to have one's tongue in one's pocket.

moulin à paroles m. (lit); windmill of speech.

sacrée tapette (avoir une) f. (lit); to have a sacred (one helluva') tongue / *Also:* **tapette** f. homosexual (derogatory).

vacciné(e) avec une aiguille de phono (être) exp. (lit); to be vaccinated with a phonograph needle.

verbe haut (avoir le) m. (lit); to have the loud (or high) verb.

verbeux, euse adj. long-winded / (lit); to be "verby" or "verbose."

BLACK EYE (œil poché)

coquard m. slang variant of **coquelicot.**

coquelicot m. (lit); red poppy.

coquelique m. abbreviated form of **coquelicot.**

œil au beurre noir m. (lit); eye of black butter.

pavoiser v. to go around with a black eye / (lit); to be ornamented.

pocher un œil à q. v. to give someone a black eye / (lit); to poach someone's eye.

BOTCH UP (ruiner)

amocher v. (lit); to make look bad or ugly / *Note:* **moche** adj. ugly.

bousiller v. to botch up / **J'ai bousillé mon exam;** I botched my exam.

cochonner v. to do a task carelessly / *Note:* **cochon** m. pig.

fusiller v. (lit); to shoot.

massacrer v. (lit); to massacre.

rater v. to goof up.

savate f. bungler / (lit); old worn out shoe.

savater v. to bungle.

savatier m. bungler / (lit); cobbler.

torcher v. to do work too quickly and carelessly / (lit); to wipe.

torchonner v. same as **torcher.**

travailler comme un sabot exp. to work carelessly / (lit); to work (nonstop) like a shoe / *Note:* **sabot** m. shoe.

BREASTS (seins)

amortisseurs m.pl. (lit); shock absorbers.

avant-scène f. (lit); the apron of the stage that protrudes past the proscenium.

blagues à tabac f.pl. (lit); tobacco pouches.

boîtes à lait f.pl. (lit); milk bottles.

boîtes à lolo f.pl. (lit); milk bottles / *Note:* **lolo** m. child's slang for milk.

gros lolos m.pl. (lit); big milkers.

il y a du monde au balcon exp. said of a woman's large breasts / (lit); there are a lot of people on the balcony.

mandarines f.pl. tiny breasts / (lit); tangerines.

nénés m.pl. humorous slang for breasts.

nichons m.pl. extremely popular for "breasts."

œufs sur le plat m.pl. tiny breasts / (lit); fried eggs on a plate.

planche à pain f. said of a very flat chest / (lit); bread board.

planche à repasser f. said of a very flat chest / (lit); ironing board.

roberts m.pl.

rondins m.pl. (lit); log (of firewood)

roploplos m.pl.

rotoplots m.pl.

tétasses f.pl. flabby breasts.

tétons m.pl. breasts / *Note:* This is where the Grand Tetons got their names.

tettes f.pl. nipples.

tripailles f.pl. flabby breasts / (lit); intestines.

tripes f.pl. flabby breasts / (lit); intestines.

BROKE, to be (être pauvre)

argenté(e) comme une cuillière de bois (être) adj. (lit); to be silvered like a wooden spoon.

côte (être à la) f. (lit); to be on the shore (or on the rocks).

court d'argent (être à) adj. (lit); to be short of money.

débine (être dans la) f. to be in a state of poverty.

décavé(e) (être) adj. to be financially ruined / *Also:* **décaver q.** v. to clean someone out.

déchard(e) n. one who is penniless / *See:* **dèche (être dans la)**.

dèche (être dans la) adj. to be in poverty, to be stone broke.

fauché(e) (être) adj. (lit); to be reaped (clean).

fleur (être) adj. (lit); to be a flower.

misère (être dans la) f. (lit); to be in misery.

mistoufle (être dans la) f. to be in a state of poverty.

mouise (être dans la) f. to be in a state of poverty.

n'avoir pas un radis exp. to be stone broke / (lit); to be without a radish / *Note:* **radis** m. centime; cent / (lit); radish.

ne pas avoir le rond exp. (lit); to be without a round / *Note:* **rond** m. centime; cent / (lit); round thing.

purée (être dans la) f. to be financially wiped out / (lit); to be in the purée (or soup).

purotin m. slang variant of **purée**.

raidard(e) (être) adj. (lit); one who is stiff.

sans un (être) adj. (lit); to be without one.

sec (être à) adj. (lit); to be dry (of money).

tomber dans la panade exp. to fall into poverty / (lit); to fall into a bread, milk, and cheese soup.

vidé(e) (être) adj. (lit); to be emptied (of one's money).

C

CAR (voiture)

bagnole f. (*extremely popular*).
bahut m. old car; taxi.
chignole f. car in poor condition.
drôle de berlingot m. car in poor condition / (lit); pimple, boil.
guimbarde f. old broken-down car.
tacot m. old broken-down car.
tas de boue m. old car/ (lit); pile of dirt.
teuf-teuf m. onomatopoeia for the sound of a car's noisy engine.
tinette f.
tire f. (lit); puller.
vieux clou m. old car in poor condition / (lit); old nail.

CARE, not to (être égal)

balancer (s'en) v. (lit); to throw it off / **J'm'en balance!**; I don't care!
battre le coquillard (s'en) exp. (lit); to bat one's eye over it / *Note:* coquillard m. eye.
battre l'œil (s'en) exp. (lit); to bat one's eye over something.
contre-fiche (s'en) v. **J'm'en fiche et m'en contre-fiche;** I *really* don't care about it!
fiche (s'en) v. not to care at all about something.
fiche comme de sa première chausette (s'en) exp. to care about something about as much as one's first sock.
fiche comme de sa première chemise (s'en) exp. to care about something about as much as one's first shirt.
moquer (s'en) v. (lit); to mock something.
moquer du tiers comme du quart (se) exp. not to give a hoot about something / (lit); to mock the third like the quarter.
tamponner le coquilllard (s'en) v. (lit); to dab one's eye (of a fake tear) / *Note:* coquillard m. eye.

CHILD (enfant)

criard m. baby / (lit); yeller.
gamin(e) n. kid.
gavroche m. child of Paris / *See:* titi.
gosse n. kid.
lardon m. little kid; brat / (lit); piece of larding bacon; lardon.
marmaille f. screaming little brats.
mioche n. kid.

môme n. kid.
morveux m. snot-nosed little boy / *Note:* This is from **morve** f. nasal mucus.
moujingue n. kid.
moutard m. little boy.
petit salé m. newborn baby.
têtard m. (lit); tadpole.
titi m. street-wise child from Paris.

CIGARETTE (cigarette)

bombarder v. to smoke / (lit); to bombard (with cigarette smoke).
cibiche f. "cig."
clope f. (*extremely popular*).
griller une (en) v. (lit); to grill one (a cigarette).
mégot m. butt of a cigarette.
orphelin m. butt of a cigarette / (lit); orphan.
pipette f. (lit); a little pipe.
sèche f. (lit); a dry thing.
tige f. (lit); stem.

COMPLAIN, to (se plaindre)

bougonner v. to grumble / *Note:* **bougon(ne)** n. grumbler / adj. grumpy.
marmonner v. (lit); to growl; grumble.
râler v. to rattle (in one's throat) / *Note:* **râleur, euse** n. bad-tempered person.
ronchonner v. to grumble.
rouscailler v. slang variant of: **rouspéter**.
rouspéter v. (lit); to resist, protest.

CONCEITED, to be (être fat)

afficher (s') v. to show off / (lit); to poster oneself.
crâneur, euse n. braggart, show-off / *Note:* **crâner** v. to show off.
croire (se) v. to be conceited / (lit); to think (a lot) of oneself.
croire sorti(e) de la cuisse de Jupiter (se) exp. to be very conceited / (lit); to believe one has come out of Jupiter's thigh.
donner des coups de pied (ne pas se) exp. to be conceited / (lit); not to give oneself any kicks.
donner des gants (se) exp. to brag, boast / (lit); to give oneself gloves.
faire du fla-fla v. to show off.
faire le flambard v. to show off / (lit); to act like a conceited person.
faiseur m. conceited person / (lit); doer.
fanfaron m. braggart.
fanfaronner v. to brag.
frimeur, euse n. braggart.
m'as-tu-vu m. show-off.
plastronner v. (lit); to throw out one's chest, to swagger.
poseur m. conceited person.

CONFESS, to (avouer)

cracher v. (lit); to spit (the truth).
cracher le morceau v. (lit); to spit the piece (of information).
déballonner (se) v. (lit); to let the air out of the balloon.
déboutonner (se) v. to get something off one's chest / (lit); to unbutton oneself.
goualer v. (lit); This is slang for "to sing."
manger le morceau v. (lit); to eat the piece (of information).
mettre à table (se) v. to confess / (lit); to set oneself down at the table.
vider son sac v. to get something off one's chest / (lit); to empty one's sack.

CRY, to (pleurer)

brailler v. to bawl; shout (of child) / *Also:* **brailler une chanson**; to sing a song.
chialer v. (*extremely popular*).
couiner v. (lit); to whimper; squeak or squeal.
ouvrir les écluses exp. (lit); to open the flood gates.
piailler v. (lit); to whimper (of children); to chirp (of small birds) / *Also:* **enfant piailleur** m. cry-baby.
piauler v. (lit); to whimper (of children); to chirp (of small birds).
pleurer comme un veau exp. to cry heavily; to blubber / (lit); to cry like a calf.
pleurer comme une madeleine exp. to cry heavily; to blubber.
verser des larmes de crocodile exp. (lit); to pour crocodile tears.

D

DARLING (chéri)

bobonne f. "honey."
chéri(e) coco n. "sweetie-pie."
cocotte f. **ma cocotte**; my darling. / *Also:* **mon coco** m.
chou m. (lit); cabbage.
chouchou(te) n. **mon chouchou**; my "honey-bunch" / (lit); one's favorite or preferred person / **Le chouchou du professeur**; The teacher's pet.
loulou(te) n. **Bonjour loulou**; Hello "sweetheart."
mon p'tit chou en sucre m. (lit); my little sugar cabbage.
mon p'tit chou en susucre m. *Note:* **susucre** m. is baby talk for "sugar."

DIE, to (mourir)

au bout de son rouleau (être) exp. to be near death / (lit); to be at the end of one's roller.
avaler sa chique exp. (lit); to swallow one's quid (of tobacco).
avaler sa langue exp. (lit); to swallow one's tongue.
avaler son extrait de naissance exp. (lit); to swallow one's birth certificate.
calancher v. "to croak."

casser sa pipe exp. (lit); to break one's pipe.

clamser v. "to croak."

clapoter v. "to croak."

claquer v. "to croak" / (lit); to slam shut.

déposer son bilan exp. (lit); to file one's petition (in bankruptcy).

dévisser son billard exp. (lit); to unscrew one's billiard / *Note:* **billard** m. head.

éteindre son gas exp. (lit); to turn off one's gas.

faire le grand saut exp. (lit); to make the big jump.

faire le grand voyage exp. (lit); to make the big trip.

faire un costume de bois (se) exp. (lit); to make oneself a costume of wood.

habiller de quatre planches (s') exp. (lit); to dress oneself in four boards.

lâcher la perle exp. (lit); to let go of the pearl.

lâcher la rampe exp. (lit); to let go of the ramp.

l'article de la mort (être à) exp. to be at death's door.

les pieds devant (s'en aller) exp. (lit); to go feet first.

manger les pissenlits par la racine exp. (lit); to eat dandelions by the root.

passer l'arme à gauche exp. (lit); to pass the arm(s) to the left.

perdre le goût du pain exp. (lit); to lose the taste of bread.

pied dans la tombe (avoir un) exp. (lit); to have one foot in the grave.

poser sa chique exp. (lit); to put down one's quid (of tobacco).

DOG (chien)

cabot m. *Also:* a bad actor.

chienchien m. term of endearment for a dog; doggy.

chiot m. puppy.

clébard m.

clebs m. (pronounced "klèps").

roquet m. dog that barks a lot; ill-tempered dog.

toutou m. baby talk for "dog."

DRESS, to (s'habiller)

accoutrer (s') v. to dress oneself ridiculously.

affubler (s') v. to dress oneself strangely and ridiculously.

attifer (s') v. to dress oneself strangely and ridiculously.

débraillé(e) (être) adj. to be dressed poorly; to have an untidy appearance.

dépenaillé(e) (être) adj. Same as **débraillé(e) (être)**.

endimancher (s') v. to dress well, in one's Sunday best / *Note:* This comes from dimanche m. Sunday.

fagoter (se) v. to dress without taste, poorly.

fichu(e) comme l'as de pique (être) exp. said of a poorly dressed individual / (lit); to be put together like the ace of spades.

fringuer (se) v. to dress oneself / *Note:* **fringues** f.pl. clothes.

mal ficelé(e) adj. poorly dressed / (lit); badly strung together.

nipper (se) v. to dress oneself / *Note:* **nippes** f.pl. clothes.

sapper (se) v. to dress oneself / *Note:* **sappes** f.pl. clothes.

DRINK, to (boire)

biberonner v. to tipple; booze it up / *Note:* This comes from **biberon** m. feed-bottle.
boire en suisse exp. to drink alone / (lit); to drink Swiss style.
boire à tire-larigot exp. to drink like a fish.
boire comme un sonneur exp. to drink a lot / (lit); to drink like a bell-ringer.
boire comme un templier exp. to drink a lot / (lit); to drink like a (Knight) Templar.
boire comme un tonneau exp. to drink a lot / (lit); to drink like a barrel.
boire comme un trou exp. to drink a lot / (lit); to drink like a hole.
boire comme une éponge exp. to drink a lot / (lit); to drink like a sponge.
boire la goutte exp. to drink a little glass of an alcoholic beverage / (lit); to drink the drop.
boire tout son soûl exp. to drink oneself under the table / *Note:* **soûl(e)** adj. drunk.
boire un pot exp. to have a drink / (lit); to drink a pot.
boire un coup exp. to have a drink / (lit); to drink a hit.
caresser la bouteille exp. to tipple / (lit); to caress the bottle.
chopiner v. to tipple / *Note:* **chope** f. beer mug.
étouffer un (en) v. to have a drink / (lit); to choke down one (a drink).
faire suisse exp. same as **boire en suisse**.
gosier blindé (avoir le) exp. to have a throat that can handle the strongest liquors / (lit); to have the numbed throat / *Note:* **gosier** m. throat.
humecter les amygdales (s') exp. to wet one's whistle / (lit); to moisten one's tonsils.
jeter un coup derrière le bouton de col (s'en) exp. (lit); to throw one (a drink) behind the collar button.
jeter un derrière la cravate (s'en) exp. (lit); to throw one (a drink) behind the tie.
lamper v. to swig.
laper v. (lit); to lap up.
lever le coude exp. (lit); to lift the elbow (with a drink).
licher v. *Note:* This slang synonym for "to drink" is often heard as **pourliche** m. waiter's tip (from **pourboire**).
picoler v. to tipple / *Note:* **pictance** f. booze.
pictonner v. same as **picoler**.
pilier de cabaret m. habitual drinker; one who is always found in bars / (lit); a cabaret pillar.
pinter (se) v. to drink a lot; to get drunk / (lit); to drink by the pint.
pocharder (se) v. to drink a lot; to get drunk.
pomper v. (lit); to pump it down.
rincer le sifflet (se) exp. (lit); to rinse one's throat / *Note:* **sifflet** m. throat.
siffler un coup exp. (lit); to whistle (up) a hit.
siffler un godet exp. (lit); to whistle (up) a glass / *Note:* **godet** m. glass.
siroter v. (lit); to sip.

DRUNK, to be (être ivre)

allumé(e) (être) adj. (lit); to be lit up.
beurré(e) (être) adj. (lit); to be buttered.

blindé(e) (être) adj. (lit); to be numbed.

bourré(e) (être) adj. (lit); to be stuffed (with booze).

brindezingue (être) adj. (lit); to be loaded.

chargé(e) (être) adj. (lit); to be loaded.

cuité(e) (être) adj. (lit); to be "baked" / *See:* **prendre une cuite.**

dalle en pente (avoir la) exp. (lit); to have the throat on a slant (in order to be able to drink constantly).

dans les vignes du Seigneur (être) exp. (lit); to be in the vines of the Lord.

ébreché(e) (être) adj. (lit); to be chipped.

éméché(e) (être) adj. to be slightly drunk, "buzzed."

émoustillé(e) (être) adj. (lit); to be exhilarated.

empoivrer (s') v. to start to get drunk / (lit); to pepper oneself / *See:* **poivrer / poivre / poivrot.**

ému(e) (être) adj. to be slightly drunk; to be "buzzed" / (lit); to be moved.

en goguette (être) adj. to be slightly drunk.

en plein cirage (être) adj. to be bombed off one's rocker / (lit); to be in complete wax.

en ribote (être) adj. to be tipsy.

entre deux vins (être) adj. (lit); to be between two wines.

gai (être) adj. (lit); to be happy.

gris(e) (être) adj. to be "buzzed"; to be on the verge of blacking out or becoming noir / *See:* **noir(e) (être).**

gueule de bois (avoir la) adj. to have a hangover / (lit); to have the mouth of wood / *Note:* **gueule** f. derogatory for "mouth"; (lit); mouth of an animal / *Also:* **avoir la G.D.B.,** *gueule de bois* (pronounced **jé, dé, bé**).

lancé(e) (être) adj. (lit); to be thrown (into a drunken state).

mal aux cheveux (avoir) adj. to have a hangover / (lit); to have a hairache.

monté(e) (être) adj. (lit); to be lifted (to a drunken state).

mûr(e) (être) adj. (lit); to be ripe.

nez piqué (avoir le) adj. to have a red nose from drinking too much / (lit); to have the nose that has been stung.

noir(e) (être) adj. to be bombed / (lit); to be black (or ready to blackout).

noircir (se) v. to get bombed / (lit); to become black (or in the blackout stage).

paf (être) adj. to be bombed.

parti(e) (être) adj. to be bombed / (lit); to be gone.

piquer le nez (se) exp. to get bombed / (lit); to get a reddened nose.

plein(e) (être) adj. to be bombed / (lit); to be full (of booze).

plein(e) comme un boudin (être) exp. (lit); to be full as a blood sausage.

plein(e) comme un bourrique (être) exp. (lit); to be full as a donkey.

plein(e) comme une huître (être) exp. (lit); to be full as an oyster.

plein(e) comme un œuf (être) exp. (lit); to be full as an egg.

pochard(e) n. drunkard / (lit); one who poaches.

poivre (être) adj. to be on the verge of getting drunk / (lit); to be pepper(ed) / *Note:* The steps of drunkness (or to becoming **noir**) are: after a few drinks one might be a little **poivre** (pepper), then **gris** (gray), and finally **noir** (black or "close to blacking out").

poivrer (se) v. to get drunk / *See:* **poivre.**

poivrot m. drunkard / *See:* **poivre**.

pompette (être) adj. to be slightly drunk / *Note:* This is from **pomper** v. to drink / (lit); to pump.

prendre une cuite exp. to get drunk / (lit); to get baked.

raide (être) adj. to be bombed / (lit); to be stiff.

rétamé(e) (être) adj. to be looped / (lit); to be re-silvered.

rond(e) (être) adj. to be drunk / (lit); to be round.

rond(e) comme une queue de pelle (être) exp. to be bombed off one's rocker / (lit); to be round (drunk) as a shovel handle.

salir le nez (se) v. to get drunk / (lit); to get one's nose dirty.

soiffard(e) n. one who is always thirsty for a drink / *Note:* This is from **soif** m. thirst.

soûl(e) (être) adj. to be drunk / (lit); to be gorged.

soûl(e) comme trente-six mille hommes (être) adj. to be dead drunk / (lit); to be gorged (drunk) as 36,000 men.

soûl(e) comme une bourrique (être) adj. to be dead drunk / (lit); to be gorged (drunk) as a donkey.

soûlard(e) n. drunkard.

soûlographie f. drunken state.

soûlot m. drunkard.

soûler (se) v. to get drunk / (lit); to gorge oneself (with booze).

sous la table (être) exp. to be dead drunk / (lit); to be under the table.

teinté(e) (être) adj. to be "buzzed" / (lit); to be tinted.

vent dans les voiles (avoir du) exp. to be slightly drunk / (lit); to have wind in one's sails.

verre dans le nez (avoir un) exp. (lit); to have a glass in one's nose.

E

EARS (oreilles)

cliquettes f.pl.

écoutilles f.pl. "listeners" / *Note:* This is from **écouter** v. to listen.

esgourdes f.pl. *Note:* **esgourder** v. to listen.

feuilles f.pl. (lit); leaves.

feuilles de chou f.pl. large ears / (lit); cabbage leaves.

portugaises f.pl. (lit); Portuguese oysters.

voiles f.pl. large ears / (lit); sails.

EASY (facile)

aller comme sur des roulettes exp. to work out smoothly / (lit); to go as if on wheels.

bête comme chou (c'est) exp. "It's easy as pie" / (lit); it's silly as cabbage.

bonne franquette (à la) exp. simply, without fuss / **dîner à la bonne franquette**; to eat simply.

ça passe comme une lettre à la poste exp. said of something that is easy to do / (lit); it goes through (as easy as) a letter to the post office.

c'est pas sorcier exp. / (lit); there is no wizardry in that.

c'est pas la mer à boire exp. (lit); it's not like drinking the ocean.

couru d'avance (c'est) exp. "It's as good as done" / (lit); it's already run.

dans le sac (c'est) exp. (lit); it's in the bag.

doigts dans le nez (les) exp. easily / **Y peut l'faire les doigts dans l'nez;** He can do it easily / (lit); the fingers in the nose.

du beurre (c'est) exp. (lit); it's butter.

du billard (c'est) exp. said of something that goes along as smoothly as a billiard ball / (lit); it's billiard.

du fromage (c'est) exp. (lit); it's cheese.

du velours (c'est) exp. (lit); it's velvet.

gâteau (c'est du) exp. (lit); it's cake.

les mains dans la poche exp. easily / **Y peut l'faire les mains dans la poche;** He can do it easily / (lit); the hands in the pocket.

sans autre forme de procès exp. without further ceremony, without further ado / (lit); without further process.

sans faire ni une ni deux exp. easily, without ceremony / (lit); without doing either one or two.

sans tambour ni trompette exp. easily, without ceremony / (lit); without drum or trumpet.

simple comme bonjour (c'est) exp. (lit); simple as good day.

sucre (c'est du) exp. (lit); it's sugar.

sur une jambe (se faire) exp. said of something easy to do / (lit); to happen on one leg.

EAT, to (manger)

(See: **FOOD)**

bâfrer v. to eat a lot; "scarf out," "pork out."

becqueter v. (lit); (of birds) to peck at something/ **E becquète sans arrêt;** She eats nonstop.

bombance (faire) f. to have a blow-out of a meal; to pork out.

bon coup de fourchette (avoir un) exp. to have a hearty appetite / (lit); to have a good "touch" of the fork.

bouffer v. *Note:* **bouffer** literally means "to bolt down food" but is now used to mean "to eat" in general and is *extremely* popular.

bouffer à s'en faire crever la peau du ventre exp. to overeat / (lit); to eat to the point of bursting the skin of the stomach.

boulotter v. to eat / *Note:* **boulot(te)** adj. fat.

bourrer (se) v. (lit); to stuff oneself (with food).

boustifailler v. to eat or eat a lot / *Note:* **boustifaille** f. good; grub.

briffer v. to eat / *Note:* **briffe** f. food; grub.

caler les amygdales (se) exp. (lit); to steady one's tonsils (by eating food).

caler les badigoinces (se) exp. (lit); to steady one's lips (by eating food) / *Note:* **badigoinces** f.pl. slang for "lips."

caler les joues (se) exp. (lit); to steady one's cheeks (by eating food).

caler l'estomac (se) exp. (lit); to steady one's stomach (by eating food).

casser la croûte exp. to break bread / (lit); to break crust.

casser la graine exp. to break bread / (lit); to break grain.

coller plein la lampe (s'en) exp. to have a huge meal / (lit); to stick lots of it (food) to the stomach / *Note:* **lampe** f. stomach / (lit); lamp / *Also:* **s'en mettre plein la lampe**.

croquer v. (lit); to crunch.

croûter v. to snack; to break bread or "crust" / *Note:* This is from **croûte** f. crust.

empiffrer (s') v. (lit); to cram, stuff (with food).

festin m. delicious meal of high elegance; feast.

festoyer v. to feast or to have a **festin**.

fourrer jusque là (s'en) exp. to eat to one's capacity / (lit); to stuff oneself with it (food) up to there.

gaver (se) v. (lit); to stuff or force feed.

goberger (se) v. to feast.

godailler v. to gormandize, to feast.

goinfrer (se) v. to guzzle, gorge / *Note:* **goinfre** m. one who overeats; "porker."

grignoter v. to nibble at one's food.

gueuletonner v. to feast, to pork out / *Note:* **gueuleton** m. huge meal.

manger sur le pouce exp. to grab a bite on the run / (lit); to eat on the thumb.

mettre plein la panse (s'en) exp. (lit); to fill up the stomach with it (food) / *Note:* **panse** f. stomach.

mettre une ventrée (s'en) exp. to eat a lot; to pork out / *Note:* **ventrée** f. belly full / This comes from **ventre** m. "belly."

picorer v. to pick at one's food / (lit); (of birds) to scratch about for food.

pignocher v. (lit); to pick at one's food.

régaler (se) v. to feast.

ripaille (faire) f. to feast; to pork out.

ripailler v. to feast; to pork out.

ronger v. (lit); to nibble, gnaw.

taper la cloche (se) exp. to eat well / (lit); to make one's bell ring (with joy from eating).

tortorer v. to eat / *Note:* **tortore** f. food, grub.

ENERGETIC, to be (être énergique)

allant (avoir de l') m. to have plenty of get-up-and-go / (lit); to have "go."

attaque (être d') f. to have plenty of get-up-and-go / (lit); to be (full) of attack.

bougeotte (avoir la) f. to be fidgety / (lit); to have the "budges" / *Note:* **bougeotte** f. This comes from **bouger** v. to move; to budge.

cracher le feu exp. to be very energetic / (lit); to spit fire.

péter le feu exp. to be very energetic / (lit); to fart fire.

dégourdi(e) (être) adj. to be wide awake / (lit); to be revived or "un-numbed."

dégourdir (se) v. to become energetic / (lit); to become revived or "un-numbed."

sang dans les veines (avoir du) exp. (lit); to have blood in the veins.

vif argent dans ses veines (avoir du) exp. (lit); to have quicksilver in one's veins.

EXAGGERATE, to (exagérer)

aller fort v. to go strongly.

aller mal v. to go badly.

allez! exclam. "stop exaggerating!"; "come on!" / *Note:* Although **allez** is commonly used as the second person plural of the verb **aller** meaning "to go," it may also be used in this context when speaking to only *one* person.

attiger v. to exaggerate.

char m. exaggeration / *Note 1:* This comes from the slang verb **charrier** meaning "to exaggerate" / *Note 2:* The noun **char** also has the literal meaning of "chariot." / *Note 3:* **Arrête ton char!** is commonly used to mean "stop your exaggerating" but since it also means "stop your chariot," the French decided to play up this double meaning by inventing the expression: **Arrête ton char, Ben Hur!**; Stop your chariot, Ben Hur! (The French pronounce "Ben" the same way as in English, and the "h" in "Hur" is silent: "Benur") This play on words is perhaps one of the most famous in the French repertoire.

charrier v. to get carried away in telling a story / (lit); to cart, carry, transport.

cherrer v. to exaggerate.

cherrer dans les bégonias exp. (lit); to exaggerate in the begonias.

EYES (yeux)

carreaux m.pl. (lit); small squares.

châsses m.pl. (lit); frame (of spectacles).

globes m.pl. (lit); globes.

lanternes f.pl. (lit); lanterns.

mirettes f.pl. *Note:* **mirer** v. to see.

quinquets m.pl. *Note:* especially used with **ouvrir** and **fermer** / **Le bébé, y a fermé les quinquets**; The baby closed his eyes.

FACE (visage)

Note:

Many of the slang synonyms for "face" are same for "head" / *See:* **HEAD**

balle f. face; head / (lit); ball.

bille f. face; head / (lit); small ball.

binette f. face; head / (lit); hoe.

bobine f. face; head / (lit); bobine, spool, reel.

bouille f. face; head / **Elle a une bonne bouille**; She has a nice face.

bouillotte f. face; head / (lit); hot-water bottle.

boule f. face; head / (lit); ball.

burette f. face; head / (lit); oil-can.

fiole f. face; head / (lit); phial, flask.

fraise f. face; head / (lit); strawberry.

frimousse f. nice, roguish little face.

gaufre f. face; head / (lit); waffle / *Note:* **se sucrer le gaufre**; to put on make-up / (lit); to sugar the waffle.

gueule f. (derogatory) head; mouth; face (lit); mouth of an animal.

hure f. face; head / (lit); head (of boar, pig).

margoulette f. "mug; kisser."

minois m. pretty face (of child, young woman).

poire f. face; head / (lit); pear.

porte-pipe m. (lit); pipe-rack.

portrait m. face; head / (lit); portrait.

trogne f. face of a drinker; bloated face.

trombine f. funny face or head.

trompette f. face; head / (lit); trumpet.

tronche f. face; head / (lit); log.

FALL, to (tomber)

casser son verre de montre exp. (lit); to break the face of one's watch.

chuter v. to fall hard / (lit); to chute.

étaler (s') v. (lit); to display oneself; to spread, stretch, sprawl oneself out (in an armchair, etc.).

fiche la gueule par terre (se) exp. to hit one's face on the ground / *Note:* **gueule** f. derogatory for "mouth" or "face" / (lit); mouth of an animal.

plaquer par terre (se) exp. to flatten oneself out on the ground.

prendre un billet de parterre exp. (lit); to take a ticket from the orchestra pit.

ramasser une bûche exp. (lit); to pick up a log.

ramasser une pelle exp. (lit); to pick up a shovel.

viander (se) v. (lit); to spread out one's "meat" (in a fall), to "meat" oneself / *Note:* This is from **viande** f. meat.

FAST, to (jeûner)

(See: **EAT**, to)

ballon (faire) m. (lit); to do the balloon / *Note:* **ballon** m. stomach / (lit); balloon.

becqueter (bouffer) des briques exp. (lit); to eat bricks / *Note:* **becqueter/bouffer** v. to eat.

becqueter (bouffer) des clarinettes exp. (lit); to eat tools / *Note 1:* **clarinettes** f.pl. tools in general / *Note 2:* **becqueter/bouffer** v. to eat.

brosser le ventre (se) exp. (lit); to brush one's stomach.

manger avec les chevaux de bois exp. (lit); to eat with the wooden horses.

serrer la ceinture (se) exp. (lit); to tighten the belt.

FED UP, to be (en avoir assez)

basta (en avoir) exp. (lit); to have had enough / **J'en ai basta!**; I've had it! / *Note:* **basta** adv. enough; This is borrowed from Italian / *Also:* **C'est basta!** or **Basta!**; That's enough! Enough!

classe (en avoir) exp. J'en ai classe!; I've had it! / *Also:* **C'est classe!**; That's enough!
marre (en avoir) exp. J'en ai marre!; I've had it! / *Also* **C'est marre!**; That's enough!
par-dessus la tête (en avoir) exp. (lit); to have had it above the head.
plein le dos (en avoir) exp. (lit); to have had a backfull.
plein les bottes (en avoir) exp. (lit); to have had a bootfull.
ras le bol (en avoir) exp. (lit); to have had it to the rim of the bowl.
sa claque (en avoir) exp. to have had it / **J'en ai ma claque!**; I've had it!
soupé (en avoir) exp. (lit); to have eaten some for dinner; "to have taken in all one can."

FEEL BLAH, to (se sentir dans un état de faiblesse)

dans son assiette (ne pas être) exp. (lit); not to be in one's plate.
dans son train (ne pas être) exp. (lit); to be out of pace.
raplapla (se sentir) adj. to feel "blah."
tout chose (se sentir) adj. to feel "out of it."
vaseux (se sentir) adj. (lit); to feel muddy.

FEET (pieds)

argasses f.pl.
arpions m.pl.
artous m.pl.
bateaux m.pl. large feet / (lit); boats.
nougats m.pl. (lit); nuggets.
panards m.pl.
patins m.pl. (lit); skates.
paturons m.pl. (lit); pastern (of horse).
pinceaux m.pl. (lit); paint-brush.
pingots m.pl. abbreviated form of **pingouins**.
pingouins m.pl. (lit); penguins
radis m.pl. toes / (lit); radishes.
raquettes f.pl. (lit); rackets.
ripatons m.pl. *Note:* **ripatonner** v. to walk.

FIGHT, to (se battre)

accrocher avec q. (s') v. (lit); to hook oneself with someone (in a fight).
avoir des mots avec q. exp. (lit); to have words with someone.
bagarrer (se) v. to fight; to scuffle, to brawl / *Note:* **bagarre** f. fight; scuffle, brawl.
baroud m. (pronounced "baroude") military slang for "fight."
battre à plate(s) couture(s) exp. to beat to a pulp / (lit); to beat to a flat fashion.
battre q. comme plâtre exp. (lit); to beat someone into plaster.
bigorner (se) v. to fight / *Note:* **bigorne** f. battle.
casser la gueule à q. exp. (lit); to break someone's face / *Note:* **gueule** f. derogatory for "mouth" / (lit); mouth of an animal.
chamailler (se) v. to fight loudly over stupid little things; to bicker, squabble.

chercher à q. des poux dans la tête exp. to look for a fight, to nitpick / (lit); to look for lice in someone's head.

chercher chicane à q. exp. to look for a fight / *Note:* **chicane** f. quibbling, quarreling.

chercher la petite bête exp. to be overcritical; to nitpick / (lit); to look for the little beast.

chercher noise à q. exp. to look for a fight / *Note:* **noise** f. quibbling, quarreling.

chercher querelle à q. exp. to look for a fight / (lit); to look for a quarrel with someone.

chicaner v. to fight / *Note:* **chicane** f. quibbling, quarreling.

colleter (se) v. to grapple, scuffle with someone.

coltiner (se) v. to fight / **Je m'suis coltiné avec un mec;** I had it out with a guy / *Also:* **se coltiner** also means "to do" or "to carry out" / **J'peux pas m'coltiner seul tout c'travail;** I can't do all this work by myself.

corrida f. free-for-all fight.

coup de chien m. free-for-all fight / (lit); dog fight.

échauffourrée f. free-for-all fight; scuffle / *Note:* This comes from **chauffer** v. to heat up.

en bisbille avec q. (être) adj. to be in a dumb little quarrel with someone / *Note:* **bisbille** f. bickering.

en venir aux coups exp. (lit); to come to blows over something.

en venir aux mains exp. (lit); to come to hands (or fisticuffs) over something.

fiche sur la gueule (se) exp. to hit someone in the mouth / (lit); to throw each other on the mouth / *Note 1:* **fiche** v. to throw; to do / *Note 2:* **gueule** f. derogatory for "mouth" / (lit); mouth of an animal.

grabuge m. big fight; squabbling / **Y aura du grabuge!;** There's gonna be a fight!

manger le nez (se) exp. to fight / (lit); to eat each other's nose / This humorous expression describes two people yelling at each other extremely close to each other's face. / *Also:* **se bouffer le nez** / *Note:* **bouffer** v. to eat.

mettre q. en capilotade exp. to knock the stuffing out of someone / *Note:* **capilotade** f. jelly.

ne rêver que plaies et bosses exp. said of a person who is always ready for a fight / (lit); to dream only of sores and bruises.

peigner (se) v. humorous for "to fight" / (lit); to comb each other's hair / **Y s'peignent comme d'habitude;** They're at it again as usual.

piler v. to beat / (lit); to pound, crush / **Notre équipe, è s'est fait piler!;** Our team got whipped!

rififi m. free-for-all fight; scuffle.

tabasser v. to beat up / *Also:* **passer q. à tabac.**

triquer v. to beat up with a stick / *Note:* This comes from **trique** f. big club used to hit.

FIRE ONE FROM OFFICE, to (mettre q. à la porte)

aller à la pêche exp. to be jobless / (lit); to go fishing.

bain (envoyer au) m. (lit); to send to the bath.

balancer v. to throw, chuck / (lit); to balance.

balanstiquer v. slang variant of **balancer.**

baller (envoyer) v. (lit); to send someone rolling like a ball.

bouler (envoyer) v. (lit); to send someone rolling like a ball.

débarquer v. (lit); to discharge, unship.

déboulonner v. to take away someone's job or **boulot** / *Note:* **boulot** m. job.

dégommer v. (lit); to ungum or unstick someone (from their job).

diable (envoyer au) m. (lit); to send to the devil.

dinguer (envoyer) v. (used only with **envoyer**) / (lit); to fling away.

flanquer q. à la porte exp. (lit); to throw at the door / *Note:* **flanquer** v. to throw, chuck.

limoger v. to fire; to demote.

paître (envoyer) v. (lit); to send someone grazing.

pelotes (envoyer aux) f.pl. (lit); to send someone rolling like a ball / *Note:* **pelote** f. ball (used in the game **pelotes**).

sacquer q. v. (lit); to sack someone.

suer (envoyer) v. (lit); to send someone sweating.

sur les roses (envoyer) exp. (lit); to send someone on the roses (with thorns).

vider q. v. (lit); to empty someone.

virer q. v. (lit); to turn someone around (in the opposite direction of their work place).

FLATTER, to (flatter)

musicien m. flatterer, softsoap artist.

passer de la pommade à q. exp. to flatter; to butter up / (lit); to give ointment to someone.

passer la main dans les cheveux exp. (lit); to give someone the hand in the air.

FOOD (nourriture)

(*See:* **EAT,** to)

bectance f. "grub" / *Note:* **becqueter** v. to eat, to chow down / (lit); (of birds) to peck at something.

bouffe f. "grub" / *Note:* **bouffer** v. to eat, "to chow down."

bouffetance f. slang variant of **bouffe**.

boustifaille f. slang variant of **bouffe** / *Note:* **boustifailler** v. to eat, "to chow down."

boustiffe f. slang variant of **bouffe**.

briffe f. "grub" / *Note:* **briffer** v. to eat, "to chow down."

croûte f. (lit); crust / *Note:* **croûter** v. to eat, to break bread (or crust in this case) / *Also:* **casser la croûte** exp. to break bread.

frichti m. "grub."

fricot m. "grub."

mangeaille f. "eats" / *Note:* This is from the verb **manger** v. to eat.

ragougnasse f. bad food / *Note:* This is from **ragoût** m. stew.

tambouille f. bad food / *Note:* Originally, this was used only as military slang.

tortore f. food in general / *Note:* **tortorer** v. to eat.

FUNNY (amusant)

(*See:* **LAUGH,** to)

bidonnant(e) adj. that which causes the **bidon** to move with laughter / *Note 1:* **bidon** m. stomach, belly / *Note 2:* **se bidonner** v. to belly laugh.

boyautant(e) adj. that which causes the **boyaux** to move with laughter; a real gut-splitter / *Note 1:* **boyaux** m.pl. guts / *Note 2:* **se boyauter** v. to laugh.

désopilant(e) adj. screamingly funny / *Note:* **se désopiler** v. to shake with laughter.

gondolant(e) adj. excruciatingly funny / **se gondoler** v. to shake with laughter / (lit); to warp; to buckle up (with laughter).

marrant(e) adj. (*extremely popular*) very funny; strange / *Note 1:* This is used in the same way as the English word "funny." Its definition is twofold, meaning "that which makes one laugh" and "that which is odd or strange" / *Note 2:* **se marrer** v. to laugh hard.

poilant(e) adj. very funny / *Note 1:* It could be loosely translated as "that which causes one's hair (**poil**) to shake with laughter" / *Note 2:* **se poiler** v. to laugh hard.

pouffant(e) adj. extremely funny / *Note 1:* A loose literal translation of this might be "that which causes one's belly to puff up (**pouffer**) as one takes in air to laugh" / *Note 2:* **se pouffer** v. to laugh hard.

rigolard(e) adj. happy, light-hearted; funny / *Note:* **rigoler** v. to laugh.

rigolboche adj. slang variant of **rigolard(e)**.

rigolo(te) adj. slang variant of **rigolard(e)**.

roulant(e) adj. extremely funny / *Note:* A loose literal translation of this might be "that which causes one to roll (**rouler**) with laughter" / **se rouler** v. to laugh hard.

tirebouchonnant(e) adj. extremely funny / *Note 1:* A loose literal translation of this might be "that which causes one to rise up and down like a corkscrew (**un tire-bouchon**) as one takes in air repeatedly in order to laugh" / *Note 2:* **se tirebouchonner** v. to laugh hard.

G

GIBBERISH (bavardage)

baragouin m. *Note:* **baragouiner** v. to jabber.

bla-bla-bla m. constant jabber.

cancan m. *Note 1:* This is usually seen as **colporter des cancans sur q.**; to spread rumors about someone / *Note 2:* **cancanier, ière** n. one who spreads rumors or gossip.

causette f. little chat / **faire la causette avec q.**; to have a little chat with someone / *Note:* **causer** v. to chat.

charabia m. jargon, gibberish / **J'comprends pas son charabia**; I don't understand his gibberish.

et patati et patata exp. yackety-yack / *Note:* This is an onomatopoeia for the sound one makes when jabbering on and on / **Et patati, et patata! Z'arrêtent jamais d'parler!**; Yackety-yack! They never stop talking!

jacasserie f. *Note:* **jacasser** v. to talk gibberish.

papotage m. idle talk; chatter / **Y perd son temps en papotages**; He spends his time gabbing / *Note:* **papoter** v. to talk gibberish.

parlotte f. little chat / **faire la parlotte avec une voisine**; to have a little chat with a neighbor / same as **causette**.

potin m. piece of gossip / **potins** m.pl. gossip / **faire des potins sur q.**; to tell little rumors about someone.

racontars m.pl. rumors / *Note:* This is from **raconter** v. to tell, to recount.

ragot m. same as **potin**.

verbiage m. nothing but talk, gibberish; hogwash / **Tu vas écouter c'te verbiage?**; You're going to listen to that bunk?

GIFTED FOR, to be (avoir le don pour)

avoir la bosse de qch. exp. (lit); to have the bump for something / **Y a la bosse du piano**; He has a knack for piano. / *Note:* This comes from phrenology: the study of the conformation of the skull based on the belief that it is indicative of mental faculties.

avoir le chic pour qch. exp. (lit); to have the skill (or knack) for something.

avoir le truc pour qch. exp. (lit); to have the "thing" for something.

GIRL (fille)

Note:

The synonyms for "girl" are all derogatory. Pay special attention to their explanations to get a good feeling for their weight.

beau brin de fille m. good-looking girl / (lit); nice little bit of girl.

beau châssis m. well-built girl / (lit); nice chassis.

bergère f. (lit); shepherdess.

bêtasse f. dumb girl / *Note:* **bête** adj. dumb, stupid.

bien balancée adj. said of a girl with a good figure / (lit); well-tossed.

bien faite de sa personne adj. said of a good-looking girl / (lit); well-made of her person.

bien fichue adj. said of a girl with a good body / (lit); well-made / *Note:* **fiche** v. to make; / past participle: **fichu(e)**.

bien roulée adj. said of a girl with a good body / (lit); well-rolled (together).

bonne femme f. (*extremely popular*) woman / (lit); good woman.

boudin m. heavy and unattractive woman / (lit); blood sausage.

cateau f. girl of easy morals; loose.

catin f. same as **cateau**.

cato f. same as **cateau**.

coureuse f. girl of loose morals who gets around / (lit); runner.

dévoreuse f. girl who is thirsty for love, who needs to devour as much love as she can / *Note:* **dévorer** v. to devour.

dondon f. fat woman or girl.

donzelle f. a pretentious, showy girl.

dragon m. shrew / (lit); dragon.

femelle f. "broad" / (lit); female.

femme à passions f. loose woman or girl / (lit); woman of passion(s).

gigolette f. girl of easy morals; loose / *Note:* This is the feminine form of **gigolo**.

gonzesse f. (*extremely popular*) woman or girl / "chick."

gourgandine f. girl or easy morals; loose.

grande bringue f. tall and lanky woman / (lit); big piece or bit.

grande perche f. tall and lanky woman / (lit); big pole.

greluche f. "chick"; pretentious girl.

grenouille f. girl of easy morals; loose / (lit); frog.
grimbiche f. young girl.
laidasse f. ugly woman / *Note:* **laid(e)** adj. ugly.
ménesse f. woman, "broad."
nana f. (*extremely popular*) "chick."
nénette f. "chick."
pépée f. (lit); doll / *Note:* This is a child's language for **poupée** f. doll.
poule f. "chick"; girlfriend; kept woman / (lit); hen.
pouliche f. young girl / (lit); filly.
poupée f. (lit); doll.
saucisson m. "blimp"; heavy woman / (lit); sausage.
sauteuse f. girl of loose morals / *Note:* **sauter** v. to jump sexually / (lit); to jump.
souris f. (lit); mouse.
typesse f. girl / *Note:* **type** m. guy.

GIVE, to (donner)

abouler v. (1) to bring / **Aboule ça ici!**; Bring that here!; (2) to hand over / **Aboule ton fric!**; Hand over your money!
fendre (se) v. to give with much pain / (lit); to split, crack, cut / **Y s'est fendu de mille francs**; He reluctantly parted with one thousand francs.
filer v. to give, to hand over.
flanquer v. (lit); to throw, chuck.
refiler v. to give someone something that is no longer wanted / **Y m'a refilé un faux billet!**; He gave me a fake bill! / **Y m'a refilé sa vieille chemise**; He handed me down his old shirt.

GOOF UP, to (faire une faute)

boulette (faire une) f. to make a blunder.
bousiller v. (1) to bungle, botch up / **J'ai bousillé mon examen**; I botched up my test; (2) to break / **J'ai bousillé ma montre**; I broke my watch.
faire quelque chose à la noix de coco exp. to bungle something up, to goof up / (lit); to do something like a coconut.
fiche dedans (se) v. to make a mistake / (lit); to throw oneself inside / *Note:* **fiche** v. to throw.
gaffe (faire une) f. to make a big mistake / *Note:* **faire gaffe** exp. to be careful / **Fais gaffe!**; Be careful!
gourer (se) v. to make a mistake.
pas de clerc (faire un) exp. (pronounced "claire") to make a blunder / (lit); to make a clerk's step.
rater v. to goof up, fail / **J'ai raté mon examen**; I goofed up my test / /*Also:* to miss / **J'ai raté l'bus**; I missed the bus.

GUY (individu)

bonhomme m. (*extremely popular*) guy.
bonne pâte f. "good egg"; person with a good personality / (lit); good dough / *Note:* **pâte molle** f. person with no personality; a zero.

chic type m. same as **bonne pâte** / *See:* **type.**

coco m. **un drôle de coco;** a strange guy.

femmelette f. weakling, sissy / *Note:* This comes from **femme** f. woman.

freluquet m. pretentious guy.

gars m. (*extremely popular*) guy.

gars bien m. same as **bonne pâte** / *Note:* It is very common in colloquial French to use the adverb **bien** as an adjective: **un film bien;** a good film, etc.

gigolo m. fancy man; gigolo / *Note:* **gigolette** f. woman of loose morals.

gonze m. "dude" / *Note:* **gonzesse** f. "chick."

greluchon m. "dude" / *Note:* **greluche** f. "chick."

lapin m. (lit); rabbit / **C't'un fameux lapin!;** He's a good egg!

mec m. (*extremely popular*) guy, "dude."

mironton m. "dude."

paltoquet m. pretentious and insignificant man.

paroissien m. (lit); parishioner.

pierrot m. (lit); sparrow.

pistolet m. (lit); pistol.

sieur m. abbreviated form of **monsieur.**

tête de pipe f. guy in general / **J'ai compté dix têtes de pipe dans la salle;** I counted ten guys in the room.

type m. (*extremely popular*) guy, individual / *Note:* **typesse** f. "chick."

zèbre m. guy / (lit); zebra.

zigomar m. "dude."

zigoto m. "dude."

zigue m. "dude."

H

HANDS (mains)

cuillères f.pl. (lit); spoons.

louches f.pl. (lit); soup-ladles.

patoches f.pl. slang variant of **pattes.**

pattes f.pl. (lit); paws.

pinces f.pl. (lit); pinchers.

pognes f.pl. *Note:* Commonly used as **passer la pogne;** to shake hands and make up.

HEAD (tête)

Note:

Many of the slang synonyms for "head" are the same for "face" / *See:* **face.**

balle f. head; face / (lit); ball.

bille f. head; face / (lit); small ball.

bobèche f. head; face / (lit); socket (of candle stick).

bobéchon m. same as **bobèche.**

bobine f. head; face / (lit); bobbin.
bougie f. (lit); candle.
bouille f. head; face.
bouillotte f. head; face / (lit); hot-water bottle.
boule f. head; face / (lit); ball.
boussole f. (lit); compass.
bulbe f. (lit); bulb.
burette f. head; face / (lit); oil-can.
cabèche f.
caboche f.
cafetière f. (lit); coffeepot.
caillou m. (lit); pebble.
carafe f. (lit); carafe.
carafon m. (lit); small carafe.
cassis m. (pronounced "kassisse") / (lit); black currant.
cerise f. (lit); cherry.
chou m. (lit); cabbage.
ciboulot m.
cigare m. (lit); cigar.
citron m. (lit); lemon.
coco m.
dôme m. (lit); dome.
gaufre m. head; face / (lit); waffle / **se sucrer le gaufre**; to put on makeup / (lit); to sugar the waffle.
gueule f. derogatory for head, mouth, or face / (lit); mouth of an animal.
lampe f. (lit); lamp.
patate f. (lit); potato.
plafond m. (lit); ceiling.
poire f. (lit); pear.
pomme f. (lit); apple.
portrait m. head; face / (lit); portrait.
timbre m. (lit); bell; gong (of clock).
tirelire f. (lit); piggy-bank.
tranche f. (lit); slice.
trompette f. head; face / (lit); trumpet.
tronche f. head; face / (lit); log.

HIT, to (frapper)

beigne f. a blow to the face / (lit) doughnut.
bourrade f. blow; thrust that one gives with the fist or elbow / **une bourrade amicale**; a friendly hit (on the shoulder).
calotte f. a hit / (lit); skull cap; calotte.
calotter v. to hit (on the head).
châtaigne f. blow, hit / (lit); chestnut.
gifle f. slap to the face / **flanquer une gifle à q.**; to slap someone in the face / *Note:* **flanquer** v. to throw.
gifler v. to slap in the face.

giroflée à cinq feuilles f. slap in the face with a wide opened hand / (lit); slap with five leaves.

gnon m. blow, punch / (pronounced "nion" as one syllable).

marron m. blow, punch / (lit); chestnut.

mornifle f. blow, punch.

pain m. blow, punch / (lit); bread / **Y lui a collé un pain;** He punched him out.

pêche f. blow, punch / (lit); peach.

prune f. blow, punch / (lit); plume.

ramponneau m. hit, punch / **recevoir un ramponneau;** to get hit.

rentrer dans la gueule à q. exp. to hit someone in the mouth / (lit); to reenter in someone's mouth / *Note:* **gueule** f. derogatory for "head" or "mouth" / (lit); mouth of animal.

rentrer dans le chou à q. exp. to hit someone in the head / (lit); to reenter in someone's head / *Note:* **chou** m. head / (lit); cabbage.

rentrer dans le lard à q. exp. to hit someone / (lit); to reenter in someone's lard.

rentrer dans le portrait à q. exp. to hit someone in the face or head / (lit); to reenter in someone's face / *Note:* **portrait** m. face; head / (lit); portrait.

sifflet m. hit, blow / (lit); a whistle.

soufflet m. hit, punch / (lit); bellows; blowing machine.

souffleter v. to box someone's ears.

HOUSE (maison)

baraque f. (*extremely popular*) / (lit); barracks.

bicoque f. (lit); house with a mediocre appearance; little house, shanty.

cabane f. (lit); hut, shanty.

cagna f.

cahute f. (lit); hut, shanty.

case f. (lit); small dwelling, hut, cabin / **une case africaine;** a (primitive) African hut.

crèche f. dwelling / (lit); manger, crib / *Note:* **crécher** v. to live.

gourbi m. (lit); hut, shack.

guitoune f. (lit); military dug-out, foxhole; tent.

hutte f. (lit); hut.

kasbah f. (from Arabic).

turne f. dirty and uncomfortable house or bedroom / *Note:* In school slang, "bedroom" or "study room."

HOW'S IT GOING? (ça va?)

bicher v. to go very well / **Ça biche?;** How's it going? / **Ça biche entre eux!;** They're hitting it off very well.

boulotter v. to go very well / **Ça boulotte?;** How's it going? / *also:* **boulotter** v. to eat a lot / *See:* **eat,** to.

boumer v. to go very well / (lit); to be booming / **Ça boume?;** How's it going?

carburer v. to go very well; said of a carburetor that is working well / **Ça carbure?;** How's it going?

coller v. to go very well / (lit); to stick / **Ça colle?;** How's it going?

gazer v. to go very well / (lit); to go full steam ahead / **Ça gaze?**; How's it going?

gazouiller v. slang variant of **gazer**.

marcher v. to go very well / (lit); to walk; to work well / **Ça marche?**; Things are going well?

ronfler v. to go very well / (lit); to snore / **Ça ronfle?**; Things are going smoothly?

rouler v. to go very well / (lit); to roll (along) / **Ça roule?**; Things are going well?

roulotter v. slang variant of **rouler**.

rupiner v. (lit); to do well (at an examination); to succeed / **Ça rupine?**; Things are working out?

qu'est-ce qu'il y a de nouveau? exp. (lit); what's new?

quoi de neuf? exp. (lit); what's new?

tourner v. to go very well / (lit); to turn / **Alors, ça tourne?**; So, how's it going?

HUNGRY, to be (avoir faim)

claquer du bec exp. to be very hungry / (lit); to smack one's lips in hunger / *Note:* **bec** m. mouth / (lit); beak of bird.

crever de faim exp. (lit); to die of hunger / *Note:* **crever** v. to die.

crocs (avoir les) f. (lit); to have the canine teeth (that are ready to bite down on food).

dalle (avoir la) f. (lit); to have the throat (that is ready to receive food) / *Note:* **dalle** f. throat / *Also:* **se rincer la dalle**; to drink / (lit); to rinse one's throat.

dent (avoir la) f. to be very hungry / (lit); to have the tooth (that is ready to bite down on food).

dent creuse (avoir une) f. to be very hungry / (lit); to have a hollow tooth.

fringale (avoir la) f. to be hungry.

les avoir longues exp. to be very hungry / (lit); to have long ones (long teeth that are ready to bite down on food).

l'estomac creux (avoir) exp. to be very hungry / (lit); to have a hollow stomach.

l'estomac dans les talons (avoir) exp. to be terribly hungry / (lit); to have the stomach in the heels.

petit creux (avoir un) m. (lit); to have a little hollow (spot).

I

IDIOT (idiot)

abruti m. idiot / *Note:* **abrutir** v. to make stupid; to drive crazy.

andouille f. nerd / (lit); sausage.

animal m. (lit); animal.

araignée dans le plafond (avoir une) exp. to have bats in the belfry / (lit); to have a spider in the ceiling / *Note:* **plafond** m. head / (lit); ceiling.

ballot m. (lit); bundle.

baluchard m.

barjot m. crazy / *Note:* This is verlan for **jobard** / *See:* **jobard**.

battre la breloque exp. to be off one's rocker; to function badly / (lit); to beat the drum.

bécasse f. stupid woman or girl.

bêta m. silly or stupid person / *Note:* This is from **bête** adj. stupid.

bêtasse f. stupid woman or girl / *Note:* This is from **bête** adj. stupid.

bête à bouffer du foin (être) exp. (lit); stupid enough to eat hay.

bête comme ses pieds (être) exp. (lit); stupid as one's feet.

bourrique f. jackass; stubborn individual / (lit); donkey.

branquignolle adj. a little crazy; touched in the head.

braque m. harebrained individual / (lit); hound.

buse f. extremely stupid person / (lit); buzzard / *See:* **triple buse**.

case en moins (avoir une) exp. (lit); to be missing one division of the brain.

cave m. gullible person, sucker.

chonosof m.

cinglé(e) (être) adj. to be cracked.

comprenette dure (avoir la) exp. to be dense; thick skulled / This is from **comprendre** v. to understand.

corniaud m. & adj. (lit); crossbred dog / **C'qu'y peut êt'corniaud, c'ui-là!**; Can he ever be a jerk!

cornichon m. (lit); pickle.

couche (en avoir une) f. to be stupid / (lit); to have a coat (of paint, etc.) on it (the brain) / *Also:* **en tenir une couche**.

cruche f. a real idiot / (lit); pitcher.

cruchon m. a real idiot / (lit); small pitcher.

détraqué(e) (être) adj. (lit); to be out of whack (said of health, mental state, machinery, etc.).

dinde f. stupid woman or girl / (lit); turkey.

dingo m. & adj. idiot; crazy, cracked.

écervelé(e) (être) n. & adj. scatterbrain; scatterbrained. / (lit); to be "unbrained."

en tenir une dose exp. to be hopelessly dumb / (lit); to hold a dose of it (stupidity).

en tenir une pochetée exp. to be hopelessly dumb / (lit); to hold a pocketful of it (stupidity).

enflé m. fat-head / (lit); swollen.

enflure m. fat-head / (lit); swelling.

étourdi(e) (être) adj. to be scatterbrained.

évaporé(e) (être) n. & adj. irresponsible, flightly, scatterbrained / (lit); to be evaporated / **C't'une petite évaporée**; She's a real scatterbrain.

fada adj. crazy, cracked.

fêlé(e) (être) adj. (lit); to be cracked.

fêlure (avoir une) f. (lit); to have a crack.

follette adj. crazy (used only for woman).

follingue adj. crazy; nuts.

fou-fou/fofolle adj. a little crazy/ eccentric / *Note:* This comes from **fou/folle** adj. crazy, mad.

ganache f. complete idiot, person with no intelligence or talent, a real "zero."

givré(e) (être) adj. (lit); to be frosted over.

gobeur m. gullible person, sucker / *Note:* **gober** v. to eat; gobble up / *Also:* **gobe-tout** m. one who believes everything he hears; sucker.

godichard(e) adj. awkward and clumsy.

godiche adj. same as **godichard(e)**.

gogo m. a person easily fooled; "sucker."

gourde f. idiot / (lit); gourd.

grain (avoir un) m. to be nuts; to be touched in the head / (lit); to have a grain (in the brain).

huître f. silly person, dope / (lit); oyster.

hurluberlu m. scatterbrain.

job m. abbreviated form of **jobard**.

jobard m. & adj. idiot; "sucker."

louf adj. *Note:* This is largonji for **fou**.

louftingue adj. *Note:* This is largonji for **fou**.

lourdeau m. & adj. thickheaded, slow / This is from **lourd** adj. heavy.

maboul(e) adj. crazy, mad.

manquer une case exp. (lit); to be missing a division in the brain / *See:* **case en moins (avoir une)**.

marteau adj. crazy; cracked / (lit); hammer.

moule f. dumbell; fat-head / (lit); mussel.

ne pas avoir de plomb dans la cervelle exp. said of an idiot; to be without gray matter / (lit); not to have any lead in the brain.

ne pas avoir inventé la poudre exp. said of an idiot / (lit); not to have invented power.

ne pas avoir inventé le fil à couper le beurre exp. said of an idiot / (lit); not to have invented the wire to cut butter.

nouille f. nerd / (lit); noodle.

onduler de la toiture exp. humorous for "to have a screw loose" / (lit); to have a roof that is buckling.

pante m. gullible guy; sucker.

perdre la boule exp. to lose one's mind / (lit); to lose the ball.

perdre la boussole exp. to lose one's mind / (lit); to lose the compass.

perdre le nord exp. to lose one's mind / (lit); to lose the north (point on the compass).

phénomène m. strange person; freak of nature / (lit); phenomenon.

pigeon m. gullible person, "sucker" / (lit); pigeon.

piqué(e) (être) adj. cracked; touched in the head / (lit); to be stung.

pocheté(e) n. idiot.

recevoir un coup de bambou exp. to become crazy / (lit); to receive a blow of bamboo.

saucisse f. idiot, nerd / (lit); sausage.

schnock m. imbecile, jerk / *Also:* **duchenock**.

sinoque (être) adj. crazy, cracked / *Also:* **cinoque**.

siphoné(e) (être) adj. crazy / (lit); siphoned (of all intelligence).

sonné(e) (être) adj. cracked; "ding-a-ling" / (lit); to be rung.

sot(te) à vingt-quatre carats n. (lit); a twenty-four-carat idiot.

souche f. silly person, dumbell / (lit); stump (of tree).

tapé(e) (être) adj. (lit); touched (in the head).

tête de linotte f. scatterbrain / (lit); head of feathers.

tête dure (avoir la) f. to be thick-skulled; dense / (lit); to have a hard head.

timbré(e) (être) adj. crazy; cracked / (lit); to be rung.

timbre fêlé m. crackpot; idiot / (lit); cracked bell.

toqué(e) (être) adj. crazy, cracked.

tordu(e) (être) adj. crazy; cracked / (lit); to be twisted.

tourte f. stupid person / (lit); tart.

tranche (en avoir une) f. (lit); to have a slice of it (craziness).

travailler de la chéchia exp. to be crazy / (lit); to work from the hat / *Note:* **chéchia** f. military cap.

travailler du chapeau exp. to be crazy / (lit); to work from the hat.

travailler du chou exp. to be crazy / (lit); to work from the cabbage / *Note:* **chou** m. head / (lit); cabbage.

triple buse m. an extremely stupid person / (lit); triple idiot / *Note:* **buse** m. buzzard.

J

JAIL (prison)

ballon m. slammer / (lit); balloon / *Note:* **ballonner** v. to throw in jail.

bloc m. "cooler."

boîte f. (lit); box.

cabane f. **être en cabane;** to be in jail / (lit); hut.

cachot m. prison cell / (lit); dark dungeon.

cellule f. (lit); cell.

frigo m. "cooler" / (lit); refrigerator.

gnouf m.

jettard m. slammer / *Note:* This comes from **jeter** v. to throw (away).

ombre m. (lit); shadow / **être à l'ombre;** to be in jail.

placard m. (lit); wall cupboard.

séchoir m. (lit); dryer.

taule m. *Note:* **taulier** m. prisoner.

trou m. (lit); hole.

violon m. violin.

JAM, to be in a (être dans une situation inextricable)

beaux draps (être dans de) m.pl. (lit); to be in pretty sheets.

bouscaille (être dans la) f. (lit); to be in the mud.

embrouillamini m. an extremely complicated and confused mess.

marmelade (être dans la) f. (lit); to be in marmalade.

mauvais pas (être dans un) m. (lit); to be in a bad step.

mélasse (être dans la) f. (lit); to be in molasses.

me voilà frais exp. "Boy, am I in a mess!" / (lit); here I am fresh.

me voilà propre exp. "Boy, am I in a mess!" / (lit); here I am clean.

mouscaille (être dans la) f. (lit); to be in mud.

pagaille f. mess / **Quelle pagaille!;** What a mess!

pastis m. (pronounced "pastisse") / (lit); an alcoholic drink with anisette.

pétrin (être dans le) m. (lit); to be in the kneading trough.

JUNK (marchandise de mauvaise qualité)

à la gomme adj. **un truc à la gomme;** a worthless piece of junk / (lit); sticky.

à la manque adj. **un truc à la manque;** a worthless piece of junk / (lit); missing.

à la noix adj. **un truc à la noix;** a worthless piece of junk / (lit); nutty.

camelote f. junk / **C'est d'la camelote!**; That's junk! / *Note:* **camelote** also means "merchandise in general" / **C'est d'la bonne camelote**; That's a nice piece of goods.

fichaise f. something worthless; junk / *Note:* This is from **fiche** v. "to do; to make" whose past tense, **fichu**, is used to mean "ruined; done for."

ne pas valoir chipette exp. said of something worthless; not to be worth a "penny."

ne pas valoir pipette exp. said of something worthless; not to be worth a "penny."

ne pas valoir tripette exp. said of something worthless; not to be worth a "penny."

ne pas valoir un coup exp. said of something worthless; not to be worth a "penny."

ne pas valoir une roupie exp. said of something worthless / (lit); not to be worth a rupee.

ne valoir que dalle exp. (lit); to be worth nothing / *Note:* **que dalle** adv. nothing.

pacotille f. junk / **bijoux de pacotille**; junk jewelry.

peau de saucisson f. (lit); sausage skin.

peau d'hareng f. (lit); herring skin.

rossignol m. (lit); nightingale.

roupie de sansonnet f. (lit); starling mucus.

roupie de singe f. (lit); monkey mucus.

toc m. junk.

tocard m. junk.

K

KILL, to (tuer)

assommer v. (lit); to knock someone senseless.

avoir la peau de q. exp. to have someone's hide / (lit); to have someone's skin.

bousiller v. (lit); to break / **Arrête ou j'te bousille!**; Stop it or I'll knock your block off!

crever v. (1) to die / **Y a crevé d'faim**; He died of hunger; (2) to kill; **Où il est? J'vais l'crever!**; Where is he? I'll pulverize him!

débarrasser de q. (se) exp. (lit); to get rid of someone.

descendre q. v. (lit); to down someone.

donner le coup de pouce à q. exp. to strangle someone / (lit); to give a blow with the thumb.

estourbir v. to kill; do in.

faire passer le goût du pain à q. exp. (lit); to make someone lose the taste of bread (as well as the other senses).

faire sauter le caisson (se) exp. to kill oneself; to blow out one's brains / (lit); to blow-up one's locker / *Note 1:* **faire sauter** v. to blow up / (lit); to make jump / *Note 2:* **caisson** m. head / (lit); locker.

fiche en l'air v. to blow someone away / (lit); to send or throw into the air.

liquider q. v. (lit); to liquidate someone.

rectifier q. v. to fix someone / (lit); to rectify someone.

refroidir q. v. (lit); to chill someone / *Note:* **refroidi** m. cadavre.

suriner q. v. to kill someone with a knife / *Note:* **surin** m. knife.

zigouiller q. v. to rub someone out.

KISS, to (embrasser)

bécot m. a kiss / (lit); a peck / *Note:* This is from **bec** m. mouth / (lit); beak of bird /
    See: **bécoter** v. to kiss.
bécoter v. to kiss, to neck.
bise f. a kiss / *See:* **biser** v. to kiss.
biser v. to kiss.
bisou m. a little kiss.
fricassée de museaux f. a whole mess of kisses and hugs / (lit); a snout or muzzel
    fricassee.
papouille f. hug, embrace; caress.

KIT AND KABOODLE, the whole (le tout)

baraque (toute la) f. (lit); to whole house / *Note:* **baraque** f. house / (lit); barracks.
barda (tout le) m. *Note:* military slang for "pack" or "kit."
bataclan (tout le) m. (lit); belongings; paraphernalia.
bazar (tout le) m. (lit); bazaar; emporium.
boutique (toute la) f. (lit); the whole boutique.
fourbi (tout le) m. (lit); soldier's kit or equipment.
saint-frusquin (tout le) m. all the wordly goods of a person / *Note:* **frusques** f.pl.
    clothes.
smala (toute la) f. (lit); the whole family / *Note:* **smala** is borrowed from Arabic.
tremblement (tout le) m. (lit); all the trembling.

L

LAUGH, to (rire)

(See: **FUNNY**)

bidonner (se) v. to laugh hard, to belly laugh / (lit); to shake one's belly (in laughter) /
    Note: **bidon** m. belly.
boyauter (se) v. to laugh hard; to laugh till you hurt / (lit); to shake one's guts (with
    laughter) / *Note:* **boyaux** m.pl. guts.
c'est pas de la rigolade exp. it's no laughing matter / *See:* **rigoler**.
désopiler (se) v. (lit); to shake or roar with laughter.
dilater la rate (se) v. to laugh hard / (lit); to swell up or dilate one's spleen (from
    laughter).
esclaffer (s') v. to laugh loudly; to burst out in loud laughter.
fendre la pipe (se) v. to split one's sides laughing / (lit); to spit one's mouth (from
    laughing) / *Note:* **pipe** f. mouth / (lit); pipe.
gondoler (se) v. to shake with laughter / (lit); to warp; to buckle up (with laughter).
marrer (se) v. *(extremely popular)* to laugh.
mourir de rire exp. (lit); to die laughing.
poiler (se) v. to laugh loudly / *Note 1:* It could be loosely translated as "that which
    causes one's hair (**poil**) to shake with laughter."
pouffer (se) v. to laugh loudly; burst out laughing / (lit); to puff up (with laughter).

rigoler v. to laugh.

rouler (se) v. to laugh hard / (lit); to roll (with laughter).

tirebouchonner (se) v. to laugh hard and continuously / *Note:* A loose literal translation of this might be "to rise up and down like a corkscrew (**un tire-bouchon**) as one takes in air repeatedly in order to laugh."

tordre (se) v. to split one's sides with laughter / (lit); to twist oneself (from laughter).

tordre comme un bossu (se) exp. same as **se tordre** / (lit); to twist oneself (from laughter) like a hunchback.

tordre comme une baleine (se) exp. same as **se tordre** / (lit); to twist oneself (from laughter) like a whale.

LAZY PERSON (paresseux)

cossard(e) n. & adj. lazy and tired / **C't'un cossard; Y est cossard**: He's a lazy bum; He's lazy / *See:* **cosse**.

cosse f. laziness / **avoir la cosse**; to be lazy.

côtes en long (avoir les) f.pl. said of a lazy person / (lit); to have long ribs.

enfiler des perles exp. said of someone who just loafs around / (lit); to string pearls.

fainéant(e) n. & adj. lazy bum; lazy.

faire le lézard exp. to do nothing but lie in the sun; to laze / (lit); to act like the lizard.

feignant(e) n. & adj. lazy bum; lazy.

feignasser v. to laze around and do nothing.

flemmard(e) n. & adj. extremely lazy person; lazy.

flemmarder v. to be lazy; to laze around.

flemme f. extreme laziness / **avoir la flemme**; to be lazy / *See:* **tirer sa flemme**.

il est venu au monde un dimanche exp. said of a person who is born lazy / (lit); he came to the world on a Sunday.

les avoir à la retourne exp. said of a very lazy person / (lit); to have them (hands) inside out.

les avoir à l'envers exp. said of a very lazy person / (lit); to have them (hands) inside out; upside-down.

les avoir palmées exp. said of a very lazy person / (lit); to have them (hands) webbed.

ne pas en fiche un coup exp. to do nothing; to be idle / (lit); to do absolutely nothing.

ne pas en fiche une datte exp. to do nothing; to be lazy / (lit); to do absolutely nothing / *Note:* **datte** f. nothing / (lit); date.

ne pas en fiche une rame exp. to do nothing; to be lazy / (lit); to do absolutely nothing / (lit); ream (of paper).

ne pas en fiche une secousse exp. to do nothing; to be very lazy / (lit); to do absolutely nothing / *Note:* **secousse** comes from **secouer** v. to shake; to jerk. This might be loosely translated as "to do nothing that would cause any movement whatsoever."

ne pas se fouler la rate exp. said of a very lazy person / (lit); not to sprain one's spleen.

ne pas se fouler le poignet exp. said of a very lazy person / (lit); not to sprain one's wrist.

ne rien se casser exp. said of a very lazy person; not to lift a finger / (lit); not to break any part of oneself.

peigner la girafe exp. to do nothing / (lit); to comb the giraffe.

rester en tas exp. to do nothing; not to move / (lit); to stay in a heap.

tirer sa flemme exp. to laze around and do nothing / (lit); to pull one's laziness (around).

tourner les pouces (se) exp. (lit); to twirl one's thumbs.

traînasser v. to loaf around.

traîner la savate exp. to loaf around / (lit); to drag around one's slipper.

traîner ses patins exp. to loaf around / (lit); to drag around one's feet / *Note:* **patins** m.pl. feet / (lit); skates.

user le soleil exp. to do nothing but lie around under the sun / (lit); to use up the sun.

LEAVE, to (partir)

arracher (s') v. (lit); to tear out; to pull out.

barrer (se) v. (lit); to cross out oneself; to strike out oneself.

briser (se la) v. to leave quickly; to leave in a breeze / *Note:* This is from **brise** f. breeze.

calter v. to leave quickly; to run away.

carapater (se) v. to leave quickly; to run away.

cavaler (se) v. to leave quickly; to run away / *Note:* **être en cavale**; to be on the lam; to be running away (from the police).

débarrasser le plancher exp. to leave quickly; to be chased / (lit); to get rid of the floor.

débiner (se) v. to leave quickly.

décamper v. to clear out fast / (lit); to pull up camp.

décaniller v. to clear out fast.

défiler (se) v. to clear out at the critical moment / **J'comptais sur lui, mais y s'est défilé!**; I was counting on him, but he left when I needed him the most!

déguiser en courant d'air (se) exp. to leave without being seen / to vanish into thin air / (lit); to disguise oneself in a breeze.

démurger (se) v. to clear out; to get away.

dérober (se) v. to slip away without being seen / **Quelle soirée horrible! On s'dérobe?**; What a horrible party! Shall we slip out?

donner de l'air (se) exp. same as **se déguiser en courant d'air** / (lit); to give oneself to the air.

éclipser (s') v. to disappear, vanish / (lit); to eclipse onself.

esbigner (s') v. to leave.

faire la malle exp. to jilt; to leave without warning / (lit); to pack up one's trunk.

faire la paire (se) exp. to run away; to disappear / (lit); to get the pair (of legs) working.

faire l'adja (se) exp. to leave quickly.

faire son baluchon exp. to pack up and leave / (lit); to fix up one's bundle (of belongings).

filer v. to "split" / (lit); to spin (off).

filer à l'anglaise exp. to "hit the road"; to take French leave / (lit); to spin off English style.

foncer dans le brouillard exp. to leave "full steam ahead" / (lit); to charge into the fog.

gagner le large exp. (lit); to gain width / *See:* **prendre le large**.

jouer des compas exp. to run away / (lit); to play the legs / *Note:* **compas** m.pl. legs / (lit); compass (needles).

jouer des flûtes exp. same as **jouer des compas** / *Note:* **flûtes** f.pl. legs / (lit); flutes.

jouer des gambettes exp. same as **jouer des compas** / *Note:* **gambettes** f.pl. legs / (lit); red- shanks.

jouer des guibolles exp. same as **jouer des compas** / *Note:* **guibolles** f.pl. legs.

jouer des quilles exp. same as **jouer des compas** / *Note:* **quilles** f.pl. (bowling) pins.

jouer rip exp. to leave quickly; to disappear.

laisser une queue exp. to leave without paying bills in full / (lit); to leave a tail.

les mettre exp. to scram / (lit); to set them (the sails) up / *Note:* **les** refers to **les voiles** (sails) / *see:* **mettre les voiles**.

lever l'ancre exp. (lit); to lift anchor.

mettre les bâtons exp. to leave quickly; to run / (lit); to put the clubs (to work) / *Note:* **bâtons** m.pl. legs / (lit); clubs.

mettre les bouts exp. to leave quickly / (lit); to put the ends (to work) / *Note:* **bouts** m.pl. legs / (lit); ends.

mettre les bouts de bois exp. to leave quickly / (lit); to put the ends of wood (to work) / *Note:* **bouts de bois** m.pl. legs / (lit); ends of wood.

mettre les cannes exp. to leave quickly / (lit); to put the canes (to work) / *Note:* **cannes** f.pl. legs / (lit); canes.

mettre les voiles exp. to leave; to pull up anchor / (lit); to set sail.

planter un drapeau v. to leave without paying the bill (in a restaurant, hotel, etc.) / (lit); to drive a flag into the ground.

plaquer v. to jilt / *Also:* **plaquouser**.

plier bagages exp. to pick up and leave / (lit); to fold baggage.

prendre la tangente exp. to leave quickly without being seen / (lit); to take the tangent.

prendre le large exp. (lit); to take width.

prendre ses cliques et ses claques exp. (lit); to take one's belongings (and leave).

sauver (se) v. to run away and escape from danger; to leave in a hurry / (lit); to save oneself.

tailler (se) v. to buzz off / (lit); to trim oneself.

tirailleur marocain (se) v. humorous for "to leave" / *Note:* **tirailleur marocain** (Moroccan gunman) is a humorous transformation of **se tirer** (meaning, "to leave") since it's one expression that suddenly leads into another / **On s'tirailleur marocain?**; Shall we take off?

tirer (se) v. to "split" / (lit); to pull oneself (away).

tirer les pincettes (se) v. to leave quickly / (lit); to pull away one's legs / *Note:* **pincettes** f.pl. legs / (lit); tweezers.

trisser (se) v. to go away; to leave.

trissoter (se) v. variant of **se trisser**.

trotter (se) v. to leave / (lit); to trot off.

trousser baggage exp. (lit); to tuck up one's baggage.

virer (se) v. to scram; to veer off / **Vire-toi!**; Beat it!

LEGS (jambes)

allumettes f.pl. thin legs / (lit); matches

bâtons f.pl. (lit); clubs.

cannes f.pl. (lit); canes.

colonnes f.pl. strong legs / (lit); columns; pillars.

crayons m.pl. thin legs / (lit); pencils.

échalas m.pl. thin legs / (lit); vine-props.

échasses f.pl. thin legs / (lit); stilts.

flûtes f.pl. thin legs / (lit); flutes.

gambettes f.pl. (lit); red shanks.

gigots m.pl. thighs / (lit); legs of lamb.

guibolles f.pl. legs.

pattes m.pl. legs; hands / (lit); paws.

poteaux m.pl. strong legs / (lit); posts.

quilles f.pl. (lit); (bowling) pins.

LOOK, to (regarder)

avoir q. à l'œil exp. to observe someone; to have an eye on someone / (lit); to have someone in the eye.

bigler v. to look.

châsser v. to look; to eye / (lit); **châsses** f.pl. eyes / (lit); frame of glasses.

chauffer v. to look / (lit); to heat (up).

faire des yeux de merlan frit exp. to gaze ecstatically at someone with wide-open eyes / (lit); to make eyes like a fried whiting (fish).

frimer v. to look at someone's face / *Note:* **frime** f. face; "kisser."

gaffer v. to look attentively at someone; to get a load of someone / (lit); to hook.

gaffouiller v. slang variant of **gaffer**.

guigner v. to eye someone or something / **Y guigne ton jeu;** He's looking at your hand (of cards).

loucher v. to look / (lit); to squint; to look cross-eyed.

mater v. to look / (lit); to master something or someone.

mirer v. to look; to eye / *Note:* **mirettes** f.pl. eyes.

mordre v. to look; to get a load of something or someone / (lit); to bite.

reluquer v. to look at something or someone at the corner of one's eye with interest and curiosity.

rincer l'œil (se) v. to look at something or someone with particular pleasure / (lit); to rinse the eye (with something nice).

viser v. to look / (lit); to aim; take sight on.

zieuter v. to look / *Note:* This comes from the word **yeux** meaning "eyes": les z'yeux = z'yeux-ter = **zieuter**.

LOVE, to (adorer)

avoir q. dans la peau exp. to have a mad crush on someone / (lit); to have someone under the skin.

chanter à v. to please / **Ça m'chante!;** I love it! / (lit); to sing to.

chipé(e) pour q. (être) v. (lit); to be stolen for someone / *Note:* **chiper** v. to steal.

coiffé(e) de q. (être) adj. to have a mad crush on someone / (lit); to be coiffed with someone.

dans la peau (avoir q.) exp. (lit); to have someone in the skin.

emballé(e) par q. (être) adj. to be infatuated with someone / (lit); to be wrapped up by someone.

entiché(e) de q. (être) adj. to be infatuated with someone / *Also:* **enticher (s') de q.**

fou/folle de q. (être) adj. (lit); to be mad about someone.

mordu(e) (être) adj. & n. to have a mad crush; to be hooked / (lit); to be bitten / **Elle est mordue du golf;** She's hooked on golf / **les mordus du tennis;** fans of soccer.

pépin pour q. (avoir le) m. to be the apple of one's eye / (lit); to have the pippin for someone.

pincer pour q. (en) v. (lit); to pinch it for someone.

raffoler de v. to be crazy about / **J'raffole du chocolat!;** I'm nuts about chocolate.

tenir à q. comme à la prunelle de ses yeux exp. (lit); to care for someone like the apple (pupil) of one's eyes.

toquade pour q. (avoir une) f. to have a little crush on someone.

LUCKY, to be (avoir de la chance)

(See: **BAD LUCK,** to have)

bidard m. happy or lucky individual.

bien loti(e) (être) adj. (lit); to be well allotted.

bol (avoir du) m. (lit); to have bowl / **Quel bol!;** What luck!

chançard(e) n. lucky individual.

embellie f. unexpected good fortune; godsend.

guigne f. bad luck / **avoir de la guigne;** to have bad luck.

né(e) coiffé(e) (être) adj. to be born under a lucky star / (lit); to be born coiffed.

pot (avoir du) m. same as **avoir du bol** / (lit); to have some from the pot / **Quel pot!;** What luck!

veinard(e) n. lucky individual.

veine (avoir de la) f. to have luck /**un coup d'veine;** a stroke of luck.

veine de coco (avoir une) f. to have great or remarkable luck.

veine de pendu (avoir une) f. to have great or remarkable luck.

verni(e) (être) adj. to always be lucky / (lit); to be varnished (with luck).

M

MEAN, to be (être mesquin)

bas(se) (être) adj. to be low and despicable / (lit); to be low.

mauvais(e) comme la gale (être) exp. (lit); to be as bad as scabies.

méchant(e) comme une teigne (être) exp. (lit); to be mean as a moth.

mauvais crin (être de) m. to be ill-tempered / (lit); to be of bad horsehair.

mauvais poil (être de) m. to be ill-tempered; in a bad mood / (lit); to be of bad hair.

mal vissé(e) (être) adj. to be ill-tempered; in a bad mood / (lit); to be badly screwed together.

MONEY (money)

(*See:* **RICH,** to be)

balle f. (*extremely popular*) one centime / **Tu peux m'prêter cent balles?**; Can you loan me a franc? / *Note:* This is an extremely popular way of saying "one franc." Of all the slang synonyms for "money," this is the most popular! / **100 balles** = 1 franc; **200 balles** = 2 francs; **1000 balles** = 10 francs; etc.

beurre m. money in general / (lit); butter.

blé m. money in general / (lit); wheat.

bougie f. 5-franc piece / (lit); candle.

braise f. money in general / (lit); live charcoal.

brique f. one million francs / (lit); brick.

cigue m. 20-franc gold piece.

fafiot m. banknote; paper.

ferraille f. change / (lit); scrap iron.

fric m. (*extremely popular*) money in general.

galetouse f. money in general.

galette f. money in general.

grand format m. 1,000-franc bill / (lit); big format.

grisbi m. money in general.

grisbinette f. 100-franc coin.

gros papa m. 1,000-franc bill / (lit); big daddy.

livre f. 100 francs / (lit); a pound.

misérable m. 500-franc bill (from the work of Victor Hugo).

mitraille f. small coins / (lit); hail of bullets.

oseille f. money in general / (lit); sorrel.

pelot m. 5-centime coin.

pépètes f.pl. money in general.

pesètes m.pl. money in general.

pèze m. money in general.

picaillons m.pl. small coins.

pognon m. money in general.

poussières f.pl. small supplementary amount of francs that is added to a basic amount / (lit); dusts / **Ce livre, y coûte 1.000 balles et des poussières**; This book costs 10 francs and some change. / *Note:* The French use decimal points in numbers whereas Americans use commas, e.g. 1,000 = **1.000,** etc.

radis m. one centime / (lit); radish.

raide m. 1,000-franc bill / (lit); stiff.

ronds m.pl. (*extremely popular*) coins / (lit); rounds.

sigue f. 20-franc coin.

sous m.pl. (*extremely popular*) coins.

thunard m. old 5-franc coin.

thune f. old 5-franc coin.

thunette f. old 5-franc coin.

ticket m. 1,000-franc bill.

MOUTH (bouche)

bavarde f. (lit); the "blabberer" / *Note:* This comes from **bavarder** v. to blabber; to chatter; to chat.

bec m. (lit); beak of bird.

boîte f. (lit); box.

égout m. (lit); sewer; drain

évier m. (lit); sink.

fente f. (lit); crack; crevice; slit.

gargoulette f. (lit); the gargler / *Note:* This comes from **se gargariser** v. to gargle.

gargue f. same as **gargoulette**.

gobeuse f. (lit); the gobbler / *Note:* This comes from **gober** v. to gobble down food; to gobble up.

goulot m. gullet; mouth / (lit); neck (of bottle).

gueule f. derogatory for "mouth" or "face" / (lit); mouth of animal / *Note:* **Ta gueule!;** Shut up!

margoulette f.

respirante f. (lit); the respirator.

N

NEVER (jamais)

à pâques ou à la trinité exp. very late; never / (lit); at Easter or at Trinity.

jusqu'à la Saint-Glinglin exp. never; "when hell freezes over."

la semaine des quatre jeudis exp. (lit); the week of four Thursdays.

quand les poules auront des dents exp. (lit); when chicken have teeth.

NOISE (bruit)

barouf m. (pronounced "baroufe") loud noise / *Also:* **barouf du diable** m. devil of a noise.

boucan m. loud noise.

bousin m. **faire du bousin;** to make a lot of noise.

chahut m. rowdiness; noise.

chahuter v. to be rowdy and loud (said of students who are partying).

chambard m. loud noise.

charivari m. loud noise.

foin m. loud noise / (lit); hay.

hourvari m. loud noise.

potin m. loud noise.

raffut m. loud noise.

tam-tam m. loud noise.

tapage m. loud noise.

tintouin m. loud and tiring noise / *Also:* **tintouin** m. a large worry / *See:* **worry,** to.

tumulte m. tumult.

vacarme m. loud noise.
zinzin m. loud noise.

NONSENSE (baliverne)

baratin m. a bunch of b.s. / *Note:* **baratiner** v. to b.s. someone.
bobard m. **les bobards d'la presse;** exaggerations of the press.
boniment m. **Quel boniment!**; What baloney!
chansons que tout ça! exclam. This exclamation signifies "baloney" / *Note:* This comes
    from **chanter** v. to sing; however, in colloquial French it takes on the meaning
    "to talk nonsense": **Mais, qu'est-ce que tu m'chantes, là?**; What are you handing
    me?
postiche f. sales talk.
sornettes f.pl. baloney / **Y m'a raconté des sornettes;** He told me all sorts of baloney.
taratata! exclam. This exclamation is used to signify disbelief in something that is
    being told.
tu veux rire! exp. This expression is used to signify disbelief / (lit); you want to laugh;
    "you've got to be kidding."

NOSE (nez)

baigneur m. (lit); bather.
betterave f. nose that is red as a beet / (lit); beet.
blair m. "schnoz" / *Note:* **blairer** v. to smell; to tolerate (used in the negative): **J'peux
    pas l'blairer;** I can't stand him (so much that I can't even smell him)!
blaireau m. slang variant of **blair**.
éteignoir m. (lit); candle extinguisher.
naze m. *Note:* This comes from **nasal** adj. nasal.
patate f. big fat nose / (lit); potato.
pif m. "schnoz" / *Note:* **piffer** v. to smell; to tolerate (used only in the negative):
    J'peux pas l'piffer; I can't stand him (so much that I can't even smell him)!
piffard m. slang variant of **pif**.
radar m. (lit); radar.
tarin m. big "schnoz."
tube m. (lit); tube.

NOTHING (rien)

balpeau m. verlan for **peau de balle** / (lit); skin of a ball.
clous (des) m.pl. zip / (lit); nails / **Combien y t'a payé? -Des clous!**; How much did
    he pay you? -Zip!
dattes (des) m.pl. (lit); dates.
nèfles (des) m.pl. (lit); medlar (fruit).
nib m. nothing.
nib de nib m. nothing but nothing.
niente m. *Note:* This is borrowed from Spanish.

nix m. (lit); nix.

peau (la) f. (lit); skin.

peau de balle f. (lit); skin of a ball.

pour la gloire exp. (lit); just for the glory of it / **J'passe pas huit heures par jour au boulot juste pour la gloire!**; I don't spend eight hours a day at work just for the glory of it!

pour des pruneaux exp. "for peanuts" / (lit); for prunes.

pour des prunes exp. "for peanuts" / (lit); for plums.

que dalle exp. nothing; zip.

que fifre exp. nothing; zip.

que lape exp. nothing; zip.

que pouic exp. nothing; zip.

que't exp. nothing; zip.

que t'chi exp. nothing; zip.

radis (des) m.pl. (lit); radishes.

tringle (la) f. nothing; zip.

vent (du) m. (lit); wind.

O

OLD PERSON (vieux/vieille)

baderne (vieille) f. old biddy.

barbe (vieille) f. (lit); old beard.

birbe (vieux) m. old codger.

bonze (vieux) m. old dodderer.

gaga (vieux) m. old dodderer.

gâteux (vieux) m. old codger.

individu vieux jeu m. person with old ideas; old-fashioned / (lit); old-game person (person who plays by the old rules).

marcheur (vieux) m. (lit); old walker.

mémère f. crotchety middle-aged woman.

noix (vieille) f. (lit); old nut.

peau (vieille) f. (lit); old skin.

perruque (vieille) f. (lit); old wig.

ramolli(e) (être) adj. (lit); to be soft.

ramollo (vieux) adj. (lit); old soft person.

toupie (vieille) f. old unpleasant woman / (lit); old top.

viocard m. old codger.

vioc m. / vioqoue f. old codger / *Note:* vioquir v. to get old.

OUT OF A FIX, to get (se débrouiller)

démouscailler (se) v. (lit); to get oneself out of the mud / *Note:* mouscaille f. mud.

dépanner (se) v. (lit); to repair something that was broken down.

dépatouiller (se) v. (lit); to get one's feet out of a mess / *Note:* pattes f.pl. feet / (lit); paws.

P

PANTS (pantalon)

bénard m.
culbutant m. *Note:* This is from **culbuter** v. to somersault.
culbute m. (lit); somersault.
falzar m.
fendart m.
froc m. (lit); frock; gown.
futal m.
grimpant m. (lit); climber / *Note:* This is from **grimper** v. to climb.
pantalzar m. combination of **falzar** and **pantalon**.

PARENTS (parents)

ancêtres m.pl. parents / (lit); ancestors.
dab m. father.
dabesse f. mother.
dabs m.pl. parents.
dabuche f. mother.
daron m. father.
daronne f. mother.
doche f. mother.
matère f. mother.
maternelle f. mother / (lit); maternal.
matouze f. mother.
pater m. father (pronounced "patère").
paternel m. father / (lit); paternal.
patouze m. father.
patron m. father / (lit); (male) boss.
patronne f. mother / (lit); (female) boss.
vieille f. mother / (lit); old woman.
vieux m. father / (lit); old man.

PARTY, to (faire la fête)

bambocher v. to party / *Note:* **bambocheur, euse** n. party animal.
casser les vitres v. (lit); to break windowpanes.
bombe (faire la) f.
bringue (faire la) f.
faridon (faire la) f.
foire (faire la) f. (lit); to do the fair.
grande nouba (faire la) f.
noce (faire la) f. (lit); to do the (wedding) celebration.
ribouledingue (faire la) f. *See:* **ribouledinguer.**
partir en bombe v. to go party.

partir en ribouledingue v. to go party.
ribouledinguer v. to party.

Q

QUICKLY (vite)

à fond la caisse exclam. Step on it! (said of a car) / (lit); all the way the car / *Note:* **caisse** f. car / (lit); case.

à la six-quat'-deux adv. quickly; in a slapdash manner / (lit); six-four-two.

à tire-d'aile adv. flying away swiftly / (lit); pull of the wings.

à toute pompe adv. "pumped out" / (lit); complete pump.

à toutes jambes adv. all out fast / (lit); complete legs.

activez! exclam. hurry. / (lit); activate.

allez, ouste! exclam. hurry!

au triple galop adv. (lit); triple gallop.

courir comme un dératé exp. to run like a maniac / (lit); to run like a spleenless person.

courir ventre à terre exp. to run like the wind / (lit); to run with the stomach close to the ground.

dare-dare adv.

donner à plein tubes exp. to hurry; full steam ahead; full power / (lit); to give full tubes.

donner plein gaz v. to hurry / (lit); to give full gas.

en cinq sec(s) adv. (lit); in five seconds.

en deux temps, trois mouvements adv. (lit); in two times and three movements.

en moins de deux adv. (lit); in less than two (shakes).

en quatrième vitesse adv. (lit); in fourth gear.

et que ça saute exp. " . . . and make it snappy!" / (lit); and let it jump.

foncer v. to hurry / (lit); to forge ahead.

gazer v. to hurry / (lit); to gas up.

gigoter v. to hurry / (lit); to shake a leg / *Note:* **gigot** m. leg / (lit); leg of lamb / *Also:* **gigoter** v. to dance.

grouiller (se) v. to hurry; "to haul"; to look alive / (lit); to swarm; to be alive with / **La branche grouillait d'insectes**; The branch was alive with insects.

illico (presto) adv. quickly / *Note:* This is borrowed from Italian.

le temps de dire ouf adv. in no time at all / (lit); the time to say "ouf."

magner (se) v. to hurry; to move it / (lit); to manipulate oneself.

magner le derche (se) exp. to "move one's buns" / (lit); to manipulate or direct one's "derrière" / *Note:* **derche** m. is slang for "derrière" / *Also:* **magner le derrière (se)**.

quatre à quatre v. (lit); four at a time / *Note:* Used in **monter l'escalier quatre à quatre**; to climb the stairs four at a time.

rapido adv. quickly / *Note:* This is borrowed from Spanish.

secouer (se) v. to hurry / (lit); to shake oneself.

R

RAIN, to (pleuvoir)

bouillon m. downpour / (lit); bouillon (broth).
dégringoler v. to fall hard / **Regarde comme ça dégringole!**; Look at it come down!
flotter v. to rain / (lit); to float / *Note:* **flotte** f. water; rain.
lancequiner v. to rain / *Note:* **lancequine** or **lance** f. rain. / *Also:* to urinate.
lancequiner à pleins tubes exp. to downpour / (lit); to rain full tubes.
pleuvasser v. to drizzle.
pleuvoir des cordes exp. to downpour / (lit); to rain cords.
pleuvoir à seaux exp. (lit); to rain buckets.
pleuvoir à verse exp. to pour.
pleuvoir des hallebardes exp. (lit); to rain spears.
rincée f. a downpour / (lit); rinsing / *Also:* **rincée** f. scolding.
saucée f. a downpour / *Also:* **saucée** f. scolding.
tomber des cordes exp. to pour down / (lit); to drop cords.
vaser v. to rain / *Note:* **vase** f. rain / (lit); mud; sludge.
verser v. (lit); to pour.

RECONCILE, to (réconcilier)

passer la pogne exp. (lit); to pass the hand (of friendship) / *Note:* **pogne** f. hand.
passer l'éponge exp. to make up and not speak about it anymore / (lit); to pass the sponge (that "soaks up" our differences).
rabibocher (se) v. (lit); to patch up / **Y se sont rabibochés;** They patched up everything (between themselves).
rafistoler (se) v. (lit); to patch up / same as **rabibocher**.

REPORT TO THE POLICE, to (signaler à la police)

donner v. to stool pigeon / (lit); to give / *Also:* **donner à la police** / *Note:* **donneur** m. stool pigeon.
faisander v. to stool pigeon / *Note:* This is from **faisan** m. pheasant / *Also:* **faisander** v. to trick; to dupe.
moucharder v. to stool pigeon; to squeal / *Note:* **mouchard** m. stool pigeon; squealer.
mouton m. police informer / (lit); lamb.
pigeonner v. to stool pigeon / *Note:* This comes from **pigeon** m. dupe; sucker / (lit); pigeon / *Also:* **pigeonner** v. to trick; to dupe.

RICH, to be (être riche)

(See: **money**)

bourré(e) (être) adj. (lit); to be stuffed (with money). / *Also:* to be drunk.
calé(e) (être) adj. to be financially set / (lit); to be wedged or set (for life).
cousu(e) d'or (être) adj. to be made of money / (lit); to be sewn up of gold.

faire son beurre exp. to make a lot of money / *Note:* **beurre** m. money / (lit); butter.
flot (être à) adj. to be financially stable / (lit); afloat.
galeteux, euse (être) adj. to have lots of **galetouse** / *Note:* **galetouse** f. money.
galettard(e) n. one who has lots of **galetouse** / *Note:* **galetouse** f. money.
gousset bien garni (avoir le) exp. (lit); to have one's pocket well garnished / *Note:* **gousset** m. small pocket on a vest or pants.
paré(e) (être) adj. (lit); to be adorned, bedecked.
plein aux as (être) adj. to be born rich / (lit); to have all the aces.
plein les profondes (en avoir) exp. to be very rich / (lit); to have lots of it (money) in the pockets / *Note:* **profondes** f.pl. pockets. This comes from **profond** adj. deep.
reins solides (avoir les) m.pl. to be financially set / (lit); to have a solid (lower) back or "to be sturdy."
rempli(e) (être) adj. to be rich / (lit); to be filled up (with money).
remplir (se) v. to get rich / (lit); to fill oneself (with money) / *See:* **rempli(e), (être)**.
remuer l'argent à la pelle exp. to have money to burn / (lit); to stir money with a shovel.
richard(e) n. one who is rich.
riche comme Crésus (être) exp. to be very rich / (lit); to be rich like Crœsus / *Note:* **Crésus** m. a very rich man.
rupin(e) n. one who is rich.
rupinos m.pl. rich people.
vivre sur un grand pied exp. to live high on the hog / (lit); to live on a big foot.

RUMMAGE, to (chercher en bouleversant tout)

chambarder v. to turn everything topsy-turvy / *Note:* **chambard** m. upheaval / **Les cambrioleurs, z'ont tout chambardé dans la baraque**; The burglars turned the whole house upside-down.
chambouler v. same as **chambarder** / *Also:* **chambouler** v. to turn one's emotions upside-down / **La mauvaise nouvelle, è m'a chamboulé!**; The bad news gave me quite a turn!
farfouiller v. to rummage without taking any care / **farfouiller dans un tiroir**; to rummage about in a drawer.
fouiller v. to rummage for something / (lit); to frisk / *Note:* **fouillis** m. jumbled mess / **Quel fouillis!**; What a mess!
fouiner v. to rummage; to nose or ferret about / **Y aime pas qu'on fouine dans ses affaires**; He doesn't like people to snoop into his things. / *Note:* This comes from **fouine** f. weasel.
fourgonner v. to poke around turning everything upside-down.
fourrager v. to rummage / **fourrager dans des papiers**; to rummage through papers.
fureter v. to nose or pry about / (lit); to ferret (about).
trifouiller v. to rummage, to turn everything upside-down / **trifouiller dans un tiroir**; to rummage in a drawer / *Also:* **trifouiller** v. to fiddle with / **Trifouille pas avec ça!**; Don't fiddle with that!

RUNT (chétif)

demi-portion m. f. half-pint / (lit); half-portion.

gringalet m. shrimp (of a man or boy); puny little fellow / **C'te gringalet, y m'fait pas peur!**; This little shrimp doesn't scare me!

mecton m. little guy / *Note:* **mec** m. guy, "dude."

petit bout d'homme m. (lit); a little bit of a man.

rabougri(e) (être) adj. (lit); to be stunted (in growth); to shrivel up.

ratatiné(e) (être) adj. (lit); to be shrunken and deformed / *Also:* **ratatiner** v. to clobber / **Reviens tout d'suite ou j'te ratatine!**; Come back right now or I'll clobber you! (. . . make you shrunken and deformed!)

S

SAD, to be (être malheureux)

bourdon (avoir le) m. to be down in the dumps / (lit); to have the bumblebee.

broyer du noir exp. to be depressed / (lit); to crush or smash the black.

cafard (avoir le) m. (*extremely popular*) to be depressed / (lit); to have the cockroach.

dans son assiette (ne pas être) exp. to feel blah; out of sorts / (lit); not to be in one's plate.

figure d'enterrement (avoir une) f. to look depressed; to have a sad face / (lit); to have a burial face.

malheureux, euse comme les pierres (être) exp. to be very sad and alone / (lit); to be as sad as the rocks.

mine d'enterrement (avoir une) f. same as **avoir une figure d'enterrement**.

ronger le cœur (se) v. to cause oneself great anguish / (lit); to gnaw at one's heart.

spleen (avoir le) m. spleen; lowness of spirits.

tête d'enterrement (avoir une) f. same as **avoir une figure d'enterrement**.

SHOES (chaussures)

bateaux m.pl. big shoes or feet / (lit); boats.

boîtes à violon f.pl. (lit); violin cases.

croquenots m.pl.

godasses m.pl.

godillots m.pl.

grolles f.pl.

pompes f.pl.

targettes f.pl.

tartines f.pl.

tatanes f.pl.

SHUT UP, to (se taire)

bouche cousue (faire) f. to close one's mouth / (lit); make the sewn up mouth.
boucler (la) v. to shut up / (lit); to buckle it (the mouth).
boucler son égout exp. to shut one's mouth / (lit); to buckle one's sewer or drain /
  Note: égout m. mouth / (lit); sewer; drain.
fermer v. to shut up / (lit); to close.
ferme ça! exp. shut up! / (lit); close it.
fermer sa gueule exp. to shut one's mouth / (lit); to close one's mouth / *Note:* **gueule**
  f. derogatory for mouth / (lit); mouth of animal.
fermer son bec v. to shut one's mouth / (lit); to close one's mouth / *Note:* **bec** m. beak
  of bird.
fermer son micro exp. to shut one's mouth / (lit); to close one's mouth / *Note:* **micro**
  m. mouth / (lit); microphone.
fermer (la) v. to shut it (the mouth) / (lit); to close it / *Also:* **La ferme!**; Shut up!
la barbe! exp. shut up! / (lit); the beard.
rideau! m. shut up!; put a lid on it! (lit); curtain.
ta bouche, bébé, t'auras des frites exp. fling at someone who is talking too much /
  (lit); your mouth, baby, you're gonna have fainting spells (from all the oxygen
  you're losing) / *Note:* **tomber dans les frites;** to faint / (lit); to fall in the (French)
  fries.
ta gueule exp. shut up! / (lit); your mouth / *Note:* **gueule** f. derogatory for mouth /
  (lit); mouth of animal.
tenir sa langue exp. (lit); to hold one's tongue.
tirer la fermeture éclair exp. (lit); to pull up one's zipper.
y mettre un bouchon exp. (lit); to put a cork on it.
y mettre un cadenas exp. (lit); to put a lock on it.
y mettre une sourdine exp. (lit); to put a mute on it.

SLEEP, to (dormir)

(*See:* **BED,** to go to)

coucher à la belle étoile exp. to sleep outside / (lit); to sleep by the pretty star.
découcher v. to sleep somewhere other than one's house.
dormir à poings fermés exp. to sleep soundly / (lit); to sleep close fisted.
dormir comme une souche exp. to sleep like a log / (lit); to sleep like a stump.
écraser (en) v. to sleep; "to crash" / (lit); to crush some / *Note:* This expression probably came to be because of the "crushing" sound that one makes when snoring.
faire dodo exp. (child's language) to go "night-night."
faire la grasse matinée exp. to sleep in / (lit); to make the fat morning.
faire une ronflette exp. to take a nap, snooze / *Note:* This comes from **ronfler** v. to
  sleep / (lit); to snore.
pioncer v. to sleep; to snooze.
romance (piquer une) f. to take a nap / *Note:* **piquer** v. to take.
ronflaguer v. to snore; to sleep.
ronfler v. to sleep / (lit); to snore.
roupiller v. to sleep; snooze.

roupillon (piquer un) m. same as **piquer une romance**.

sieste f. a little nap / *Note:* This is borrowed from Spanish.

SNAG (point difficile)

accroc m. the snag, hitch / (lit); hook / **Voici l'accroc** . . . ; Here's the hitch. . . .

chiendent m. the snag, hitch / (lit); couch grass.

hic m.

pépin m. (lit); pip (of apple), seed.

rembourré(e) avec des noyaux de pêches (être) exp. said of something difficult to do / (lit); to be stuffed with peach pits.

SPEAK, to (parler)

(*See:* NONSENSE)

avoir voix au chapitre exp. to have one's say / (lit); to have voice to the chapter.

babiller v. to chatter on about nothing / (lit); to babble (of brook).

bafouiller v. to talk nonsense, to speak incoherently / *Note:* **bafouille** f. letter.

baliverner v. to talk nonsense; to b.s.

baragouiner v. to talk gibberish; to jabber / *Note:* **baragouineur, euse** n. one who talks about nothing.

bavasser v. to talk about nothing / *Note:* This is a slang variant of **baver** v. to dribble, to drool.

bredouiller v. to speak quickly and indistinctly / **bredouiller une excuse**; to jabber out an excuse.

cancaner v. to gossip / *Also:* **colporter des cancans sur q.**; to spread rumors about someone.

débiter v. to spout / **débiter une longue harangue**; to spout a long speech / *Note:* **harangue** f. long and endless story / *See:* **haranguer**.

débloquer v. to talk nonsense.

déjanter v. (*extremely popular*) to talk nonsense.

déménager v. to talk nonsense.

dérailler v. to talk nonsense / (lit); to derail.

dévider v. to talk nonstop / (lit); to unwind; reel off (thread, etc.).

divaguer v. to talk nonsense.

fariboler v. to talk nonsense / *Note:* **faribole** f. nonsense.

haranguer v. to spout a long and boring speech / (lit); to harangue.

jaboter v. to speak.

jacasser v. to chatter; jabber.

jacter v. to speak, to chatter / *Note:* **jactance** f. talking; speech.

jaspiner v. to chatter; speak.

laïusser v. to jabber; to talk on and on / *See:* **piquer un laïus**.

palabrer v. to talk nonsense / (lit); to palaver.

papoter v. to talk a lot about insignificant things; to blabber.

parler à bâtons rompus exp. to talk by fits and starts / (lit); to talk with broken clubs.

parler à tort et à travers exp. to talk without knowledge of one's subject / (lit); to speak randomly.

parler affaires exp. (lit); to talk business.

parler dans le vide exp. to talk without being listened to / (lit); to speak in a vacuum.

parler de la pluie et du beau temps exp. to chat / (lit); to talk about the rain and nice weather.

parler en l'air exp. to talk idly / (lit); to talk in the air.

piquer un laïus exp. to make a long-winded speech.

prêcher à un sourd exp. to talk without being listened to / (lit); to preach to a deaf person.

ragoter v. to gossip / *Note:* **ragots** m.pl. piece of gossip.

raisonner comme un sabot exp. to talk nonsense / (lit); to reason like a shoe.

raisonner comme un tambour mouillé exp. to talk nonsense / (lit); to reason like a wet drum.

raisonner comme une pantoufle exp. to talk nonsense / (lit); to reason like a slipper.

tailler une bavette exp. to chat / (lit); to trim a bib.

tenir le crachoir exp. to have the floor (in a discussion) / *Note:* This is from **cracher** v. to spit.

travailler du pick-up exp. to talk a lot; to talk like a broken record / (lit); to work on the record player.

user sa salive exp. to waste one's breath / (lit); to use one's saliva.

SPILL THE BEANS, to (trahir le secret)

couper (se) v. to let the cat out of the bag / (lit); to cut oneself (and let the truth leak out).

éventer la mèche v. "to snuff off the project" / (lit); to air the wick of the candle.

lâcher le paquet exp. (lit); to let go of the package.

vendre la mèche exp. (lit); to sell the wick.

STEAL, to (voler)

barboter v. to swipe / *Note:* **barboteur** m. thief.

casser v. to break in / (lit); to break / *Note:* **casseur** m. thief.

chaparder v. to steal small things / *Note:* **chapardeur** m. thief.

chiper v. to swipe / *Note:* **chipeur** m. thief.

choper v. to swipe / *Note:* **chopeur** m. thief.

décrocher v. (lit); to unhook.

dégraisser v. (lit); to degrease.

dépouiller v. (lit); to skin.

écorcher v. to rip off / (lit); to skin / **Je m'suis fait écorcher!**; I got myself ripped off!

entôler v. to steal by deceiving; to swindle / *Note:* **entôleur** m. swindler.

estamper v. to swindle / (lit); to stamp / *Note:* **estampeur** m. swindler.

faire main basse sur quelque chose exp. to swipe / (lit); to do the low hand on something.

faucher v. to swipe / (lit); to reap / *Also:* **être fauché(e)** adj. to be broke / (lit); to be reaped clean.

lever v. (lit); to lift.

piquer v. (lit); to take.
plumer v. to rip off / (lit); to pluck / **Je m'suis fait plumer!**; I got myself ripped off!
roustir v. to steal / *Note:* **roustisseur** m. swindler; crook.
tirer v. to pull / *Note:* **tireur** m. pickpocket.
truander v. to rip off / **Je m'suis fait truander!**; I got myself ripped off! / *Note:* **truand** m. a rip-off artist / **Quel truand!**; What a rip-off artist!

STINK, to (puer)

cocoter v.
cogner v. (lit); to hit.
coincer v. (lit); to stick.
corner v.
emboucaner v.
fouetter v. (lit); to whip.
repousser v. (lit); to repel.
schemecter v.
schlingoter v. slang variant of **schlinguer**.
schlinguer v.
schlipoter v.
taper v. (lit); to tap, strike, hit.

STOMACH (ventre)

bedaine f. paunch; round belly.
bedon m. paunch; round belly.
bide m. belly.
bidon m. belly / (lit); can, drum (for oil).
bocal m. (lit); goldfish bowl.
buffet m. (lit); buffet.
burlingue m.
estome m. abbreviated form of **estomac**.
globe m. (lit); globe, sphere.
panse m. belly.
tiroir m. (lit); drawer.

STORY (histoire)

bien bonne (une) f. a good and interesting story, a "good one."
des vertes et des pas mûres exp. risqué or raw and dirty stories, "stories that are not cleaned up enough to be told" / (lit); green and not ripe.
galéjade f. tall story / *Note:* **galéjer** v. to tell tall stories.
histoire à dormir debout f. a long and boring story / (lit); a story that makes one sleep standing up.
histoire abracadabrante f. cock-and-bull story.
histoire de bonnes femmes f. old wive's tale.

histoire marseillaise f. tall story / (lit); a Marseillaise story.

rengaine f. repetitious story / **C'est toujours la même rengaine;** It's always the same old story.

STROLL, to (se promener)

badauder v. to walk slowly and sightsee; to rubberneck / *Note:* **badaud(e)** n. rubbernecker.

baguenauder v. to stroll with no destination / *Also:* **être en baguenaude.**

balader (se) v. (*extremely popular*) to stroll, to wander, to saunter / *Note:* **baladeur, euse** n. wanderer.

déambuler v. to stroll about, to wander.

flânocher v. slang variant of **flâner** v. to stroll.

glander v. to stroll.

glandouiller v. slang variant of **glander.**

vadrouiller v. to stroll with no destination / *Also:* **être en vadrouille.**

virée (être en) f. to be on a quick little jaunt.

STUBBORN PERSON (personne obstinée)

tête de cochon f. (lit); pig-head.

tête de lard f. (lit); fat-head.

tête de mule f. (lit); mule-head.

tête de pioche f. (lit); pickax-head.

STUPEFIED, to be (être stupéfait)

aplati(e) (être) adj. to be floored / (lit); to be flattened.

assis(e) (en être) adj. to be floored / (lit); to be seated.

en boucher un coin exp. to be flabbergasted.

en boucher une surface exp. to be flabbergasted.

en être comme deux ronds de flan exp. to be flabbergasted / (lit); to be like two rounds of flan (or custard) about something.

en être comme deux ronds de frites exp. to be flabbergasted / (lit); to be like two rounds of fries about something.

en rester baba exp. to be so stunned with amazement or surprise that the sound "bah-bah" is all that can be uttered.

en rester comme une tomate exp. to be flabbergasted / (lit); to stay there like a tomato (and be red with shock) about something.

en rester comme une tourte exp. to be flabbergasted / (lit); to stay there like an idiot about something / *Note:* **tourte** f. idiot / (lit); (fruit) tart.

épater v. to flabbergast; to bowl over.

époustouflé(e) (être) adj. to be flabbergasted.

estomaquer v. to flabbergast; to take one's breath away / (lit); to affect one's **estomac** (stomach).

sidérer v. to flabbergast.

tomber de haut exp. to fall over with surprise / (lit); to fall from a height.

tomber des nues exp. to fall over with surprise / (lit); to fall from the high clouds / *Note:* **nues** f.pl. is an old term for "clouds."

T

TELEPHONE (téléphone)

bigophone m. *Note:* **bigophoner** v. to telephone (someone).

cornichon m. (lit); pickle (since it resembles the shape of the receiver).

phonard m.

téléphon m.

THIN (maigre)

maigre comme un clou exp. (lit); thin as a nail.

maigre comme une lame de rasoir exp. (lit); thin as a razor blade.

maigrichon(ne) adj. a little thin.

maigriot(te) adj. a little thin.

manche à balai m. (lit); broomstick.

n'avoir que la peau sur les os exp. to be nothing but skin and bones / (lit); to have nothing but skin on the bones.

sac d'os m. (lit); sack of bones.

sec comme un coup de trique exp. (lit); to be as dry as a heavy stick.

THIRSTY (avoir soif)

cracher blanc exp. (lit); to spit white.

gosier sec (avoir le) m. (lit); to have a dry throat / *Note:* **gosier** m. throat.

pépie (avoir la) f. to be very thirsty / *Note:* **la pépie** (lit); a disease of the tongue of fowl.

sécher (la) v. (lit); to have it (the throat) dry.

THRASHING (volée de coups)

(See: **BAWL SOMEONE OUT,** to / **FIGHT,** to*)*

carder le cuir exp. to tan one's hide / (lit); to card leather.

correction f. (lit); correction.

danse f. (lit); dance / **filer une danse;** to give a thrashing / **recevoir une danse;** to get a thrashing.

dégelée f. (lit); defrosting, thawing out.

dérouillée f. (lit); "derusting."

distribution f. (lit); distribution.

floppée f. (lit); a large quantity (in this case) of hits.

fricassée f. (lit); a fricassee.

frottée f. (lit); a rubbing.

moucher v. to give someone a thrashing / (lit); to wipe / **se faire moucher;** to get oneself severely reprimanded.

passer à tabac v. to give someone a thrashing; to chop someone up like tobacco / (lit); to make into tobacco; / *Note:* **passage à tabac;** thrashing / *See:* **tabasser.**

pâtée f. (lit); mash; mush.

peignée f. (lit); a combing.

pile f. thrashing.

purge f. (lit); purge.

raclée f. (lit); scraping.

ramasser v. to give a thrashing / (lit); to collect / *Note:* **ramassée** f. a thrashing.

ramener v. to give a thrashing / (lit); to bring someone back again.

ratatouille f. (lit); stew.

rincée f. (lit); a rinsing out.

rosser v. to thrash someone / *Note:* **rossée** f. thrashing.

schlague f. military slang for "flogging."

sonner les cloches (faire) exp. to get severely reprimanded / (lit); to make the bells ring.

tannée f. (lit); a tanning.

tanner le cuir exp. to tan one's hide / (lit); to tan leather.

tatouille f. thrashing.

tisane f. (lit); infusion (of herbs, etc.).

tortignole f. thrashing.

tournée f. (lit); a round (of drinks, etc.).

trempe f. (lit); a tempering.

trempée f. (lit); a soaking.

trifouillée f. (lit); a "rummaging."

tripotée f. thrashing.

triquée f. thrashing; beating / *Note:* This comes from **trique** f. heavy stick.

THROAT (gorge)

avaloir m. (lit); swallower / *Note:* This comes from **avaler** v. to swallow.

col m. (lit); collar. -

colback m. (lit); collar.

corridor m. (lit); corridor.

couloir m. (lit); hallway.

gargane m. (lit); the "gargler" / *Note:* This comes from **se garagariser** v. to gargle.

gargoulette f. same as **gargane.**

gosier m. (lit); gullet.

goulot m. (lit); neck of bottle.

quiqui m. *Also:* **kiki** / **serrer le kiki à q;** to squeeze someone's throat, to strangle.

sifflet m. (lit); whistle.

tube m. (lit); tube.

TIRED, to be (être fatigué)

ciboulot qui se coince (avoir le) exp. to be very tired / (lit); to have the head that is jamming.

battre de l'aile exp. to be exhausted / (lit); (of wounded bird) to flutter; to beat the wing.

canuler v. to tire or wear someone out / **Y m'canule avec ses histoires!**; He's wearing me out with his stories!

claqué(e) (être) adj. to be "wiped out."

claquer v. to tire someone.

coltar (être dans le) adj. to be exhausted.

coup de barre (avoir le) exp. to be suddenly exhausted / (lit); to have a sudden bar or rod (that is weighting one down).

coup de pompe (avoir le) exp. to be suddenly exhausted / (lit); to have a sudden pumped-out-of-energy feeling.

crevé(e) (être) adj. to be dead tired / (lit); to be dead / *Note:* **crever** v. to die.

éreinté(e) (être) adj. to be exhausted; to be "wiped out."

éreinter v. to exhaust.

esquinté(e) (être) adj. to be exhausted / (lit); to be ruined.

esquinter v. to exhaust / (lit); to ruin.

flapi(e) (être) adj. to be exhausted.

fourbu(e) (être) adj. to be tired out; dead tired.

guibolles en accordéon (avoir les) exp. to be exhausted; to be hardly able to stand from fatigue / (lit); to have legs like an accordion.

lessivé(e) (être) adj. to be drained of all one's energy; to be "wiped out" / (lit); to be washed (out).

moulu(e) (être) adj. to be exhausted / (lit); to be powdered.

nettoyé(e) (être) adj. to be drained of all one's energy; to be exhausted / (lit); to be cleaned (of all one's energy).

piné(e) (être) adj. to be exhausted; pooped.

pompé(e) (être) adj. to be pooped / (lit); to be pumped (of all one's energy).

pomper v. to tire one out / (lit); to pump someone (of all his energy).

ramasser à la petite cuillère (être à) exp. to be completely exhausted / (lit); to be picked up with a little spoon.

raplapla (être) adj. to feel blah.

rendu(e) (être) adj. to be "wiped out" / (lit); to be rendered.

rincé(e) (être) adj. to be "wiped out" / (lit); to be rinsed (of all one's energy).

rompu(e) (être) adj. to be "wiped out" /(lit); to be broken.

sentir à plat (se) exp. to feel blah / (lit); to feel flattened out.

sur les genoux (être) exp. to be "wiped out" / (lit); to be on the knees.

sur les rotules (être) adj. to be "wiped out" / (lit); to be on the kneecaps.

vanné(e) (être) adj. to be "wiped out" / (lit); to be fanned, winnowed.

vanner v. to tire one out / (lit); to fan or winnow.

yeux en capote de fiacre (avoir les) exp. to have tired and swollen eyes / (lit); to have eyes like the bonnet of a horse-drawn carriage.

yeux qui se coincent (avoir les) exp. to be exhausted; to be unable to see straight due to excessive fatigue / (lit); to have eyes that are jamming or "crossing."

U

UGLY (laid)

gueule à caler les roues de corbillard (avoir une) exp. said of a very ugly person / (lit); to have a face that could stop the wheels of a hearse / *Note 1:* **gueule** f. derogatory for "face" or "mouth" / (lit); mouth of animal / *Note 2:* any synonym for "face" could be used in place of **gueule** in this expression / *See:* FACE.

gueule d'empeigne f. ugly face / (lit); a face that looks like the upper part of a shoe.

laidasse f. ugly woman / *Note:* This is from **laid(e)** adj. ugly.

mochard(e) n. & adj. ugly / **Quel mochard!**; What an ugly person! / **Y est mochard;** He is ugly.

moche adj. *(extremely popular)* ugly.

mochetée f. ugly woman.

remède contre l'amour m. humorous for "ugly" / (lit); remedy for love.

tarte adj. ugly.

tarterie f. ugly woman.

tartignolle adj. slang variant of **tarte.**

tartouillard(e) adj. same as **mochard(e).**

tartouse adj. slang variant of **tarte.**

tête à coucher dehors avec un billet de logement dans sa poche (avoir une) exp. said of a very ugly person / (lit); to have a face that should be made to sleep outside even with a billeting order in his/her pocket.

toc adj. ugly.

tocard(e) n. & adj. same as **mochard(e).**

tocasse adj. slang variant of **toc.**

tocasson adj. slang variant of **toc.**

UMBRELLA (parapluie)

chamberlain m.

paralance m. *Note:* **lance** f. rain.

pébroc m.

pépin m.

riflard m. (lit); plastering trowel.

UP TO DATE, to be (être au courant)

à la coule (être) exp. (lit); to be in the flow.

à la hauteur (être) exp. to be up on what's going on / (lit); to be at the height.

à la page (être) exp. to be with it / (lit); to be at the page.

au parfum (être) exp. to be with it / (lit); to be in the perfume.

dans la note (être) exp. to be with it / (lit); to be in the note.

dans le mouvement (être) exp. to be with it / (lit); to be in the movement.

dans le train (être) exp. to be with it, in the swing of things / (lit); to be in the movement, pace.

dans le vent (être) exp. (lit); to be in the wind.

UPPER SOCIETY (haute société)

l'aristo m. abbreviation of **aristocratie** meaning "aristocracy."
l'artistoche m. slang variant of **l'aristo.**
le gratin m. the *upper crust* of society / *Note:* This is from **au gratin** m. (cooked) with
    breadcrumbs and grated cheese.
le Tout Paris m. the upper society of Paris.

W

WIFE (épouse)

bérgère (ma f. (lit); my shepherdess.
bourgeoise f.
cinquante-pour-cent (mon) m. (lit); my fifty percent.
gouvernement (mon) m. (lit); my government.
légitime f. (lit); legitimate.
moitié (ma) f. my better half / (lit); my half.
panthère f. (lit); panther.
régulière f. (lit); regular one.

WORK, to (travailler)

bosser v. to work hard, to slave / *Note:* **bosseur, euse** n. worker.
boulonner v. to work / *Note:* **boulot** m. (*extremely popular*) work.
bricoler v. to do small jobs; to tinker / *Note:* **bricoleur** m. handyman.
bûcher v. to work hard; to study hard / *Note:* **bûcheur, euse,** n. one who works or
    studies hard.
chiader v. to work; to prepare for an examination.
décarcasser (se) v. to work one's butt off / (lit); to "decarcass" oneself.
démancher (se) v. to work hard; to bend over backwards / (lit); to disjoint oneself.
gratter v. to do a lot of paper work / (lit); to scratch.
job m. job / *Note:* See Unit II; English Words That Are Commonly Used in Colloquial
    French.
labeur m. work / (lit); labor; toil.
marner v. to work hard / *Note:* **marne** m. work.
masser v. to work / (lit); to massage / *Note:* **masseur, euse** n. worker.
piocher v. to work or study hard / (lit); to dig with a pick / *Note:* **piocheur, euse** n.
    worker.
suer sang et eau exp. to work extremely hard / (lit); to sweat blood and water.
travailler pour des prunes exp. to work for "peanuts" / (lit); to work for plums.
travailler pour des pruneaux exp. to work for "peanuts" / (lit); to work for prunes.
travailler pour la peau exp. to work for nothing / (lit); to work for skin.
trimer v. to work terribly hard, to drudge, to toil.
turbiner v. to work hard, to toil / *Note 1:* **turbin** m. work, grind / *Note 2:* **turbineur,**
    euse n. worker.

WORRY, to (s'inquiéter)

biler (se) v. to worry; to get all worked up and upset / *See:* **se faire de la bile**.

bileux, euse n. & adj. one who worries a lot; worried / **C't'un bileux;** He's a worrywart / **Y est bileux;** He's worried.

cent coups (être aux) exp. to be extremely worried / (lit); to be at the one hundred blows.

chiffonner v. to worry; to make feel uneasy / (lit); to crumple (a piece of paper, etc.).

faire de la bile (se) exp. to worry; to get all worked up and upset / (lit); to make oneself bilious.

faire du mauvais sang (se) exp. to get all worked up and upset / (lit); to make oneself bad blood.

frapper (se) v. to worry greatly / (lit); to hit oneself.

mettre martel en tête (se) exp. to worry / (lit); to put a hammer in the head / *Note 1:* This expression conjures up an image of a person who is so worked up over something that he can hear his own pulse banging like a hammer in his head / *Note 2:* **martel** m. old term for "hammer"; current term is **marteau** m.

tintouin m. worry; trouble / **Tu t'fais du tintouin;** You're making yourself problems.

turlupiner v. to plague with worry.

GLOSSARY

This glossary contains all the slang words and expressions used in the first unit.

à brûle-pourpoint adv. point-blank, bluntly.

à cran (être) adj. to be on the verge of getting angry

à la coule (être) exp. to be up to date on something

à l'article de la mort (être) exp. to be at death's door

à l'œil exp. free; "for nothing"

à tout casser adj. to best, "that beats all"

à zéro exp. completely and absolutely

affurer v. to spend

agrafer (se faire) v. to arrest

aller en eau de boudin (s'en) exp. said of something that does not turn out

allez! exclam. stop exaggerating!; come on!

amener (s') v. to arrive

apéro m. cocktail

archi- prefix very, really

attrape-pognon m. casino

attriquer v. to buy

au poil exp. terrific; first-rate

badigeon m. makeup

badigeonner (se) v. to put on makeup

badour(e) adj. very pretty or handsome

bâfrer v. to eat a lot; "to pork out"

bagarre f. a fight

bagatelle f. small sum of money; a trifle

bagnole f. car

bagos m.pl. abbreviation of **bagages**

balader (se) v. to stroll

balancer v. to give; to throw

balle f. one centime

baragouiner v. to jabber

baragouineur, euse n. one who jabbers

baraque f. house

baratin m. lie; nonsense; "bull"

barboter v. to steal; "swipe"

barbouze f. slang variant of **barbe** meaning "beard"

barder v. to turn to violence, to get "heated up"

barman m. barman

barrer (se) to leave

basta adv. enough

bath affure f. good bargain; great buy

battant m. heart

battre le pavé exp. (lit); to pound the pavement (in search of a job)

bazarder v. to sell

beau/belle adj. considerable, "one big..."

beau-dab m. father-in-law; "beau-père"

beauffe m. brother-in-law; "beau-frère"

beaux-vieux m.pl. parents-in-law; "beaux-parents"

bécot m. a kiss.

bécoter v. to kiss; to "neck"

becquetance f. food; "grub"

belle-doche f. mother-in-law; "belle-mère"

béquiller v. to walk

bête à bouffer du foin (être) exp. "to be dumb as an ox"

bidoche f. meat

bidonner (se) v. to laugh hard; to belly-laugh

bien roulé(e) (être) adj. to have a good body

bigler v. to look from the corner of one's eye

bigophone m. telephone

blairer v. (used only in the negative) to be unable to stand or tolerate someone

blaze m. name

bled m. place in general

bombarder v. to smoke

bon débarras! exp. good riddance!

bonir v. to tell, to recount

bonne femme f. (*extremely popular*) woman

bosse de qch. (avoir la) exp. to be gifted at something

bosser v. to work hard

bouchon m. youngest member of the family

boudin m. tire

bouffe f. food; "grub" / **bouffer** v.

bouffer le nez (se) v. to fight

boui-boui m. bad restaurant; "dive"

bouille f. face; "kisser"; head

boule (se mettre en) exp. to get very angry

boulot m. work

boume f. big party; "bash"

bouquin m. book

bourguignon m. sun

bourre (être à la) f. late

bourre (de première) f. excellent

bourré(e) (être) adj. to be very drunk

bousculade f. hustling and jostling crowd

bousiller v. (1) to break; (2) to botch up

boustifaille f. food; "grub"

boutanche f. bottle

brancher v. to talk to someone

brème f. playing card

brindezingue adj. drunk; "bombed"

broquille f. minute

brouille-ménage m. humorous for red wine

brûler le dur exp. to ride the train without a ticket

brûler les planches exp. said of an actor who performs with great energy

cabot m. bad actor; ham actor

cafouiller v. to go about things in an unsure manner

cafouilleur adj. & n. one who works in an unsure manner and makes lots of mistakes

cagnotte f. (of games, etc.) kitty; pot

cailler v. to be extremely cold

ça j'te dis! exp. of agreement "I'm telling you!"

calé(e) (être) adj. to be very smart at something

cancaner v. to spread rumors

cancans m.pl. rumors

canulard m. orderly; hospital worker

caouah m. coffee

carapater (se) v. to leave quickly; to scram

carburer v. to be going very well

carrément adv. completely

cartonner v. to ace a test

ça saute aux yeux exp. said of something that is obvious

casser v. to break in and rob

casser la baraque exp. to bring the house down

casser la gueule (se) exp. to break one's "neck"

casser les oreilles à q. exp. to tire one's ears with excessive talking

casser les pieds à q. exp. to annoy someone a great deal

casseur m. robber

ça va pas non? exp. it doesn't make any sense; one just doesn't do that

cave m. a real "sucker"; one who lets himself be easily duped

c'est pas tes oignons exp. it's none of your business

champignon m. gas pedal

changer de disques exp. to change topics

chapeau! exclam. congratulations!

char m. exaggeration

charivari m. loud noise, racket

châsse f. eye

châsser v. to look, "to eye something"

châsses en capote de fiacre (avoir les) exp. to have swollen eyes

chauffard m. bad driver

chialer v. to cry

chiquer v. to chew tobacco

chômedu m. unemployment

chouchou(te) n. teacher's pet

chouette interj. terrific, neat

cinglé(e) (être) adj. to be cracked; off one's rocker

cinoche m. cinema

clamser v. to die; "to croak"

clope f. cigarette

colle f. a difficult question to answer

collant(e) (être) adj. said of someone who is hard to get rid of

comprenette dure (avoir la) exp. to be dense; slow

connobrer v. to know

contredanse f. ticket (issued by a policeman)

coquard m. black eye

corbuche f. ulcer

cornichon m. telephone

cossard m. a lazy individual

couper à v. to avoid

coûter les yeux de la tête exp. to cost an arm and a leg

cradingue adj. filthy

cramer v. to burn

crâneuse f. conceited woman or girl

crèche f. room or bedroom

crêper le chignon (se) exp. humorous expression said of two women who are having a fight

crève f. bad cold; "one's death"

crever v. to die

crispé(e) (être) adj. to be uptight, on edge

crocs (avoir les) exp. to be very hungry

cuisiner v. to interrogate

cuit(e) être adj. to be done for; "to get one's goose cooked"

cuver son vin exp. to sleep off one's booze

d'acc abbreviation of **d'accord** meaning "okay"

dans ses cordes (être) exp. to be up one's alley

dans son assiette (ne pas être) exp. to be out of it; out of sorts

daron m. father

débarquer v. to arrive without notice

déboiser la colline (se faire) exp. to get a haircut

décambutage m. to exit

décambuter v. to exit

décarcasser (se) v. to work one's butt off

déchanter v. to sing a different tune

défendre (se) v. to get by

dégoiser v. to talk a lot; to spout off

dégoter v. to find, discover

dégringoler v. to tumble down

déjanter v. to talk nonsense

de malheur adj. darned

de mauvais poil (être) exp. to be in a bad mood

dénicher v. to find something (where it was hiding)

dérailler v. to go crazy; "to lose it"

déveine (avoir la) f. to have bad luck

dingue adj. crazy

dire ses quatre vérités à q. exp. to tell someone off

donner du fil à retordre exp. to cause someone difficulty

douloureuse f. bill (in a restaurant)

draguer v. to cruise (for sexual encounters)
driver v. to drive
duraille adj. hard

éclipser (s') v. to leave quickly; to vanish
écoper v. to receive something that is unwanted
écraser (en) v. to sleep; "to crash"
embellie f. stroke of luck
encarrer v. to enter
enfiler des perles exp. to laze around and do nothing
engueuler v. to yell (at someone)
entendre (s') v. to get along with someone
entifler v. to enter
entraver v. to understand
entre quat'z'yeux exp. between you and me
éponges f.pl. lungs
esgourder v. to listen
étendre (se faire) exp. to blow (a test)
et patati et patata onom. and so on and so forth; etc., etc.
éventer la mèche exp. to "spill the beans"
exam m. abbreviation of **examen**

faire (s'en) v. to worry; to get all worked up over something
faire de la bile (se) exp. to get all worked up; to worry
faire écorcher (se) v. to get oneself ripped off; taken
faire sur une jambe (se) exp. said of something easy to do
faire tout un plat (en) exp. to make a big deal about something
farfouiller v. to rummage (without taking much care)
fiche comme de sa première chaussette (s'en) exp. to not care at all
faire la gueule exp. (1) to pout, frown; (2) to give someone the cold shoulder

faire la pige exp. to surpass someone; to "beat"
faire un douze exp. to trick the adversary
fair-play adj. said of one who plays fairly
fauché(e) (être) adj. to be broke
fendre la pipe (se) exp. to laugh hard
ficelé(e) (être mal) adj. to be poorly dressed
fiche v. (1) to give; (2) to put; (3) to do
fiche le camp exp. to leave quickly; to "beat it"
fiche une rame (ne pas en) exp. to do absolutely nothing
figaro (faire) v. "to stiff a waiter"
filer v. to give
fissa adv. quickly
fiston m. son; "fils"
fistonne f. daughter
flambeur, euse n. (of games) player
flambe f. game
flamber v. to play a game
flâneuse f. chair
flic m. cop
flicaille f. the police
flotte f. water
fourrer v. to cram; to stick
frangin m. brother
frangine f. sister
frangin-dab m. uncle
frangine-dabuche f. aunt
frelot m. brother
fric m. money
fringues f.pl. clothes
frite (avoir la) exp. to be hyperactive; hyped up
frit(e) (être) adj. to be done for
fromage m. a cushy job (that's as soft as cheese)
froussard(e) n. scaredy-cat
frousse (avoir la) f. to be frightened
fumantes f.pl. socks
fusiller v. to spend

gaffe (faire) exp. to pay attention; be careful
galerie f. public (in general)

galure f. hat
gargue f. mouth
gâteau (c'est du) exp. said of something
    easy to do
G.D.B. (avoir la) exp. to have a
    hangover / **Avoir la gueule de bois**
génial(e) adj. terrific
goinfrer (se) v. to pork out
gonze m. guy; "dude"
goualeuse f. female singer
graillonner v. to cough hard; to hack
graisseur, euse n. cheater
grenouiller v. to drink water
griller v. to run a red light
grisbi m. money; dough
grisole adj. expensive
grouiller (se) v. to hurry, "to haul"
gueuleton m. a huge meal
guindal m. glass (of water)

hosto m. hospital
humecter les amygdales (s') exp. to
    drink; to wet one's whistle

il y a du monde au balcon exp. said of
    a woman with large breasts
impec adj. abbreviation of "impeccable"
itou adj. also, same / **moi itou**; me too

jardiner v. to play cards, etc.
j'en parlerai à mon cheval exp. "bull";
    nonsense
jeter un derrière la cravate (s'en) exp.
    to drink
jetons (avoir les) exp. to have the jitters
journaille f. day
jus m. gasoline
juste adv. just

la barbe! exclam. shut up!
lancequine f. rain
lancequiner v. to rain
la vache! exclam. **Oh, la vache!**; Wow!
lécher les babines (s'en) (exp). To lick
    one's lips over something
lessivé(e) (être) adj. to be exhausted
lézarder (se) v. to bake in the sun

ligoter v. to read
lourde f. door

machin m. thing
magner le derche (se) exp. to "move
    one's buns"
mal fichu adj. sick
mal vissé(e) (être) adj. to be in a bad
    mood; to be all worked up
maquiller v. to cheat; to cover up
marrant(e) adj. funny; bizarre
marre (en avoir) exp. to be fed up
marron m. punch to the face / (lit);
    chestnut
marquet m. month
martel en tête (se mettre) exp. to worry
mater v. to look
maths m.pl. abbreviation of
    "mathematics"; math
mauvais sang (se faire du) exp. to
    worry; to get all worked up
mec m. guy; "dude"
méganote f. a high grade
melon déplumé (avoir le) humorous exp.
    to be very bald
merlan m. barber
mettre au clou (exp.) to hock
mettre le paquet exp. to shoot the wad
    of money
mettre les bouts exp. to leave quickly
mettre sur les roses exp. to fire one
    from the office
mettre un bouchon (y) exp. to shut up
mirer v. to look
mirettes f.pl. eyes
mironton m. individual; "dude"
moche à caler les roues de corbillard
    (être) humorous exp. (lit); to be
    ugly enough to stop the wheels of a
    hearse
moins de deux (en) adv. quickly
moisir v. to wait
mon vieux exp. "my pal"; "my (old)
    friend"
moucher (se faire) v. to get oneself
    severely reprimanded
moussante f. beer
moutards m.pl. children; "kids"

nana f. girl; "chick"
neuille f. night
nickel adj. spotlessly clean
nippé(e) (être bien) adj. to be well
  dressed

oignon m. watch
opinel m. pocketknife
oseille f. money; "dough"
ouais interj. "yeah"

pageot m. bed
pageoter (se) v. to go to bed
paluche f. hand
paquet m. a lot; a pile
partie de sœurs f. checkers
pas mal adv. a lot; many
passer sur le billard exp. to undergo an
  operation
patin m. brake pedal
patraque adj. broken down; worn out
paumer v. to lose
payer cash exp. to pay cash
payer une tranche (s'en) exp. to have a
  great time
pébroc m. umbrella
peinard(e) adj. "mellow(ed out)"
penses-tu! exp. the idea!; how could
  you think of such a thing?!
pépie (avoir la) f. to be very thirsty
pépin m. trouble; complication
perdre la boule exp. to lose one's mind,
  to lose "it"
pétrin (se fourrer dans le) exp. to get
  into a mess
pharmaco m. a slang variant of
  pharmacien meaning "pharmacist"
piaf m. bird
picoler v. to drink alcohol
picoleur m. one who drinks a great deal
pige f. year
pincer pour quelqu'un (en) exp. to have
  a mad crush on someone
pioncer v. to sleep; snooze
poincer à la belle étoile exp. to sleep
  outside
piquer v. to get; to take (illegally)

piquouser v. to inject
placard m. jail
plancher v. to be called to the blackboard for questioning
planquer v. to hide
plein les bottes (en avoir) exp. to be fed
  up
plombe f. hour
plumard m. bed
pognon m. money; loot; dough
poil dans la main (avoir un) exp. said
  of a person who is very lazy
pointer (se) v. to arrive
poireauter v. to wait; "to take root"
poisse f. bad luck
poke m. an abbreviation of **poker**
  meaning "poker"
pompes f.pl. shoes
portrait m. face
potache m. student
potasser v. to study hard; to bone up
pourliche m. tip
pouvoir voir q. en peinture (ne pas)
  exp. to be unable to stand
  someone
prendre la tangente exp. to slip away
  without being seen
prendre une culotte exp. to lose heavily
  (at cards)
prof m. & f. teacher; professor

quand les poules auront des dents
  humorous exp. never; "when hell
  freezes over"
que t'chi adv. nothing; "zip"

radiner v. to show up, arrive
rappliquer v. to show up; to come back
raquer v. to pay; to "fork out"
réchauffé m. old news; "news that has
  been heated up again"
réchauffer v. to bring up old news again
refiler v. to give something away that
  one no longer wants
régulière f. wife
remède contre l'amour (un) exp. said of
  an ugly person

remonter la pente exp. to get better, to recuperate

rencarder v. to inform

rendre ses clous exp. to quit

rengaine f. repetitious story

rentrer dedans v. to crash into something

repérer v. to spot someone

reprendre le collier exp. to get back to work or school

resquiller v. to enter without paying or invitation

rester baba (en) exp. to be stunned with amazement

resto m. abbreviation of "restaurant"

revenir (ne pas en) v. to disbelieve

revenons à nos moutons exp. " . . . let's get back to what we were talking about"

rigolard adj. funny

rigoler v. to laugh

rond comme une queue de pelle (être) exp. to be totally bombed

roublard(e) adj. sneaky, clever

rouler v. to rip off, cheat someone

rouler sa bosse exp. to travel

roupane f. dress

rouquin(e) adj. & n. red; redhead

rupin(e) adj. rich

sacré(e) adj. big (when placed before a noun), "blessed"

salade (en faire toute une) exp. to make a big deal about something

salé(e) (être) adj. to be expensive

salut interj. "hi"

saucée f. (1) downpour; (2) thrashing

schlinguer v. to stink

sécher v. to voluntarily miss something

signer un bail v. to get married

singe m. boss; "big cheese"

smala f. (large) family or household

soûlard(e) adj. drunkard

sur le carreau (être) exp. to be out of work

sympa (être) adj. nice

tailler une bavette exp. to chat

taper la cloche (se) v. to eat well

taper sur les nerfs à quelqu'un exp. to get on one's nerves

tarte adj. ugly

tartine f. endless speech

téloche f. television

temps de chien m. bad weather

terrible! exclam. (*extremely popular*) fantastic; wonderful

tête près du bonnet (avoir la) exp. to be on the verge of getting angry

tickson m. ticket (other than that issued by a policeman)

tifs m.pl. hair

tirants m.pl. stockings

tire f. old car

tirer (se) v. to leave; "split"

toc m. junk

tomber dans les pommes exp. to faint; pass out

tomber des cordes exp. to rain heavily

torchon m. the curtain of a theater

tord-boyaux m. very strong alcohol; rot-gut

toubib m. doctor

tournée f. round (of drinks)

toute flambant neuve adj. brand spankin' new

tranche-lard m. surgeon

trouille (avoir la) f. to be scared silly.

truc m. thing

tu parles! exp. you said it!

tu rigoles exp. you're kidding

tu veux rire! exp. you've got to be kidding!

type m. guy; "dude"

typesse f. girl; "chick"

un d'ces mat' exp. one of these days

un d'ces quat' exp. one of these days

user sa salive exp. to waste one's breath

vacciné(e) avec une aiguille de phono (être) exp. humorous expression for

one who talks a lot / (lit); to be
    vaccinated with a phonograph
    needle
vanterne f. window
veine (avoir de la) exp. to be very lucky
vieille f. mother
vieux m. father
vieux m.pl. parents

vingt-deux! exclam. watch out!
virée (faire une) exp. to take a spin; a
    quick jaunt

zieuter v. to look; to see
zigue m. guy; "dude"
zinc m. (1) airplane; (2) counter or bar

A Special Offer From Wiley

Introducing *MORE Street French* which contains additional slang and colloquialisms not found in book one, *Street French*.

In addition, *MORE Street French* contains an entire section dedicated to the extremely popular usage of sexual slang, insults, and name calling that one is bound to hear used in movies, in school, among friends, and most definitely behind the wheel!

To place your order, fill out the form below and mail it along with your payment to:

John Wiley & Sons, Inc.
Order Department
1 Wiley Drive
Somerset, NJ 08875-1272

- - - - - - ✂ -

Please send me _____ copy(ies) of **MORE Street French** (0-471-50771-7) @ $12.95 plus applicable sales tax.

NAME _____

COMPANY _____

ADDRESS _____

CITY _____ STATE/ZIP _____

Method of Payment (please make payment to John Wiley & Sons)

❒ Payment Enclosed (Wiley pays postage)   ❒ Bill me   ❒ Bill Company
                                                       P.O. # _____

❒ VISA   ❒ MASTERCARD

(Sales tax, postage and handling will be added)

Expiration Date _____/_____/_____   Card no._____

SIGN HERE: _____
Order invalid if not signed. Offer good in U.S. and Canada only.